The Polit
of Fandom

The Politics of Fandom

Conflicts That Divide Communities

HANNAH MUELLER

McFarland & Company, Inc., Publishers
Jefferson, North Carolina

This book has undergone peer review.

Library of Congress Cataloguing-in-Publication Data

Names: Mueller, Hannah, 1978– author.
Title: The politics of fandom : conflicts that divide communities / Hannah Mueller.
Description: Jefferson : McFarland & Company, Inc., Publishers, 2022. |
Includes bibliographical references and index.
Identifiers: LCCN 2021030117 | ISBN 9781476676005 (paperback : acid free paper) ∞
ISBN 9781476643557 (ebook)
Subjects: LCSH: Fans (Persons) | Subculture—Political aspects. | Mass media—
Political aspects. | BISAC: SOCIAL SCIENCE / Popular Culture
Classification: LCC HM646 .M68 2021 | DDC 306.1—dc23
LC record available at https://lccn.loc.gov/2021030117

British Library cataloguing data are available

ISBN (print) 978-1-4766-7600-5
ISBN (ebook) 978-1-4766-4355-7

Front cover images © 2022 Shutterstock

Printed in the United States of America

*McFarland & Company, Inc., Publishers
Box 611, Jefferson, North Carolina 28640
www.mcfarlandpub.com*

For Deryn Storm,
tiny superhero and big fan

Table of Contents

Acknowledgments

Many, many people and institutions have contributed to the creation of this book in a multitude of ways. It would be impossible to list all the individuals who have supported my work over the years, and thus any list will inevitably be incomplete. Still, I do want to highlight some names and their contributions specifically. Thanks go to:

McFarland for believing in my project and in particular my editor, Layla Milholen, for her patience and support; the anonymous peer reviewers for providing constructive criticism and for helping make the work just this much better; my friends Carly Kaloustian, Alex Phillips, and Leigh York for their help with copyediting; my dissertation advisory committee at Cornell University, Professors Elke Siegel, Jane Juffer, Sabine Haenni, and Geoffrey Waite, for their invaluable advice and expertise and their continuous belief in my work; also at Cornell University, the Department of German Studies, the Program of Feminist, Gender, and Sexuality Studies, the American Studies Program, the Department of Performing and Media Arts, the John S. Knight Institute for Writing in the Disciplines, the Society for the Humanities, and Cornell University Library for providing institutional and financial resources; *Science Fiction Studies* for awarding me with the R.D. Mullen Research Fellowship, and the Eaton Collection as well as Professors Sherryl Vint and Nalo Hopkinson in the Speculative Fiction and Cultures of Science Program at UC Riverside for their interest in my work; the Fandom-Related Collections at University of Iowa, in particular library staff member Peter Balestrieri, and the Rare and Manuscript Collections at Cornell University for letting me dig through their archives; my graduate cohort, Nathan Taylor, Anna Horakova, and Matteo Calla, for making me feel like I wasn't going through it alone; the members of the Popular Culture Reading Group and the Popular Culture Dissertation Writing Group at Cornell, Jane Glaubman, Seth Soulstein, Leigh York, Lee Tyson, Aya Saiki, and Anaar Desai-Stephens, for the wonderful conversations and for sharing my belief in the academic and societal relevance of all things pop culture; my conferencing buddies Bärbel Göbel-Stoltz, Isabel Pinedo, Kriszta

Pozsonyi, Lauren deCarvalho, and Maria San Filippo for making various academic conferences a lot less overwhelming; my childcare providers, including my mother, Brianna Hammond, Megan Mikonowicz, Viola Miller, and the entire staff at Acorn Academy and Discovery Kingdom for taking such good care of my child; other life-saving members of my social support network over the years, in particular my family in Lahr and Ulm, but also Carolyne Strain, Eliza Allen, Diana Hamilton, Lena Krian, Barbara Eichenauer, Jessica Goldring, Matt Stoltz, Johannes Wankhammer, Carl Gelderloos and Agatha Okulicz-Kozaryn, Elena Liskova and Alexey Zayak, Heidi Nees, Julia Brunner, and Carolin Deggelmann. Lastly, I want to commemorate those who have passed away and cannot witness the publication of this book: my friend and mentor Alison van Dyke, my friend and movie buddy Florian Weiland, and my grandparents.

Fandom Divided

An Introduction

Nation of Geekdom, States of Fandom

In July 2012, acclaimed science-fiction author and fan favorite John Scalzi posted an opinion piece on his professional blog *Whatever* with the title "Who Gets to Be a Geek? Anyone Who Wants to Be."[1] In his essay, which prompted more than 700 comments and circulated widely online, Scalzi painted a rather utopian picture of Western fandom's sprawling landscape, describing it as a diverse affinity community bound together through the mutual sharing of love. "Many people believe geekdom is defined by a love of a thing," he wrote,

> but I think—and my experience of geekdom bears on this thinking—that the true sign of a geek is a delight in sharing a thing. [...] When a geek sees someone else grooving on the thing they love, their reaction is to say "ZOMG YOU LOVE WHAT I LOVE COME WITH ME AND LET US LOVE IT TOGETHER."

Scalzi's vision of fandom aligns with what long has been the persistently dominant narrative revolving around the cluster of affective communities that make up self-organized fandom in the 20th and 21st centuries. Accounts written by fans and analyses published by scholars alike have historically tended to describe fan communities as both tight-knit communities made up of dedicated connoisseurs, and as havens of tolerance for social outsiders and misfits. Even though fan studies scholars have since acknowledged that this emphasis on the inclusive community was at least in part a conscious choice, with the goal to counteract the widespread bias against consumers of popular culture in general and fans in particular,[2] the perception of fandom as a diverse but supportive and unified community persists.

1

Yet, a closer look at the history of self-organized fandom reveals that fans' understanding of community has always been highly contested and complex, and that their efforts toward tolerance and diversity are frequently at odds with communitarian ideals. In fact, Scalzi's essay and the context it emerged from illustrate this tension quite well. In his article, Scalzi describes fandom as "a nation with open borders,"[3] praising fandom's accessibility even as he defines it as a political body, a constituency, a *nation*—that is, an entity with laws, social norms, and clearly defined citizenship. Indeed, the publication of his own essay was prompted by a negotiation over the laws and the citizenship requirements in this very nation: Scalzi's opinion piece was a direct response to the complaints of a fan who demanded the exclusion of certain female cosplayers from the nation of geekdom.[4] Thus, the description of harmoniously co-existing fans in "Who Gets to Be a Geek?" is not so much a reality but rather a utopian ideal. In reality, fandom is far from being the "nation with open borders" that Scalzi envisions, but is, in fact, an uneasy alliance of states whose borders are well-guarded and highly contested at the same time.

As they have always been. Neither the definition of fandom as a political entity, nor the negotiations over its borders are phenomena specific to fandom in the 21st century. In fact, the idea of fandom as a quasi-political constituency shaped fans' self-conception even in the earliest days of science-fiction fandom, and efforts to define and strengthen the borders of this constituency are not limited to lone resentful individuals, as Scalzi's essay might want to make us believe. Rather, conflicts over the laws, norms, and inhabitants of the "States of Fandom" are a recurrent theme throughout the history of Western fan communities, and many of these controversies have revolved around what role fans should play as political actors, or whether politics should have a place in fandom at all.

Fans and Political Discourse

Until very recently, fan studies scholars concerned with fans' sociopolitical consciousness and the role of politics in fandom tended to skirt the topic of inner-fandom controversies. Early fan studies pioneers such as Camille Bacon-Smith, Henry Jenkins, and Constance Penley still had to show that there was more to fan communities than the stereotypical images of the lonely science-fiction nerd and the crowds of screaming fan girls. Heavily influenced by cultural studies scholars like John Fiske and Stuart Hall, they focused primarily on fans' practices of popular consumption in order to highlight the resistant-subversive potential of creative fan practices, such as the appropriation of copyrighted materials or the production of transformative fanworks, in particular the (traditionally women-centric) labor of writing fanfiction.[5]

Yet in the past decade, fan studies scholars have increasingly moved away from the consideration of fandom as a *private* practice of resistant consumption, and toward an analysis of fans as actors in the *public* sphere. This disciplinary shift happened in response to the increased public visibility of fans since the beginning of the 21st century. Scholars such as Tanya Cochran, Ashley Hinck, Henry Jenkins, Neta Kligler-Vilenchik, and Sangita Shresthova[6] became increasingly interested in fans' self-conception as public actors who are not only concerned with the fate of their favorite television characters, but also with issues of general societal relevance. They observed an apparent proliferation of fan-organized activism with a focus on various sociopolitical issues from gender equality to poverty to environmental issues, such as the *Harry Potter* fans who set out to convince entertainment giant Warner Bros. to use fair-trade products for their *Harry Potter* merchandise.[7]

Much of this research is grounded, on the one hand, in the premise that fandom's political turn in the 21st century was triggered by the rise of participatory online culture. For Henry Jenkins, fan-organized activism is "what democracy looks like in the 21st century."[8] He and other scholars have explained the apparent increase in fan-organized activism as a consequence of shifting political structures and processes in a digitally networked global world: "Fan-based citizenship," Ashley Hinck writes, "has emerged as a new mode of citizenship at a time when the whole of citizenship seems to be in flux."[9] On the other hand, most of the scholarship on fandom-based activism continues to rely on the notion that fan groups are tight-knit communities whose activist potential is fueled and sustained by their communal spirit. "Fannish civics," Neta Kligler-Vilenchik argues, "is strongly rooted within the practices of a preexisting fan community, which includes not only a connection to a primary text, but a strong social bond between community members."[10]

There is no doubt about the significance of this research, which has theorized the relationship between fan communities and politics in the 21st century as a politicization of fandom resulting from the cross-pollination between communal attachment and participatory culture. However, it has since become clear that the body of scholarly work celebrating fan-organized activism as the manifestation of a new form of progressive democratic action was responding to a specific brief period in the history of Western fandom, marked roughly by the beginning and the end of Barack Obama's appointment as President of the United States from 2009 to 2017. Against the backdrop of Obama's election (and re-election), the wave of fan-organized sociopolitical engagement was interpreted as hopeful sign that seemed to contradict the often-repeated complaints from older generations about millennials/post-millennials and their presumed indifference toward political and social concerns. The spotlighted examples of fan-organized activism seemed to imply that those born post–1980 were certainly willing and ready to put effort into the fight for social change, even if their agendas and strategies diverged from approaches that had traditionally been associated with the political sphere.

"While we are skeptical of change occurring in the short term through the mechanisms of institutional politics," Jenkins writes in 2016, "we are intrigued by political, social, and cultural changes occurring around the edges of the dominant institutions, as young people work together to address issues that matter to them."[11] Jenkins and others like him argued that young voters and fans might not look for moral and political inspiration primarily in political manifestos or established party candidates, but instead in the texts, objects, and symbols of mass-produced popular culture. And rather than becoming involved in local party politics, they might be found in their living rooms and favorite coffee shops, wired into the digital communication and distribution networks of the 21st century, where they would put their advanced media literacy to good use in order to spread information and connect with like-minded others.

Accordingly, some of the presidential candidates in the 2016 election explicitly tried to tap into the discourses of young fan-activists. In early 2016, the official Twitter account of Democratic candidate Bernie Sanders tweeted the picture of a young woman holding up a sign that compared Sanders to the "Mockingjay," the symbol of political revolution in Suzanne Collins' young adult trilogy *The Hunger Games*. The photograph was accompanied by the caption: "Casey knows a political revolution when she sees one. She Voted Early in Wisconsin!"[12]

Yet a mere six months after young Casey had proudly raised her sign that called for revolutionary change with a reference to a young adult fantasy novel, global political developments seemed to contradict the "cautious optimism"[13] which Jenkins and his fellow researchers had expressed regarding the increase in youth-centric participatory politics and the complex, but tentatively hopeful examples of political discourse, community work, and civic engagement emerging from within fan organizations. In November 2016, populist Republican candidate Donald Trump won the electoral vote in the United States presidential election. As unexpected as this development was for many people in America and worldwide, in other ways it was merely the continuation of a global political shift. Trump's victory came at the end of a year in which, for example, the citizens of the United Kingdom of Great Britain and Northern Ireland had decided, in a referendum known as Brexit, to leave the European Union; and a right-wing populist candidate only narrowly failed to become the next Austrian Federal President. The same dissatisfaction with established political institutions that had led fans to engage in the sociopolitical activism praised by fan studies scholars had also led to a rallying around populist candidates on the right.

This global political shift was mirrored by accompanying developments in the fandom landscape. In 2014, two years after Scalzi had celebrated fandom as a "nation with open borders," politically reactionary fans launched vicious attacks on female, queer, and POC fans and creators in the gaming and the science-fiction communities in altercations that went down into fandom history under the politically charged names Gamergate and Puppygate.[14] As it turned out, right-wing politicians and agitators of the alt-right had also discovered the political potential of fan organizations. While Democratic Socialist Bernie Sanders appealed to fans of *The Hunger Games*, future White House Chief Strategist Steve Bannon rallied supporters of Donald Trump among the fans of *World of Warcraft*.[15]

These recent developments have not made the work of fan studies scholars interested in fandom-based civics obsolete, quite the contrary. However, they do point toward a need for the further exploration of areas that have so far been somewhat overlooked, and perhaps even more importantly the interconnection of several questions that have been studied mostly as separate phenomena by scholars in the field: (a) a historical perspective on political consciousness in fandom, (b) the role of politicized conflict within fan communities, and (c) the appropriation of user-generated content and fandom-based activism by political actors and the entertainment industry.

Fans and Politics: A Historical Perspective

To date, the majority of fan studies scholarship, especially scholarship engaging with fan-based citizenship and activism, has focused on communities and movements in the late 20th and the early 21st centuries. In this book, I argue for the necessity of tracing political discourse and civic engagement in fan communities back to the roots of self-organized fandom in the early 20th century. The reasons behind this move toward a historical perspective on fandom are twofold. First, it shows that fans' engagement with political questions did not begin, as is often implied, with the migration of fan communities to the internet, but is in fact the result of a long history of fans conceptualizing their organizations as quasi-political publics and constituencies. Far from being a product of 21st-century global digital networks, Scalzi's notion of fandom as a political constituency—a "nation," to use his term—has been part of fan communities' self-conception since the beginnings of science-fiction fandom in the early 20th century. In fact, as Chapter 1 of this book will reveal, not only were many prominent players in the early decades of science-fiction fandom intensely invested in the formal unification of fandom; the controversy over the ideal organizational structure of fandom also mirrored the ideological tensions and political conflicts playing out simultaneously on a global scale. Yet early science-fiction fans were not only concerned with the political foundations of their own community, they also contemplated the role fans might play in shaping or changing the world. The fans who founded the first science fiction clubs in 1920s America, inspired by the futuristic visions they encountered in Hugo Gernsback's professional fanzine *Amazing Stories*, "saw themselves as world-making agents, harbingers of progress"[16] who envisioned themselves as an educated elite that was going to bring about a better future for Western society, if not the entire world.

Second, a historical approach to fandom is meant to counteract the trend of universalizing statements about fans and fan culture in fan studies scholarship. To historicize fandom means to show that various fan groups differ not only in regard to their objects of interest and their fan practices, but also in how they conceive of themselves as communities, which in turn affects how they think of their roles as political actors within their constituencies and in the broader public sphere. Fandom, it turns out, is not so much a unified nation but rather a network of states, each of whom has its own historically and culturally specific rules, expectations for citizenship, alliances and conflicts with other constituencies. Thus, political disagreements and controversies are common not only within, but also between these different fannish states.

Controversies in Fandom: A Political Perspective

Although Derek Johnson already called in 2007 upon fan studies to engage in "more expansive theorizations of constitutive, hegemonic antagonisms,"[17] it has only been in the last couple of years that an increasing number of fan studies scholars have started to move beyond the emphasis on fandom as unified community. Even so, much of the recent work on disagreements and conflict in fandom has centered around "anti-fandom," an expression used to describe the passionate antipathy directed at certain popular texts and objects, which has received attention from scholars such as Bethan Jones, Melissa Click, and Jonathan Gray.[18] Anti-fans' negative engagement with popular culture is primarily directed at the works they despise, although anti-fandom can also lead to heated battles between the fans of a text and its anti-fans. Chapter 3 touches on the example of *Twilight* anti-fandom to show that anti-fannish sentiments are not necessarily just a matter of personal taste but often fueled by more deep-seated reservations, such as the widespread bias against certain audience demographics.

Some fan studies scholars have also begun to delve into an investigation of "toxic fan practices"[19] or what CarrieLynn Reinhard has called the "dark side of fandom"[20]: fan behaviors such as harassment, bullying, or trolling which negatively affect both individual fans and the peace within communities. Some scholars interpret negative fan behaviors ultimately as the consequence of individual psychological dysfunctions. Buckels et al., for example, understand the practice of online trolling as an expression of online users' sadistic predispositions: "Sadists just want to have fun … and the Internet is their playground!"[21] Other scholars are more interested in exploring toxic fan behaviors as a breakdown of communicative norms. Reinhard sees conflicts between fans as "manifesting from and being exacerbated by communication problems"[22] which could potentially be solved through different communicative strategies. Similarly, J. Richard Stevens and Rachel van der Merwe argue that "[t]oxic disagreements tend to disrupt dialogue, undermining the community's ability to productively discuss differences,"[23] thus suggesting that toxic rhetoric is standing in the path of what could otherwise be a productive dialogue.

However, by focusing primarily on the communicative aspects of toxic fan practices rather than the political values and ideological differences at stake in these conflicts, these scholars risk veering into both-sideism and the normalization of oppressive ideologies. For example, Matt Hills laments that a focus on the "culture war discourse" at the heart of recent fandom controversies "makes it difficult for scholars and critics not to have to take sides"[24]—but his argument perpetuates the notion that a politically neutral observer position is actually possible, when in fact any critical analysis is automatically situated within existing political power structures. Mel Stanfill argues that to "position fandom as resistant (rightly or wrongly) is to stake a case for it as political."[25] Looking at politically charged conflicts and controversies within fan communities therefore requires a serious engagement with the political values and power dynamics at play.

The most relevant studies in this context are those by scholars who have investigated how prejudice, discrimination, and inequalities are not only punctually affecting fans on an individual level but are woven into the very fabric of fan communities. Lisa Nakamura's early work on racism in online gaming[26] has more recently been joined by the research of scholars such as Rukmini Pande and Benjamin Woo, both of whom have critiqued the structural whiteness of Western fan communities.[27] Meanwhile, Sarah

Banet-Weiser, Megan Condis, and Anastasia Salter and Bridget Blodgett have taken on the significant influence that toxic masculinity and misogyny have on gaming and geek culture.[28]

While most of their work has focused on contemporary developments in a global digitally networked environment, this book connects their analyses of exclusionary and discriminatory structures in fan communities to the historical analysis of political consciousness in fandom. As it turns out, negotiations over the borders of fannish nations, communal decisions about who gets to be a card-carrying geek with a voice in his or her fannish constituency, have throughout the history of fandom played out frequently with an eye toward questions of politics. More specifically, many of these conflicts have been framed as a disagreement between those fans who believe that fandom should be "apolitical," and those who insist on bringing politics into fandom, or rather point out that fandom without politics does not exist. However, it will become apparent that the line between what is considered "political" and "apolitical" has historically been determined by dominant groups and shaped by hegemonic ideas. In the 1930s, for example, members of the centrist-conservative wing in science-fiction fandom conceived of themselves as apolitical and were strongly opposed to the fans with socialist leanings who argued that the science-fiction community should take an explicit stance against fascism, in other words, "become political." Eighty years later, participants in the Gamergate controversy were similarly arguing for a gaming community that should remain free from politics, even as the instigators of the movement were rather obviously enabled by political actors from the circles around the alt-right.

Fan Practices, Appropriated: An Industrial Perspective

The example of Gamergate points toward another site of conflict that increasingly influences fans' self-conception as political actors: the appropriation and cooption of fan practices and user-generated content by corporations and political movements. Fans' role as consumers and their inevitable complicity with the capitalist structures of the entertainment industry complicates their agency as public actors. However, many fan studies scholars have argued that the more immediate contact between fans and creators/producers in the era of media convergence and online participatory culture has actually prepared the ground for fan-based civics and fan-organized activism. Participatory online culture, they have argued, has empowered fans because digital culture has given them easier access to and control over their own means of media production, communication, and distribution, which has made their opinions and practices more visible to creators/producers and the general public alike. In 2006, Jenkins argued that these "elite consumers exert a disproportionate influence on media culture in part because advertisers and media producers are so eager to attract and hold their attention."[29]

To a certain degree, this description has held true. As Kristina Busse says, "[f]ans are everywhere and at the center of attention from the academy, journalism, and industry."[30] As such, they are courted as consumers by an industry that used to treat them at best with benevolent neglect. Online culture has also provided fans with unprecedented opportunities to create their own networks and independent communication platforms. In order to navigate their inevitable entanglement in the entertainment industry, to stay under the radar, or to keep technology both accessible and affordable, fans have often consciously worked to build communication networks and platforms with as little reliance on corporate providers as possible, from the amateur presses of early science-fiction fandom to the independent non-profit online archives of contemporary transformative fandom. Among the latter is the Organization for Transformative Works (OTW, founded in 2007), which hosts Archive of Our Own (AO3), one of the largest online archives for fanfiction. In the context of fans' engagement with politics, these networks gain a renewed significance, since alternative media are not "merely oriented towards the creation of content and infrastructures," but "inherently political. Indeed, these media create spaces that oppose the dominant cultures in a direct manner, and, hence, challenge mainstream and mass media power that have the monopoly over the naming of realities."[31]

However, corporations and political actors have predictably reacted to these developments with efforts to regulate, commercialize, appropriate, and infiltrate fannish spaces, practices, and content for their own interests. Scholars such as Matt Hills and Suzanne Scott have shown how transmedia franchises purposefully expand into media platforms frequented by fans and tap into fan practices in order to ensure consumer loyalty, regulate transformative fan practices, and capitalize on fan-generated content.[32] The case studies on *Glee* and *The Hunger Games* in this book (Chapters 4 and 5) show how recent transmedia marketing strategies in the entertainment industry both facilitate and complicate fan-organized activism. While the heavy use of participatory elements in transmedia marketing can support civic participatory engagement by boosting the fans' sense of agency, transmedia marketing campaigns also increasingly appropriate and commercialize fan platforms, practices, and interests. This already precarious and complex relationship between fan-organized activism and capitalism has become even more fraught with the efforts from political actors to infil-trate fannish platforms and exploit and steer politicized energies within fan communities. As we will see, in the lead-up to the 2016 U.S. presidential election, the entanglement of fan culture and national politics contributed to the promotion of a political climate in online spaces that directly affected the outcome of the election.

Fandom Divided: The Book

This book, then, delves into the connections and intersections between the history of political discourse in fan communities on the one hand, and the role of conflict within fan communities (between different fractions of fandom, and between fans and creators) on the other. The trajectory of this book is both chronological and dialectic: the five chapters trace the his-tory of fandom from the 1930s to the year 2020, but also map out a narrative of perpetually returning similar conflicts that play out in slightly different ways.

The case studies assembled in this book expand on previous scholar-ship about fan-based civics and fan-organized activism both by extending the historical focus beyond 21st-century online participatory culture and by complicating the dominant narrative of fan-based citizenship as inherently progressive. I argue that political discourse has always been negotiated in the different communities of self-organized fandom, but that much of this discourse has been omitted from historiographies of fandom: because hegemonic groups of fans have tended to obscure their own ideological interests by framing them as "apolitical," and because fans and fan stud-ies scholars have long prioritized depictions of fandom as cohesive, unified communities. Throughout the chapters of this book, it will become clear that ever since the early 20th century, fans have conceived of themselves as members of quasi-political bodies, even if the types of civic formation fans most strongly identify with vary based on the specific historical and cul-tural context of the respective groups. As members of *communities*, fans are always at work to establish the borders of their invisible townships, and to regulate the rules of inclusion and exclusion that determine access to their communities. As participants in alternative *public spheres*, fans constantly engage in the negotiation of public opinion and in the (re)evaluation of communal consensus. As members of *constituencies*, fans establish author-ities and hierarchies, develop processes of decision-making, and determine courses of action in order to resolve conflicts within their groups.

In the process of reading this book, it will also become apparent that conflicts and controversies between different players and groups in the fandom landscape are not singular occurrences or instigated by individual troublemakers; but rather, that they are often crucial moments in the development and transformation of different fan communities. That doesn't mean that these conflicts are necessarily positive, or even productive—in fact, they often reveal the gaping ideological rifts and deep-seated animosities between different groups of fans that tend to be glossed over in narratives of cohesion and communal spirit. The controversies that will be discussed throughout this book play out on different fronts: between different fractions of the same community, between affirmative and transformative fans, between fanboys and fangirls, between fans and creators, between the left and the right wings of fan communities, between those who consider fandom to be an inherently political space and those who demand that fandom should be kept free from politics. These fronts are not always clear but rather continuously in flux; different lines intersect and overlap in various controversies playing out in the fannish field, and they shift in response to these conflicts and over time.

Methodologically, this book combines critical perspectives on the production, representation, and consumption of cultural texts and is thus firmly situated within the scholarly tradition of cultural studies. To some degree the material itself lends itself to this specific approach: in the phenomena considered across the following chapters, the realms of production, representation, and reception are often so closely entwined that it seems almost impossible—and certainly counterproductive—to study them independently from each other. In fact, in many cases it can be difficult to determine under which of these categories (production, representation, reception) a certain cultural practice should be considered. Consequently, while this book employs methods of textual analysis, my understanding of "text" is a very broad one that encompasses various forms of cultural production, including mass-produced entertainment, independent works created by individual authors, fanzine contributions, derivative texts like fanworks, but also advertising and marketing campaigns, activist initiatives, and social media discourses.

This method of applying textual analysis to a broad spectrum of materials has two significant implications. First, this approach does not erase the category of "identity"; in fact, questions of race, class, gender, and sexuality (among others) are repeatedly brought up throughout the book. However, it shifts the focus toward the cultural and social practices that generate *discourses of identity* instead of relying on an understanding of identity as fixed and defining notion of the self. For that reason, archival and online-ethnographic research undertaken for this book engages with issues of identity primarily within the context of communicative and discursive practices and for the most part does purposefully not rely on specific demographic data about particular fan groups. Second, the inclusion of and emphasis on various cultural practices allows me to better capture the complex and shifting flows between the discourses of popular culture, alternative media, online communication platforms, marketing campaigns, institutional politics, grassroots activism, and interpersonal relationships that shape and in return are shaped by the practices and self-perceptions of fans and their communities.

The first part of the book, "Platforms and Conventions: (Hi)stories of Conflict and Community," explores different political conflicts that have divided fan communities at different points throughout the history of self-organized fandom in order to explore how fans' understanding of their communities as quasi-political bodies has formed and changed over time. The first chapter, "'Preserving harmony in all the fan field': The Great Exclusion, the Breen Boondoggle and the Debate Over Community," focuses on literary science-fiction and fantasy fandom in the early/mid–20th century. The chapter discusses two events that drastically divided the fan community into different camps at the time of their occurrence: the "Great Exclusion Act" of 1939, in which the conservative fraction of the fan community on the North-American East Coast barred a group of socialist-leaning fans from attending the World Science Fiction Convention in New York; and the "Second Great Exclusion" (also called "The Breen Boondoggle") of 1964, during which Marion Zimmer Bradley's husband Walter Breen, a well-connected member of the fan community, was excluded from Pacificon II in Oakland because he was known for molesting children in fannish circles. I use these two controversies to discuss how science-fiction fandom at the time saw itself as community and political constituency, how public discourse functioned within the community, and how decisions were made regarding the in- or exclusion of entire groups or individual members. I argue that this male-dominated and highly educated fan group maintained a communitarian ideal in which exclusion was determined by how much the controversy affected the balance of the community, not by the risk it posed to individual members. This dominant notion of community also provides an explanation for the fan community's slow and reluctant acceptance of feminist thought as well as the influx of fans with an interest in film and television in the 1970s; a development that ultimately led to a splintering between traditional science-fiction fandom and a new community of feminist and media fans which over the decades developed into what is now known as "transformative online fandom."

This fan group is at the focus of the second chapter, "'For the first time, we got to do some shouting back': RaceFail '09, or: Journal-Based Fandom as Alternative Public Sphere." Using the example of another inner-fandom dispute, this chapter shows how the discursive practices of transformative online fandom significantly diverge from those in the literary science-fiction community. In the far-reaching online debate generally known as "RaceFail '09," writers and fans from the literary science-fiction community and from transformative online fandom clashed in what has perhaps been the most extensive discussion about race and racism in science-fiction culture to this day. Because the internet allowed these different groups to directly interact with each other on social media platforms like LiveJournal and Dreamwidth, the debate not only highlighted their different positions regarding inclusivity, discursive norms, the meaning of public and private, and the relationship between author, reader, and text; it also exemplified the role journal-based online platforms played for the emergence of new forms of public discourse. At the same time, RaceFail '09 also revealed the limitations of this new alternative public, which promoted inclusivity yet also perpetuated the notion of whiteness as default in online fandom.

Chapter 3, "'Yep, the Hugo award might be RUINED!' Geek Masculinity, Puppygate and the Reputation of the Hugo Awards," takes the investigation of hegemonic politics in fandom further by shifting the gaze to active fan engagement fueled by conservative politics. In the discussion of two recent controversies surrounding the prestigious Hugo Awards for science fiction and fantasy, Chapter 3 shows how some of the contemporary controversies between different segments of fandom turn out to be astonishingly similar to those led by early science-fiction fans in the 1920s and 1930s. However, rather than grow closer together, as fans during the early days of self-organized fandom had hoped, the fannish landscape has become increasingly splintered, with some ideological rifts growing deeper instead of closing over time. The controversies surrounding the Hugo Awards also demonstrate that fandom has experienced a noticeable shift regarding the interrelation between fannish and nonfannish politics. Where previously politically interested fans had carried their ideas and projects into their fan communities, now political groups, in particular right-wing organizations, target fan communities explicitly to exploit existing tensions and animosities within fandom for their own ideological agendas.

The second part of the book, "Fiction and Reality: Between Transmedia Marketing and Social Critique," interrogates how transmedia marketing strategies in contemporary entertainment franchises have affected fans' self-understanding as public actors, and how transmedia marketing both encourages and complicates fans' engagement with sociopolitical concerns. In Chapter 4 "'A Loser Like Me': A Community of Outsiders, Fan Activism and Transmedia Marketing in *Glee* Fandom," I show how the politicized discourse emerging from online transformative fandom interrelates with fans' investment in specific fictional texts and subsequently translates into forms of fan-organized social activism. Focusing on the high school dramedy series *Glee,* the chapter explains why and how *Glee* fans became concerned with LGBTQ rights activism. The chapter shows that fans were inspired by what they considered the essential ethical message of the fictional text but also by a transmedia marketing campaign that created the illusion of a sphere in which diegetic and extra-diegetic reality overlap, thus instilling in fans a heightened sense of agency. Ironically, this very sense of empowerment also encouraged fans to direct their criticism at the show (and its creators) when the text seemed to violate the ethical ideals they had come to believe in. Thus, the discussion of *Glee* fans and their investment in LGBTQ rights also points toward the perpetual tension between the resistant potential stemming from fans' critical engagement with popular culture, and the ways in which fannish practices are appropriated by entertainment companies striving to contain those resistant elements.

Chapter 5, "'We Are the Districts': Fans' Reactions to Lionsgate's *Hunger Games* Transmedia Marketing Campaign," further problematizes the relationship between the entertainment industry and fans invested in sociopolitical issues. The chapter studies Lionsgate's controversial viral transmedia marketing campaign for the *Hunger Games* movies, which relied heavily on fannish online platforms and practices, and focused on the glamorous world of the Capitol, thus seemingly neglecting and disavowing the critical message of the text. I discuss the different responses to the marketing campaign and show that fans' perception of the campaign heavily depended on their initial reception of the text itself: fans who disliked the campaign showed themselves concerned with issues of social inequality and considered the original texts a call for action; by contrast, other fans saw the novels as an absolution from social responsibility and embraced the marketing campaign because it supported their personal reading of the text. The divided response to the marketing campaign among *Hunger Games* fans seriously complicates common assumptions about alternative readings and resistant politics. Certain fans aligned themselves with an alternative reading of the text that nevertheless reflected hegemonic politics, showing that alternative readings are certainly not automatically politically resistant and might in fact affirm hegemonic positions, even as they resist the dominant reading of the fictional text.

This perhaps uncomfortable realization confirms what is already outlined in the previous chapters: the fact that the historical trajectory of fandom-based political discourse is not a linear narrative toward a more politically conscious, more progressive, more inclusive fandom. Rather, the different case studies in the book reveal the pattern of a much more dialectic fan history, in which similar battles continue to be fought by different actors over a variety of stakes, over and over again. At the same time, fandom in the 21st century looks different than it did a century ago, and this also affects the way fans are perceived, and perceive themselves, as public actors of political weight. While the advent of online participatory culture in the era of media convergence has made fans more visible as actors in the public sphere and has provided them with an increased sense of agency, this growing visibility has also made them more vulnerable to attempts at infiltration and cooption by major entertainment companies and by various political interest groups.

Platforms and Conventions
(Hi)stories of Conflict and Community

1

"Preserving harmony in all the fan field"

The Great Exclusion, the Breen Boondoggle and the Debate Over Community

Introduction

> "It never fails to amaze me that people regard fandom as an entity, something to be cherished, protected and prolonged at all cost."—Gregg Calkins, February 1965[1]

Calkins' observation seems to be a rather broad statement that could be easily applied to any number of situations in the history of self-organized fandom. However, at the time it was printed and distributed in a Fantasy Amateur Press Association (FAPA) mailing from early 1965, it was not meant as a general commentary, but voiced in reaction to a situation that had kept large parts of the North American science-fiction community in uproar for the previous year. The controversy had initially erupted over the decision of the Pacificon II[2] organizing committee to ban "Big Name Fan" Walter Breen from the 1964 convention because he had a known history of molesting children. Yet the subsequent discussion extended far beyond the question of whether the committee had been right in stopping this particular fan from attending the convention. Instead, the conversation turned toward questions such as: What might be the most democratic form to organize a fan community? Who should have the right to make decisions for fandom in its entirety? What kind of decisions would benefit fandom as a whole?

Of course, to return to Calkins' above-cited statement, these questions already presume that it makes sense to speak of fandom as a unified entity in the first place. And in fact, even if the controversy that erupted over the exclusion of a fan from Pacificon II showed clearly that the fan community was far from a united front, most fans involved in the discussion seemed to believe that it very well *should be*. The members of mid–20th century science-fiction fandom did indeed see their community as an "entity, something to be cherished, protected and prolonged at all cost."[3] Therefore, conflicts erupting among different fractions of the fan community, as it happened in the case of the Pacificon II ban, were often discussed not only in regard to their subject matter, but also with an eye toward how they affected fandom as a community. Controversies over general interest topics (ranging from foreign politics and the Equal Rights Act to the benefits and risks of pornography to religion and childrearing) frequently circled back to discussions about the fan community's organizational structure, its internal hierarchies, rules of discourse, processes of decision-making, and the in- and exclusion of individual members. In fact, fans were often concerned primarily with whether the issue at hand, as well as the conflict surrounding it, put the cohesion of the community at risk.

The invocation of the "ideal community" in controversies among science-fiction fans is what this first chapter focuses on. Against the backdrop of theoretical discourses on "community," I discuss the negotiation of community in early science-fiction fandom in the context of two major controversies that divided the fan community at the time of their occurrence and for years after: the so-called "Great Exclusion" of 1939, in which the conservative wing of the fan community stopped a group of socialist fans from attending the First World Science Fiction Convention (Worldcon) in New York, and the "Second Great Exclusion" in 1964, wherein the fan community argued over the exclusion of well-known fan Walter Breen from Pacificon II and the Fantasy Amateur Press Association in response to his repeated sexual abuse of children and teenagers. It will become apparent that the discourse about community in early/mid–20th century literary science-fiction fandom was dominated by a strongly communitarian ideal, which in turn was fueled by a climate of intellectual elitism that positioned science-fiction fans as intellectually superior to the average population. This ideal of community was reiterated over decades through a perpetual evocation of crisis or threat from the outside, which made the push toward a unified fandom appear particularly urgent. Within this discursive environment, the unity and growth of the science-fiction community generally took priority over individual interests, and the exclusion of members tended to be determined primarily based on how much their actions affected the balance of the community, rather than their perceived transgressions or the danger they posed to individual members. At the same time, the fan community's self-conception as an intellectual, progressive group fostered an ethos of tolerance that was in conflict with fandom's communitarian ideal. This tension erupted repeatedly during disagreements among members of the group, because despite the ruling discourse of cohesion and unity, the history of science-fiction fandom throughout the 20th century was full of rather serious controversies between different fractions of fans. These conflicts often revolved not so much around fan-specific questions such as the interpretation and evaluation of cultural texts, but rather around matters of general social and political significance such as socialism or the women's rights movement. Fans did not see these controversies as unrelated to their identity and interactions as fans. In fact, science-fiction fans often felt that national or world politics affected them not just as individuals or national citizens but also specifically as fans, and they saw themselves and their fellow fans as playing their own role in the (inter)national public sphere.

Conflict and Community

It may at first glance seem counterintuitive to approach a study of community by focusing on moments of conflict and controversy. After all, theoretical approaches to the idea of community, both affirmative and critical, have for the most part focused on communities' potential for creating unity, cohesion, and consensus. In one of the earliest sociological texts about the question of community, the 1881 monograph *Community and Society* (orig. *Gemeinschaft und Gesellschaft*, first transl. 1957), Ferdinand Tönnies describes the emergence of (local) communities as an organic evolution of immediate kinship relations, like those between mother and child or husband and wife, into broader networks of solidarity: "The study of the home is the study of the Gemeinschaft."[4] For him, functioning communities—just like families—are perfectly balanced systems of reciprocity, and social hierarchies within these communities are not detrimental to community cohesion, but necessary and working in perfect unison to everyone's benefit.

In many ways, this concept of community was propagated fairly consistently by other theorists over the next 150 years. In his 1991 *The Dance with Community*, an overview on the discourse about community in Western political thought, Robert Booth Fowler still describes the idea of community as deeply rooted in a quasi-spiritual experience of togetherness:

> The concept of community invariably invokes the notion of commonality, of sharing in common, being and experiencing together. This is the root concept implied in most uses of the word. [...] That the sharing implies an affective or emotional dimension is a usual assumption. It is not that advocates of community spurn rationality [...]; it is, rather, that community is and must be a deeply felt experience. That is inherent to what it is.[5]

Tönnies and Fowler have in common with many other theorists of community not only that they emphasize the community's interest in consensus and unity, but also that they consider this sense of community as difficult to grasp analytically. Instead they describe it as a natural, subjective, even spiritual force that resists theorization. In the introduction to the 1991 anthology *Community at Loose Ends*, a collection of poststructuralist critiques of community, Georges Van Den Abbeele calls this belief an "element of demagoguery or mystification at work in the seductive appeal to community," to which scholars on both sides of the political spectrum tend to succumb easily: "both the New Left and the New Right claim for themselves the enthusiastic appeal the notion still garners."[6]

In his much-discussed *Bowling Alone: The Collapse and Revival of American Community* (2000), Robert Putman shares this perception of community as, if not explicitly anti-rational, at least rooted in instinctive, affective attachment. At the same time, however, he mentions "bonding" and "bridging" as specific strategies of socializing which he considers necessary for maintaining this supposedly natural balance:

> Some forms of social capital are, by choice or necessity, inward looking and tend to reinforce exclusive identities and homogeneous groups. Examples of bonding social capital include ethnic fraternal organizations, church-based women reading groups, and fashionable country clubs. Other networks are outward looking and encompass people across diverse social cleavages. Examples of bridging social capital include the civil rights movement, many youth service groups, and ecumenical religious organizations.[7]

For Putnam, these are positive and necessary inclusionary networking strategies with the purpose of holding communities together. Other scholars however, although in the minority among those theorizing community, see this striving for consensus more critically. Miranda Joseph's *Against the Romance of Community* (2002) describes the darker side of communities' seemingly inclusionary strategies and shows that they can in fact turn communities into sites of oppression and exclusion. In her study of what many might consider the prototype of an inclusive community, a gay and lesbian community theater, she analyzes the exclusionary rhetoric influencing the community's self-definition.

> [T]he invocation of community served to articulate what might be called homosexism—that is, the prioritization of gayness over other identity features. [...] [It] functioned here to exclude people of color and transgendered people for whom, though they might in fact also be gay, sexuality was not an isolated or primary identity.[8]

What scholars from Tönnies to Putnam perceive as the quasi-magical glue holding communities together creates for Joseph an atmosphere that excludes those not fitting comfortably into the group's self-conception, and leads to the suppression of open discourse within the group, because critical voices might be considered a threat to the community's unity. Iris Marion Young had already voiced a similar criticism in 1986 by suggesting that rather than overcoming difference, the ideal of community actually cements prejudice and bias: "The desire for community relies on the same desire for social wholeness and identification that underlies racism and ethnic chauvinism, on the one hand, and political sectarianism on the other."[9]

This brief review shows clearly that scholarship on community—whether affirmative or critical—has focused consistently on the ideal of consensus and unity. It is also noticeable that in many of these theoretical accounts, the emphasis on cohesion goes hand in hand with the evocation of crisis. From the 19th century to the present, authors on the political left and right equally introduce their works by voicing concerns about the "state of community," which they perceive to be threatened by social and cultural change. Jean-Luc Nancy states 1983 in *The Inoperative Community* (*La communauté désœuvrée,* first transl. 1991):

> The gravest and most painful testimony of the modern world, the one that possibly involves all other testimonies to which this epoch must answer [...] is the testimony of the dissolution, the dislocation, or the conflagration of community.[10]

Nancy attributes this sentiment to the specific political climate at the end of the 20th century. However, a similar rhetoric has appeared repeatedly in discourses about community ever since the 19th century, even if the perceived reasons for this crisis change over time. For Tönnies, it is late 19th-century modern urban society which threatens the traditional community of the village. Almost a century later, Fredric Jameson describes the destructive effect capitalism has had on organic communities: "The historically unique tendential effect of late capitalism on all such groups has been to dissolve and to fragment or atomize them into agglomerations (Gesellschaften) of isolated and equivalent private individuals."[11] In 1991, Fowler explains why "modern communitarian thinkers"[12] (including himself) blame liberalism for the downfall of community: "Liberalism not only neglects our need for community, it is often downright hostile to it."[13] And at the turn to the 21st century, Putnam blames individualism in contemporary America for the decline of communal engagement.

The narratives that communities develop to define themselves often mirror this constant fear of a threat from the outside. In particular communities' founding myths tend to revolve around moments of crisis, as Joseph points out: "Communities are frequently said to emerge in times of crisis or tragedy, when people imagine themselves bound together by a common grief or joined through some extraordinary effort."[14] Yet, the evocation of a crisis is not limited to communities' myths of origin—in fact, a driving force behind ongoing narratives of community appears to be a recurrent threat or crisis.

This recurring narrative of community in crisis never fails to invoke, if sometimes implicitly, a (distant) past in which the cohesion of community was presumably given and secure. It is noticeable that unity and consensus never really appear as actual features of real-existing communities, but are usually introduced as a lost or fading ideal that is constantly under fire from outside threats. Nancy points out the problematic implications of such a narrative:

> But it is here that we should become suspicious of the retrospective consciousness of the lost community and its identity [...]. We should be suspicious of this consciousness first of all because it seems to have accompanied the Western world from its very beginnings: at every moment in its history, the Occident has given itself over to the nostalgia for a more archaic community that has disappeared, and to deploring a loss of familiarity, fraternity and conviviality.[15]

Rather than merely being a nostalgic sentiment, however, the evocation of crisis actually serves a crucial function for narratives of community, because it creates the sense that community is a threatened sanctuary in need of saving. By claiming that the spirit of community is in decline, the narrative of a constant crisis can actually work to establish and maintain continuity, while highlighting, in the face of a perceived threat, the importance of overcoming difference. Ultimately, then, the evocation of crisis has a stabilizing and unifying effect on the community.

At the same time, this permanent sense of crisis leads to an atmosphere in which any serious controversy within the community is treated as a threat to the cohesion of community. Unlike the threat from outside, which becomes a recurrent element of communities' self-narratives, internal conflicts are more likely to be suppressed or, in retrospect, downplayed or completely excluded from a community's history.

This stabilizing pattern of emphasizing external threats while suppressing internal conflict appears to emerge in a broad range of communities, but it is perhaps particularly crucial for social formations whose self-definition as community is based primarily on shared interests, communities that Tönnies describes as invisible townships:

> Thus, those who are brethren of such a common faith feel, like members of the same craft or rank, everywhere united by a spiritual bond and the cooperation in a common task. [...] [S]piritual friendship forms a kind of invisible scene or meeting which has to be kept alive by artistic intuition and creative will.[16]

While Tönnies doesn't explicitly rank these affinity-based communities lower than other forms of community, his statement that they have to "be kept alive" makes them appear fragile and vulnerable in comparison to other examples he employs, such as the "organic" familial household and the village. In the absence of stabilizing factors like biological kinship, spatial proximity, shared territory (like the village or the nation state[17]) or even a shared identity category (like the queer community Joseph describes), communities that are "based on affinity rather than identity"[18] appear more arbitrary in their composition, and thus are less likely to be seen as "natural" or necessary formations. It stands to reason that this perception might lead to a greater investment in securing the stability of the community by its members through a discourse that combines the insistence on internal cohesion with the reminder of an external threat.

Science-fiction Fandom as Literary Community

One such kind of invisible township held together by shared affinity are literary circles, some of which rely on spatial proximity (like local book clubs) while others have developed a practice of communicating across spatial distance. Into the latter category falls the literary science-fiction community, which from its early beginnings relied on letter-writing and the circulation of newsletters and fanzines to maintain a connection among its members. Despite the fact that literary communities appear to be bound together "merely" by their shared interest in literature and reading, literary circles have often been attributed major significance for the emergence of public discourse and civic participation in Western modern society. Theorists tend to see the shared act of reading as both an intellectual and a communal practice that fosters political and social awareness and engagement. For Jürgen Habermas, author of the influential 1962 *The Structural Transformation of the Public Sphere* (*Strukturwandel der Öffentlichkeit*, first transl. 1989), the Western-European bourgeois public sphere of the 18th century emerged from the culture of literary salons. He understood public communication as grounded in cultural consumption, and explained the emergence of the public sphere resulting from the increasing political engagement of an originally literary public.[19] In *Bowling Alone*, Robert Putnam attributed similar importance to reading circles in 19th-century America, which he credited with the proliferation of civic engagement: "From such groups and such moments were born the suffrage movement and numerous other civic-minded initiatives of the Progressive Era [...] by converting a solitary intellectual activity (reading) into one that is social and even civic."[20] In *Imagined Communities*, Benedict Anderson emphasized the importance of print-capitalism and the proliferation of newspapers in the 18th and 19th centuries for individuals' identification as citizens of a nation state. The nationwide consumption of newspapers is for Anderson a "mass ceremony" that

> is performed in silent privacy, in the lair of the skull. Yet each communicant is well aware that the ceremony he performs is being replicated simultaneously by thousands (or millions) of others of whose existence he is confident, yet of whose identity he had not the slightest notion.[21]

This idealized notion of intellectual reading circles as the foundation of national citizenship and a hearth of civic or political engagement stands in stark contrast to an equally widespread, much more skeptical perspective on social formations around the consumption of *popular* texts. T.W. Adorno and Max Horkheimer's early critique of mass culture in their 1944 *Dialectic of Enlightenment* (*Dialektik der Aufklärung*, first transl. 1972) depicted the consumers of popular culture as passive recipients and mindless victims of the ubiquitous culture industry. Decades later, readers of popular fiction are still frequently accused of apolitical affective irrationality.[22] While social formations dedicated to "serious reading" are considered birthplaces of political discourse, groups convening around what is considered "trivial consumption" have been deemed unreceptive to enlightened thought. In his article on Marxist influences in early science fiction, Sean Cashbaugh criticizes this academic attitude toward readers of popular literature, and remarks that "studies of the American literary Left frequently ignore lesser-known writers and less traditional forms, namely those of popular culture (including SF)." He suggests that "[w]hen scholars ignore such spaces of production and forms in studies of American leftist culture, casting them as marginal or ephemeral, large spheres of leftist cultural activity escape critical examination."[23] The insistence on an often arbitrary distinction between serious and trivial reading (with "trivial" frequently standing in as a synonym for "feminine," "lower-class," or "juvenile") allows scholars to ignore sites of political discourse simply because are associated with low or popular culture.

In response to this dismissive stance toward popular consumption, which continues to be perpetuated by both academic and public discourses, historiographers of fandom and fan studies scholars have worked (increasingly so since the 1990s) to highlight the sophisticated discursive practices, the efficient communication networks, and the communal spirit of fan communities. Liesbet Van Zoonen suggests that fan groups "rest on emotional investments that are intrinsically linked to rationality and lead to 'affective intelligence.'"[24] Her use of the term "affective intelligence" undercuts the distinction between "serious readers" and "popular consumers" and indicates that while their interests might be different, their discourses and practices of community formation are more similar than generally assumed. Thus, fan communities can fulfill a role very similar to that of the traditional middle-class reading circles in the 18th and 19th centuries. "We see fan communities as performing similar functions today, with the added value that they provide shared mythologies that can inspire acts of civic imagination,"[25] as Neta Kligler-Vilenchik explains.

This necessary and intentional active defense of fan communities has also meant, however, that much of fan studies scholarship and fannish historiography has followed the community-oriented pattern of dismissing internal conflicts in favor of a focus on consensus and cohesion. Derek Johnson laments that accounts of conflict and controversies have been mostly omitted from historiographies of fan communities:

> While early works like Bacon-Smith's *Enterprising Women* (1992) stressed unity within fan communities, Jenkins's *Textual Poachers* acknowledged rifts among fans, producers, and even other fans [...]. However, Jenkins too deflected attention from conflict and dissent, emphasizing the consensual [...]. As Jenkins later explained, he "accented the positive" to distance fandom from perceptions of it as immature, deviant, and ultimately immaterial to academic study [...].[26]

Camille Bacon-Smith's *Science Fiction Culture,* a monograph on 20th-century science-fiction fandom, is a good example for this take on fandom in fan studies scholarship, both in its focus on cohesion and in its narration of the founding myth of science-fiction fandom. Bacon-Smith describes the emergence of the science-fiction community in the early 20th century in a moment of socioeconomic crisis as a reaction to the lack of professional and social prospects young men in the United States faced in the aftermath of the Great Depression.[27]

> Those young men, raised to expectations of employment and status that the worldwide Great Depression took away, created in their clubs and organizations the complexly structured hierarchical forms of the corporate middle class to which they aspired.[28]

Bacon-Smith carefully analyzes the science-fiction community's cohesion-building strategies, both inward- and outward-facing, in her ethnography of fan conventions during the 1980s and 1990s. The strategies she discusses share noticeable similarities with the practices of "bonding" and "bridging" that Putnam describes only a couple of years later in *Bowling Alone*. She concedes, for example, that newer members may find it difficult to initiate change within fandom and are often met with resistance to new ideas, but argues that there is a good reason for the community's tendency to hold on to tradition:

While this inertia can be frustrating to new members in times of fast change in the world and the science fiction community, it does provide a base of continuity that transcends the memory of the individual and passes the traditions from generation to generation of incoming fans.[29]

Similarly, she argues that the fan community is justified to be concerned with maintaining the borders between members and non-members, particularly in convention spaces where their world intersects with other social groups: "A convention sharing space with outsiders must defend the boundaries of its realities more rigorously [...]. [A]ll conventions must provide a defended space for the playing out of events and the safe practice of community."[30] Her repeated use of the word "defend(ed)" implies that she sees the community's efforts of maintaining traditions and borders as an understandable reaction to an apparently real threat from outside. Just as Putnam sees the strategies of "bonding" and "bridging" as necessary for maintaining the unity and harmony of a community, Bacon-Smith justifies the science-fiction community's resistance to change and the exclusion of outsiders by stressing the significance of these strategies for fandom's continued survival as a community.

In this context, it is an important detail that Bacon-Smith's ethnographic study relies heavily on interviews with fans. This means that her account of the community's historical development is based to a large degree on eyewitness accounts and memories. In that regard, her monograph shares some similarities with other historical accounts of science-fiction fandom, many of which were written by community members, often prominent fans and/or authors, like Sam Moskowitz's *The Immortal Storm: A History of Science Fiction Fandom* (1954), Damon Knight's *The Futurians* (1977), and Lester Del Rey's *The World of Science Fiction, 1926-1976: The History of a Subculture* (1980).[31] The prevalence of published accounts of science-fiction fandom by fans likely is due to fans' proclivity for historiography and self-documentation as much as to the fact that fan communities were ignored as the subject of research by academic scholarship until fairly recently. These insider reports are detailed and deeply insightful because they demonstrate an intimate knowledge of the community, but they also tend to gloss over some of the intra-communal controversies within the fan community. Disagreements which at the time of their occurrence shook the fan community at its core are often granted barely a mention or dismissed as interpersonal antipathy. Following the general tendency to emphasize consensus in narratives about communities, fan studies scholarship on science-fiction fandom and historiographies of the fan community have in common that they tend to present fandom as more of a united front than it necessarily was.

Shifting the gaze away from traditional publications about fandom toward fan-produced materials, it is noticeable that the dominant outsider perspective on consumers of popular literature is quite at odds with readers' own understanding and explanation of their interests. Science fiction may only fairly recently have been accepted as a "serious" literary genre of noteworthy cultural and political impact, but since the emergence of science-fiction fandom in the early 20th century, its consumers have very consistently considered themselves serious readers and part of a highly intellectual community.

One likely consequence of this self-perception is the science-fiction fan community's remarkably prolific investment in publication, documentation, and historiography, which manifested in an immense archive of printed documents, including amateur press mailings, fanzines, newsletters, brochures, leaflets, pamphlets, guidebooks, and convention materials. Numerous publications such as Donald Franson's 1962 booklet *Some Historical Facts About Science Fiction Fandom*[32] demonstrate fans' early interest in historicizing their own community. The wealth of archival material available to scholars today is not only an indication of fans' eagerness to print-publish in the decades from the 1920s to the 1980s (and even later, beyond the rise of the internet), it also demonstrates the considerable significance fan collectors at the time attributed to the articles, illustrations, and conversations in fanzines when they chose to preserve them for future generations.

At the same time, the production and circulation of fanzines and other fan-produced publications in which fans engaged by writing, editing, reading, sharing, or collecting, was not simply a way to document and preserve the community's practices but also a significant communal practice itself that shaped fans' experience and understanding of participation in their community. Rather than (merely) a way of communicating across distance to keep the community alive, it was a practice that in itself created and sustained a sense of community. Invoking (perhaps coincidentally) Tönnies' concept of the invisible township, Camille Bacon-Smith describes science-fiction fandom as "a community whose geography exists primarily in the minds of its members";[33] however, this mental geography was in fact mapped out and thus shaped by the publications that science-fiction fandom produced, spanning decades and wide spatial distances.[34]

Therefore, the sustenance and maintenance of community was a dominant discourse in fanzine conversations throughout the decades. One continuous, easily recognizable pattern is the frequent oscillation between the idealization of consensus within fandom and the fear of an outside threat to that very same community. On the one hand, there is a heavy focus on the unifying power of science fiction that goes far beyond a simple shared pleasure drawn from a certain kind of fiction. In his speech at the Chicago Worldcon in 1940, guest of honor and science-fiction author Edward E. Smith described the science-fiction fan community as follows:

> It seems to me, then, that what brings us together and underlies this convention is a fundamental unity of mind. We are imaginative, but with a tempered, analytical imaginativeness which fairy-tales will not satisfy. We are critical— sometimes we have been called hypercritical. We are fastidious. We have a mental grasp and scope which does not find sufficient substance in the stereotyped, the cut-and-dried. We feel intensely, and we are not always either diplomatic or backward in putting our feelings into words, and sometimes into action.[35]

Smith justifies his emphasis on community cohesion by highlighting a notion of exceptionalism that understands fans not only as a group of people with similar literary interests but also as a specific type of human being. He is not alone in this perspective on fandom. In fact, especially fanzine articles from the 1930s and 1940s often speak about science-fiction fans as an avantgarde elite with the potential to significantly influence Western society, even as a superior type of human with qualities that surpass those of the general population: "Fans saw themselves as an elite cadre of science fiction literati, typically male, with the unique social authority and power associated with scientific knowledge."[36]

In later decades of the 20th century, this idea of science-fiction fans' superiority is not articulated quite as frequently and explicitly, but it does keep reemerging in fanzine conversations. In 1979, a group of fans proposed in their contribution to an APA-55 mailing that the government should have an interest in encouraging procreation among science-fiction fans: "What we said was that fans should be paid by the government to have children, so that intelligent women will not find it so unprofitable, moneywise and emotionally, to have children."[37] Of course, the classist trajectory of their argument, which calls for educated upper-/middle-class women to have more and for lower-class women to have fewer children, is not unique to fandom. However, the fact that they identify female fans as a group of well-educated professional women who should be encouraged to become mothers is certainly telling in its implications for the self-understanding of science-fiction fans at the time.

This insistence on shared mentality and superior intellect among science-fiction fans appears in fanzines side by side with the perpetual diagnosis of crisis that fandom appears to suffer from at any given time. As early as 1939, when self-organized science-fiction fandom in the USA was barely entering its second decade, Leslie A. Crouch expressed this experience of crisis, combined with a nostalgic look backwards, in an article called "The Good Old Days" in the fanzine *Ad Astra:*

> How long, dear readers of AD ASTRA, have you opened an S-F mag and in the readers' department saw letters with phrases like these: "Remember the good old days when so and so wrote whosis and whatsis on the whirliwig?"; and "The stuff you print today ain't as good as what you gave us in the good old days of '28, '29, '30"; and "Remember such and such and this and that? Why can't we have stories like those today?"[38]

Four decades later, another fanzine article once again gave voice to the perception of a community in crisis, albeit for different reasons. For Paul Abelkis in 1979, it was the growing popularity of science fiction in television and cinema that threatened to ruin science fiction's good name and drew readers away from the literature he considered serious science fiction:

> Science fiction is presently experiencing its gravest crisis ever; while most "sci-fi" enthusiasts / fans is too generous a term / are losing themselves in "Superman," S.W., and "Battlestar Booboobtica," few trufen[39] even realize what is occurring.[40]

Beyond this reiteration of internal unity vs. external threat, however, the fanzines and brochures from the early decades of science-fiction fandom also provide detailed insight into the internal conflicts within the group over time. Unlike scholarly accounts, which have tended to gloss over many of these internal controversies in favor of creating the image of a unified community, the immense archive of print materials left by science-fiction fans of previous decades has the significant benefit of providing a close look at the various conflicts and controversies within the community. Due to the countless conversations and debates in fanzines and amateur press publications led by numerous people across considerable spatial distances and over extended time periods, disputes within the community are painstakingly documented by those who witnessed them happening at the time of their unfolding.

Derek Johnson proposes that there are good reasons to pay closer attention to the role of controversy in fan communities, in particular at a point in time when fan studies has become a relatively stable field of research within media/cultural studies and is not constantly forced to justify its own existence. Media studies, he argues, "would benefit from more expansive theorizations of constitutive, hegemonic antagonisms."[41] However, when Johnson pushes for greater attention to the controversies within fandom, he is primarily concerned with the debates over different interpretations of cultural texts: "I propose that ongoing struggles for discursive dominance constitute fandom as a hegemonic struggle over interpretation and evaluation."[42] In contrast, this book focuses on the controversies within fandom that do not touch only on presumably fan-specific topics such as interpretations of fannish objects, but instead are concerned with the functioning and structure of the community itself. I propose that internal controversies, often neglected in fan historiographies, are precisely the moments which best reveal the discursive practices within a community, since they force members to engage in fundamental negotiations about issues of inclusion/exclusion and consensus/disagreement. This becomes clearly visible, for example, in Julian Dibbell's influential article "A Rape in Cyberspace" from 1993. Dibbell describes the case of an avatar in an online MOO[43] sexually assaulting other players within the game, and relates the heated discussion that erupted among the participants after the details of the incident became known:

> It's the story of a man named Mr. Bungle, and of the ghostly sexual violence he committed in the halls of LambdaMOO, and most importantly of the ways his violence and his victims challenged the 1000 and more residents of that surreal, magic-infested mansion to become, finally, the community so many of them already thought they were.[44]

At first, Dibbell's statement might bring to mind the familiar foundational narrative of a community that finds itself bonding during difficult times. However, it is important to note that the debate among MOO players in the wake of a sexual assault against several group members did not end in a shared consensus, but was rather full of vehement disagreement and unsolvable differences. And yet it ultimately led to the implementation of a complaint system allowing the group to deal with similar cases of inappropriate behavior in the future. So when Dibbell writes that Mr. Bungle's actions forced the members of LambdaMOO to come together as a community, he does not suggest that they closed ranks in the aftermath of an assault, but rather that this internal crisis forced the members of an already-existing group to think about solutions for a shared problem; that is, they were forced to think about the structure and organization of their own community, to define themselves as an organization, a constituency, a political body with specific responsibilities and powers. Thus, I would argue that it is precisely in the moments when a community's structures and beliefs seem to be questioned or shaken that they become visible the most clearly—and, in fact, might actually be shaped.

The Great Exclusion

If one trusts Lester Del Rey's account of the history of science-fiction fandom, the controversy that fans at the time referred to as the "Great Exclusion Act" was barely worth a mention. He describes the event in the following, rather dismissive way:

Long before the convention, feuding had broken out between some of the Futurians and others working to hold the affair. When the convention opened, some of the Futurians who had been most active—Pohl, Wollheim and Lowndes, among others—appeared; after considerable hassling, they were denied admittance by Moskowitz. This was blown up into a major action by many of the partisan fans.[45]

What Del Rey attributes in his throw-away comment to a merely personal feud, however, was at the time discussed in hundreds of articles and comments in various fanzines over several years, and was considered a matter of great significance for the future of science-fiction fandom. In a pamphlet with the title "The Futurians and New Fandom," published in 1939 by the Futurian Society, Robert W. Lowndes writes:

A short time ago a fan remarked to me his belief that the future of fandom would be settled here at this conference—either the Futurian way or the New Fandom way would prevail, once and for all. [...] Between Futurians and New Fandom stands a word—democracy.[46]

This grave statement, which interpreted the controversy around the "Great Exclusion" as nothing less than a fight over democracy itself, indicates that the people involved in the controversy considered it far more than a personal feud; in fact, they felt that it was closely tied to world-political matters at the time. This idea might very well have a somewhat megalomaniac ring to it, but becomes understandable if one considers the "Great Exclusion Act" not as an isolated event but in connection to two other concurrent developments, one fandom-specific and one of global political concern. On the one hand, the "Exclusion" happened within the context of a broader discussion among fans regarding the establishment of a permanent Worldcon organizing committee and the foundation of a nationwide science-fiction fan organization, both of which were geared toward making science-fiction fandom an established, unified, centralized organization, rather than the sprawling, growing, and ever-changing landscape of local clubs, chapters, and fanzines it was at the time. On the other hand, the controversy leading up to the "Exclusion" was very much influenced by the global political climate during the era of the National Socialists' rule in Germany at the beginning of World War II. The "Great Exclusion," therefore, was the result of a controversy over the political future of the 20th century as much as it was a negotiation over the organizational future of the fan community.

Ultimately, the event called the "Great Exclusion" was the high point of a controversy between two groups of fans that were both part of science-fiction fandom in the New York area during the late 1930s/early 1940s, but differed significantly in their internal organization as well as their perspective on fandom and politics. The mid–1930s saw much fluctuation and regrouping in the fannish landscape around New York due to both personal and ideological tensions that eventually culminated in the formation of two fan groups which proceeded to engage in a severely antagonistic back-and-forth over the following years. The tensions first came to a head at the 1937 Third Eastern Science Fiction Convention in Philadelphia,[47] when New York fan John Michel presented a now infamous speech with the title "Mutation or Death" (read aloud by his friend Donald Wollheim), in which he called for the political awakening of fandom. In this speech, he demanded that

> the Third Eastern Science Fiction Convention, shall place itself on record as opposing all forces leading to barbarism, the advancement of pseudo-sciences and militaristic ideologies, and shall further resolve that science fiction should by nature stand for all forces working for a more unified world, a more Utopian existence, the application of science to human happiness, and a saner outlook on life.[48]

The speech addressed the political climate in Europe, where the rise of fascism presented an increasingly imminent threat, but it also attacked the prevalent attitude toward politics and science in science-fiction fandom at the time. Hugo Gernsback's[49] professional science-fiction magazines had provided the point of origin around which self-organized science-fiction fandom had initially formed, and so the majority of fans seemed to more or less share the "largely apolitical, if not conservative"[50] mentality promoted by these magazines. Of course, the attribute "apolitical" is to be taken with a grain of salt: this dominant mindset, which Cashbaugh calls "Gernsbackian ideology,"[51] represented a modernist type of utopianism fueled by faith in technological and scientific progress, and grounded in a socially conservative and economically capitalist worldview. Fans outspokenly believed in the ideal of "American modernity," the "celebration of American corporate and industrial success";[52] they were "apolitical" mainly in the sense that they believed science, technology, and industrial capitalism to be objective and untainted by politics.

This attitude is precisely what John Michel took offense with in his explicitly political speech "Mutation or Death," which was met with much resistance and even outrage from other fans. The fallout over his presentation at the "Third Eastern" consequently led to the formation of the two groups that eventually became the major antagonists in the events around the "Great Exclusion." On one side of the controversy was the Queens Science Fiction League (QSFL), a New York–based science-fiction club which was headed at the time by the influential fans Will Sykora, James Taurasi, and Sam Moskowitz, and shortly after gave rise to the movement of New

Fandom. On the other side stood the group of Futurians around fans like Robert W. Lowndes, John Michel, and Donald Wollheim.

Their ideological differences were reflected already on the level of organizational structure. With clear bias, Del Rey later describes the QSFL as "a real club" led by "important fans," and the Futurians as "more like a group of friends,"[53] but despite his obvious partiality, his distinction nevertheless points to actual structural differences between the two groups. Like many clubs and chapters at the time, the QSFL had a rigid, hierarchical structure with official functions and protocols. In contrast, the Futurians purposefully rejected "the complexly structured hierarchical forms of the corporate middle class,"[54] which many science-fiction clubs at the time were modeled after. Instead, they preferred a much more loosely organized group structure, and even experimented with attempts at other forms of community-building like the "Futurian House," a commune of sorts in which several fans cohabitated in 1939.[55] While the members of New Fandom explicitly insisted on keeping politics out of science fiction, the Futurians believed that science-fiction fans, whom they saw as educated, future-oriented people, were responsible for taking an openly political stance against fascism. In their fanzines and pamphlets, the group was outspoken in their socialist leanings and frequently expressed concern over both the rise of fascism in Europe and the demonization of communism in the Western world. In 1938, the Futurians founded the "Committee for the Political Advancement of Science Fiction (CPASF)," about which founding member John Michel wrote:

> From the deliberations of this group were evolved these concrete resolutions: That the world is rapidly approaching an international crisis, the nature of which shall be armed conflict between the mutually antagonistic forces of Fascism and Democracy; That science-fiction fans, by the nature of their outlook as visionaries and speculators, are inevitably and vitally concerned in the future development of international affairs; [...] That science-fiction fans as progressive people must therefore lend their immediate aid to the cause of Democracy in an active and aggressive struggle to smash its enemies; That a committee be formed to rally, organize and direct science-fiction fans toward the fulfilment of that purpose.[56]

In its expression of intellectual elitism at least, this statement was actually fairly typical for the mentality of science-fiction fans at the time; yet many fans, like the members of QSFL, considered the pamphlet's particular political trajectory and rhetoric to be a betrayal of science-fiction fandom's core values, namely, the ideals of objective science and technological progress. The explicit introduction of politics (aka socialism) into fannish discourse was seen as a diversion and disruption of the community's cohesion. In fact, the Futurians' publications and activities, such as the foundation of the

CPASF, were considered such a threat that some members of the QSFL saw the need to start a counter-movement, the so-called New Fandom: "Fearful of the Wollheim-Michel clique, the dynamic young Moskowitz convinced Sykora of the need to create a counter force called 'New Fandom'"; with the self-declared purpose of saving "fandom from the former tyranny of Wollheim and Communism."[57]

The animosities between the two groups had had time to boil for a full year when the Fourth Eastern Science Fiction Convention[58] came around in 1938. At the convention, the organizing team, consisting mostly of New Fandom members, brought forth a motion to appoint themselves as the temporary planning committee for the First Worldcon, which was scheduled for 1939. Members of the Futurian fraction expressed their dissatisfaction with the process leading up to the decision: "Unless the majority is permitted to decide things for itself, then you do not have democracy regardless of what else you have."[59] In protest, they withdrew themselves from any activities related to the organization of the Worldcon. The situation remained tense during the following preparations for the convention, with the Futurians criticizing New Fandom's organizational style as undemocratic, while New Fandom members were concerned that the Futurians might plan to boycott or disrupt the Worldcon with their political agenda.

As a consequence, reports of the escalation at the convention itself vary greatly depending on the commentator's loyalties. What most convention reports in fanzines agree on is that six fans, all affiliated with the Futurians, attempted to enter the convention space and were rejected by the organizing committee, which resulted in a series of rather tumultuous encounters at and around the location. At some point, the organizers called the police, who appeared at least twice during the back-and-forth, although they never arrested anyone.

The bone of contention leading to the exclusion was a number of publications the Futurians had brought to the convention to distribute among fans, which included Lowndes' 1938 "Dead End"[60] about the suicide of a fellow science-fiction fan, and "An Amazing Story" about Gernsback's magazine *Amazing Stories*; a print version of British fan Douglas W.F. Meyer's speech "The Purpose of Science Fiction"; Upton Sinclair's literary review "Science-fiction Turns to Life," and Michel's pamphlet "The Foundation of the CPASF."[61] The convention organizers considered these materials political propaganda, which they had preemptively banned from the convention, and accused the Futurians of purposefully stirring up trouble. The Futurians, on the other hand, insisted that the materials they had brought were harmless and not meant as an affront to the organizing team. David Kyle, another fan who was loosely affiliated with the Futurians, took responsibility for the disagreement in 1989 and argued that it wasn't the Futurians' brochures that caused the exclusion, but a pamphlet of his own making with the headline "A Warning!,"[62] in which he called out the undemocratic leadership of New Fandom and criticized the Worldcon organizing team:

> I, for better or worse, was the trigger for the banning of those six fans from the meeting. I published the infamous "yellow pamphlet" which provoked the incident. It reflects the times in so many ways, both fannishly and internationally.[63]

Right after the convention, the organizers blamed the altercation on the Futurians' actions, insisting that their behavior at the convention had left them with no choice but to exclude them: "Wollheim and his compatriots were not expelled by New Fandom or anyone associated with the organization. They actually <u>expelled themselves</u>."[64] In contrast, Donald Wollheim, one of the banned Futurians, voiced suspicions that their exclusion hadn't been a spontaneous decision, but had actually been planned far in advance[65]; and in his later monograph, Sam Moskowitz admits that an exclusion had at least been discussed: "the triumvirate felt serious consideration should be given to excluding them."[66]

The exclusion from the Worldcon did not curb the feud between Futurians and New Fandom; quite the contrary, the tension between the groups was refueled by biting exchanges in fanzines and erupted in several personal encounters, like a QSFL meeting in early 1941, more than a year after the convention:

> Queens, January 5, 1941: A fist fight which ended with William S. Sykora lying on the floor brought the January meeting of the Queens Science Fiction League to a hasty end and precipitated a near riot. In a physical attempt to expel two invited guests, William S. Sykora and two aides—James V. Taurasi and Sam Moskowitz—found that their bullying tactics, engaged in without the knowledge or consent of the duly elected officers of the club, had backfired. The result was that the manager of the meeting hall turned the entire gathering, one of the largest yet, out into the streets.[67]

Contrary to Del Rey's account, the intensity of these interactions makes the controversy leading up to and surrounding the "Great Exclusion" appear as far more than just a result of personal dislike. The "Great Exclusion" pitched two groups against each other who were certainly part of the same community—the New York area science-fiction fandom—but differed considerably in regard to their political views, as well as their ideas about the right way to organize a fan community. On both sides, the controversy was noticeably framed in absolute terms. Their rhetoric in speeches and fanzine articles reflects both groups' conviction that nothing less than the future of fandom was at stake in the fight. Fandom, according to the message in both camps, needed to be "saved"—either from communism or an undemocratic dictatorship, depending on the side. Their controversy about the organization of fandom also gained an added urgency because it fell into a period when fandom was explicitly looking for ways to both solidify and expand the community's borders. The necessity to unify fandom in particular was a dominant theme in broader fannish discussions at the time, and it is reflected in writings by both Futurians and New Fandom members: both sides felt that coming to a consensus was crucial if fandom was to persist at all.

At Philcon[68] 1939, for example, Futurians and New Fandom clashed over the discussion of a national science-fiction organization, after New Fandom had proposed a constitution for this potential organization which the Futurians rejected as dictatorial:

> In the constitution [*sic*] which New Fandom will take as its law, NF openly declares its intention of controlling all stf dictatorially, of declaring who are fans and who are not, of 'preserving harmony in all the fan field' whether in or out of NF which means a declaration of war [...] on all fans who will not bow to the dictation of the unspeakable Trio.[69]

Of course, that the Futurians rejected New Fandom's proposed constitution of a national science-fiction organization didn't mean that their side did not equally long for a united fandom—in 1941, Damon Knight called for the foundation of a National Fan Federation in an article with the title "Unite or Fie":

> One of the queerest things about fandom which has to date come to my attention, during the year-and-two-months I have been a fan, is the fact that fandom as a whole, is not, and apparently has never been, organized for its own defense and welfare. It is obvious that a need for such an organization exists.[70]

The desire for a unified fandom also extended beyond the two parties involved in the feud. At the 1940 Worldcon in Chicago, Edward E. Smith alluded, in his aforementioned speech, to the controversy between Futurians and New Fandom precisely in order to appeal to fans' sense of unity:

> [N]ow, if as I believe, the basic causes of those local warfares have been elucidated, it should not be an impossible task to remove them. I hope not, for in such a group as ours, co-operation is, or should be, decidedly of the essence.[71]

And really, the following year, fans' repeated calls for a united national fan organization resulted in the foundation of The National Fantasy Fan Federation (N3F)—complete with a constitution, a president, a directorate, and an overseas bureau, geared at establishing relations with fan communities in other countries and thus unifying fandom beyond the national borders of the USA.

Still, the fight around the "Great Exclusion" indicates that fans differed greatly in their positions on how such cohesion should ideally be realized.

New Fandom believed in a stratified and hierarchical form of organization, in which decisions were to be made by appointed officials and committees, whose position would grant them the authority to speak for fandom as a whole. They also believed that the influx of socialist politics into fandom in the 1930s upset the consensus about a shared mindset among fans (the belief in technological and economic progress, and the objectivity of science) to the point where Worldcon organizers perceived the presence of the Futurians and their published materials as a threat to the cohesion of the fan community that needed to be contained, or rather excluded. The Futurians, on the other hand, were skeptical of the rigid organization that New Fandom envisioned and questioned the (un)democratic process of elections within the fan community. In this context, their exclusion from the Worldcon only seemed to prove their point that New Fandom members were heading toward a dictatorial rule of fandom which would eliminate processes of direct democracy from the community. But they, too, clearly hoped for fandom to stand with the anti-fascist movement as a united front, and for a national or even worldwide fan organization, even if they imagined its organizational structure in a different way.

The intense desire for the ideal of a united fandom did not come to rest with the foundation of N3F; indeed, it continued to reappear throughout the fandom's history. Donald Wollheim recounts a meeting with Will Sykora in the early 1950s, during which Sykora asked him to overcome their old differences and reconcile, so that they could "reorganize fandom, reorganize the clubs, and go out there and control fandom. […] Somebody should do it, somebody should, you know, *unite fandom*."[72] Sykora's proposal, addressed at his former antagonist, reflects the drive toward cohesion in the literary science-fiction community even years after the controversy between New Fandom and Futurians had long simmered out.

The Second Exclusion, or the Great Breen Boondoggle

From the very beginning, this desire for unity within the fan community, which seemed to foreclose the possibility of diverse standpoints, was noticeably at odds with another part of fandom's self-conception. Science-fiction fans' self-definition as an intellectually superior group of people implied an image of fans as enlightened, progressive, and tolerant—not the least because science-fiction fans saw themselves as misunderstood by society and therefore had a certain immediate sympathy toward outsiders and misfits. This expectation of tolerance and open-mindedness tended to clash with the longing for a community that shared the same convictions and beliefs. In a fanzine-based letter exchange between two fans in 1964, this tension became visible in yet another argument over the presence of socialist fans in the community. Science-fiction fan John Boston reacted with heavy sarcasm to a previous statement by Edward Bryant, who had demanded the exclusion of socialist-leaning fans from the science-fiction community:

> According to Ed Bryant, a member should be kicked out if he should be kicked out [*sic*] if he shows "overt signs of the Communist faith." This fatuously vulgar asininity is exemplary of the bigotry that fandom is usually free from. [...] One of the most desirable features of fandom and the N3F is the relatively free exchange of ideas among its members.[73]

This correspondence shows not only that 25 years after the "Great Exclusion," communism was still a controversial issue within science-fiction fandom, but also reveals the double-sided face of a community that on the one hand was concerned with maintaining the cohesion of a spatially spread-out community of affinity, and on the other hand prided itself in being open-minded and progressive.

In 1964, the very year Bryant and Boston discussed censorship and communism in a fanzine letter exchange, another major conflict within science-fiction fandom also put a spotlight on the tension between the conflicting ideals of tolerance and consensus. This controversy went down into fannish history as "The Second Great Exclusion," a clear reference to the "Great Exclusion Act" of 1939. Even though at first glance, the two events don't seem to have all that much in common, in fannish discourse the two events became very much linked as different variations of the same communal issues: the question of in-/exclusion, the problem of authority, and the price to be paid for the community's unity.

While the "Great Exclusion" has occasionally been downplayed by historiographers of fandom, the "Second Great Exclusion" has barely received any mention at all in historical accounts of science-fiction fandom. This may have to do with the sensitive nature of the conflict, or possibly also with the fact that from the distance of several decades, the conflict shines a somewhat unflattering light on the picture of the united, but tolerant fan community that is often painted by historiographers of fandom. Within the recent history of science-fiction fandom, the controversy around the "Second Great Exclusion" did not really become a public topic of debate until 2014, and only indirectly, when Walter Breen's daughter Moira Greyland came forward to accuse her late mother Marion Zimmer Bradley of child abuse.[74] But even the following discussion revolved primarily around Zimmer Bradley's role in the case, with Breen remaining an afterthought. This omission of Breen's role from the historiography of science-fiction and fantasy fandom is even more remarkable considering that two other communities affected by the scandal, the Pagan community and numismatic circles, have made admittedly sparse but at least explicit attempts at working through the problematic aspects of their history with the Breen case.[75]

The controversy revolved around Walter Breen, an active and well-connected member of the fan community in the Berkeley area. Breen participated in science-fiction fandom as a writer, coordinator, and editor of the fanzine FANAC[76]; he later gained additional influence through the growing fame of his wife, fantasy author Marion Zimmer Bradley, whom he married in 1964. They moved to Staten Island in 1968, where they joined the New York area fan community.[77] At the same time, Breen was involved in several other affinity communities: he was a passionate coin collector with a considerable reputation among the numismatic community; through his wife he became involved with the Pagan community; and he moved in circles with an interest in "greek love," that is, sexual relationships between men and young boys. It was this latter proclivity that led to the controversy remembered in fandom as the "Second Great Exclusion." Among science-fiction fans on the West Coast who interacted with Breen on a regular basis, it appears to have been fairly common knowledge that Breen was not only preoccupied with the theme of pederasty in his writings and his correspondence,[78] but also acted on these desires continuously and frequently.[79] In 1964, the discussion about Breen in the Berkeley fan community gained enough urgency that Bill Donaho, himself a well-known fan and member of the approaching Pacificon II's organizing committee, felt it necessary to write a long letter with the title "The Great Breen Boondoggle,"[80] recounting in detail the controversy around Breen's behavior toward children in science-fiction fandom. Donaho discusses several incidents involving Breen and different children (of which four are identified by name and several others are mentioned in passing), as well as the respective parents' reactions, which seem to have ranged from simply telling their children to keep their distance to banning Breen from their homes. The purpose of Donaho's letter was to gather opinions and advice from a group of friends on how to deal with Breen in regard to his presence at the upcoming convention and within fandom in general. It is apparent that Donaho himself didn't claim to know how to handle the situation. He brought up several options, which included informing the police, letting parents handle the issue themselves as they saw fit, and excluding Breen from fandom by banning him from clubs and conventions, including the upcoming Pacificon II. The document was addressed merely to a number of friends, accompanied by the explicit disclaimer: "This article is most emphatically a Do Not Print, Do Not Quote and Most Especially Do Not Blab My Name When You Mention This Letter Substitute." It may speak to the efficiency of science-fiction fans' communication channels that the letter nevertheless circulated among a much larger group of fans rather quickly so that "The Great Breen Boondoggle" became a hot topic in the wider fan community.

Two organizations took action against Breen in reaction to Donaho's report, and in both cases, their measures were met with very mixed reactions. In the decision that gave the "Second Great Exclusion" its name, the Pacificon II organizing committee did indeed decide to ban Breen from attending the conference. They were concerned that they might be held liable if Breen's behavior at the convention would prompt someone to press charges. The committee set a hearing to which Breen didn't appear, then proceeded to distribute a mailing to inform the fan community of the reasons for the exclusion. To protest this decision, eight fans announced that they would boycott the Worldcon,[81] and at the convention itself, supporters and critics of Breen got into a physical altercation that strongly resembles the brawls between Futurians and New Fandom 25 years earlier:

> In what has been _inaccurately_ described as a fistfight but was actually a shoving, wrestling, and (on the Schwenn woman's part) a clawing match, Bob grabbed her wrists to keep her from scratching him any more. […] Things calmed down at last—in part because the people standing close kept the struggle from spreading by neither joining in nor letting anyone near who might like to join in—and HaLevy finally persuaded the trio to leave.[82]

Shortly after the Pacificon committee announced their decision, a number of FAPA members also signed a "blackball" that effectively removed Breen from the FAPA membership waitlist and prevented him from joining the amateur press association. This blackball, however, was overturned almost immediately via two petitions launched by other FAPA members who opposed Breen's exclusion.

The actions taken against Breen and the subsequent counter-actions show clearly how much the Breen issue divided the fan community. And just like the "First Great Exclusion," the "Second Exclusion" was controversial not merely because of its subject matter—whether Breen was guilty of the things he had been accused of, and if so, whether this warranted any kind of action from the side of fandom—but also because of the communal procedures and practices employed in the process.

Many felt there was plenty of evidence to show that Breen had molested children, although not everyone agreed on how to react: "As I said in SAPS last week, I am convinced that enough evidence exists to convict Walter Breen of child molestation, were those in possession of the evidence willing to put it forward."[83] But there were also a considerable number of fans who doubted the truth of the accusations. Even among those who admitted that Breen didn't make a secret out of being attracted to children, not everyone wanted to believe that he had actually acted on those desires, like Breen's fellow scientologist Prentiss Choate:

> So Walter Breen is attracted to children. What of it? A damn sight more of us have sexual attractions to children than we normally admit to each other or even to ourselves. The entire issue is, how much does a person have <u>control</u> over his impulses? And, in all the dirt that has flied so thick, I don't recall ever hearing Walter accused of molesting a child in the face of express disapproval on the part of the child, parents, or anyone else close to the scene.[84]

The sides in this controversy were anything but clear-cut and, as many fans pointed out, did not necessarily run along political lines of left-wing/right-wing. Still, the sociopolitical climate in mid–1960s America clearly influenced fans' reactions. On the one hand, the experience of McCarthyism and the denunciatory tendencies that came with it had made many fans reluctant to trust accusations of a certain kind against members of the community. On the other hand, public and medical discourses in the 1960s falsely tended to equate homosexuality with pedophilia/pederasty, and science-fiction fandom was no exception in this regard. Therefore, fans' opinion of Breen's actions was often influenced by their attitude toward homosexuality—some fans who deemed themselves progressives defended Breen because they saw him first and foremost as a homosexual or bisexual man; others critiqued him harshly not primarily for abusing children, but for openly displaying his presumed homosexuality.

Noticeable is that the vast majority of fans were clearly very reluctant to involve the authorities, and highly critical of Bill Donaho and Alva Rogers' decision to approach the Berkeley police with their collected evidence (which apparently did not convince the police to take action). Fans were concerned that drawing the authorities' attention to Breen would also draw unwanted attention to the fan community in general and the Worldcon in particular—in their statement on the Breen case, Richard Brown and Dave Van Arnam pointedly retitled Pacificon II "Copcon."[85] The fan community had a vested interest in not becoming subject to the scrutiny of the police, a concern that was tied to the reputation of fans outside their community. While fans themselves might have considered themselves intellectually superior to the average citizen, the general public tended to perceive them as "freaks." In addition, there were occasional worries about materials distributed in fan mailings being affected by obscenity laws, such as fanzines featuring drawings of (half)naked women on covers and in illustrations. Fan conventions were also a place where fans might have extramarital sexual encounters, another reason why police presence at conventions would have been unwelcome. In addition, it appears that in the late 1950s some prominent fans were in fact investigated by the FBI regarding a potential affiliation with communism.[86]

The concern about potential negative consequences for the fan community apparently outweighed the arguments in favor of turning Breen over to the authorities. Overall, it is clear that fans saw the Breen problem as an internal issue that should be solved, one way or another, by the fan community itself. But while the community seemed to be united in the desire to handle this problem within the community, they were far from reaching an agreement on what the community should do. First, fans argued over whether this matter should be of any concern to the fan community at all. Some fans suggested that Breen should not be penalized by the community as long as his digressions didn't relate to specifically fannish matters, among them Richard Bergeron, who spoke out against the FAPA blackball: "On the basis of past performance I cannot see how Breen can do anything but make FAPA more stimulating. [...] I do not see how a person's personal life will have any effect on my enjoyment of his membership in FAPA."[87] Others refused to consider such a separation of fannish and non-fannish life: "I see no basis whatsoever for an attitude that proclaims someone unacceptable in one facet of society—the In Person facet—and perfectly all right in another facet, the Correspondence facet—the amateur presses."[88]

The more urgent question for many fans, however, was the question of whether, and under what circumstances, a committee like the Worldcon organizing committee or the FAPA leadership had the right to exclude members based on what they considered a danger to the community. Even those who attempted to remain neutral on the topic of Breen's guilt (because they did not feel informed enough) usually had an opinion about the representative rights and duties of committees within the fan community. The most adamant defenders of Breen were very critical of both the convention committee and the FAPA board's decision to exclude Breen. Brown/Van Arnam called for the convention committee to resign, claiming that they had somehow shirked their responsibility to the community by banning Breen from the convention.[89] For Breen's defenders, the convention committee had done injustice not only to Breen, but more importantly, to the community as a whole: Choate blamed the committee for having "driven many people away from the convention and caused a deep rift in fandom both locally and nationally that is likely to be very slow in healing"[90]; Rusty Hevelin raised his voice to "say that it has not been established that the best interests of fandom and the convention are served by revoking the membership of any given fan in a convention society."[91]

Other fans, whether they believed in Breen's guilt or not, defended the committee's right to exclude people from the convention if there was any reason to assume that perhaps they might cause difficulties for the convention or the fan community as a whole.

> [A]s far as that specific statement of the power of the Committee goes, I'm all for it. In fact, I can't see that there is any question about the point. The Convention Committee is responsible for the convention; therefore it has the power to run the convention and to remove anyone who proves undesirable. The question in this case is whether or not the Pacificon Committee misused its authority; that it had the authority is demonstratable fact. The Con Committee is chosen by fandom to run the convention. Once chosen, they are in charge.[92]

Others again were fine with the convention committee's decision to ban Breen, but used the occasion to question the blackball amendment in the FAPA constitution, which stated that if ten members opposed the admittance of another fan, that fan would automatically be taken off the waitlist.

Chuck Hansen, albeit hesitant to make any statements about Breen's guilt, had insisted on the committee's right to exclude Breen from the convention for liability reasons. He was equally clear that he felt the blackball was within the official rules of the FAPA constitution: "The cold facts are that the Fapa blackball was not monstrous, unethical, nor immoral. It was a perfectly decent, ethical legal act under the Fapa constitution."[93] But he went on to say that perhaps the concept of the blackball rule in itself was flawed and should be reconsidered:

> Personally I do not feel that it is very democratic that the vote of such a small minority of the membership can reject an applicant. I have considered submitting an amendment to require a majority of the membership for this purpose.

In the end, despite the fact that many fans seemed to feel uneasy about Breen's presence in fandom and supported the convention committee's decision to ban him from attending Pacificon II, the fallout from the "Great Breen Boondoggle" became so dramatic that Bill Donaho felt the need to publish an official apology for plunging fandom into uproar in August 1964:

> The Pacificon II committee has cancelled the membership of Walter Breen. The committee feels this to be a necessary and desirable action. But it could have been done differently. It should have been done differently. [...] I should not have published the BOONDOGGLE. [...] The BOONDOGGLE was essentially true of course. But that's no excuse. [...] Let's look at it from a purely practical point of view for a moment. We are going to get nowhere. [...] There are too many people on both sides. And leave [sic] us face it, some of our best friends are evial [sic] monsters on the other side. Some friendships are already irreparably [sic] gone. Let's don't [sic] send any more down the drain.[94]

Donaho's public apology shows that even those who had initially pushed for Breen's exclusion from fandom came to feel that his exclusion was not worth the toll the controversy had taken on the community. Restoring the harmony of the community as fully as possible ultimately appeared to take priority over the best solution for the Breen problem. Since it seemed impossible to resolve the controversy to everyone's satisfaction, the only reasonable solution for Donaho was to simply put the matter to rest and move on. Consequently, Breen remained an active member of the fan community for the following decades.

Conclusion

From today's perspective, the "Great Exclusion" and the "Breen Boondoggle" might not intuitively seem to offer themselves up for comparison. However, the two events highlighted similar aspects of science-fiction fandom's understanding of community. Sam Moskowitz, one of the major players in the "Great Exclusion" of 1939, drew a direct connection between the two events when he wrote a retrospective piece about Pacificon II and the Breen controversy from the distance of several decades in 1989:

> This [that is, Breen's exclusion from the convention] opened up a new perspective on the action taken by the committee of The First World Science Fiction Convention in 1939 in barring six Futurians from entry for fear, "with overwhelming cause," that they might disrupt the convention.[95]

As a convention organizer who had faced criticism for excluding the Futurians from the convention in 1939, he now suggested that if Breen's exclusion in 1964 had been justified, then surely that meant the Futurians' exclusion in 1939 had been the right thing to do as well: in both cases, the convention committee had claimed to act with the community's best interest in mind, since they were primarily concerned about potentially disruptive occurrences in the convention space. Regardless of whether one agrees with Moskowitz' conclusion, his argument indicates that the fan community perceived both cases as examples that raised questions regarding the organizational and representational structure of the community: What was in the best interest of the community as a whole? Who had the right to speak for the community? And how far did their authority ultimately reach? Even though the heated controversies in both cases demonstrated that these questions were highly contested territory over decades of fannish history, their negotiation in fanzines showed that the "common good" and the unity of the community were often given priority over the rights of individual members. This does not mean that fans necessarily agreed on what was best for the community, merely that their argumentation was usually grounded in communitarian rather than individualist ideals.

This ideal of community continued to have consequences for the negotiation of different conflicts within the science-fiction community, and ironically the focus on community cohesion is what ultimately caused part of the community to effectively split off from literary science-fiction fandom in the early/mid–1970s. The 1960s saw an increase in television programs and films with science-fiction themes, which led to what Paul Abelkis in 1979, as mentioned earlier in this chapter, called fandom's "gravest crisis ever." Around the same time, female writers like Joanna Russ and Ursula Le Guin started to develop a specifically feminist tradition within science-fiction literature, all the while female fans began pushing for a more inclusive atmosphere in the fan community. Up to that point, fandom had certainly accepted women as participants (often the wives and girl-friends of male fans), but had not taken them into consideration as equal members of the community, as comments like the following convention report from 1974 show:

> But doesn't the New Orleans group know that people's wives go to the convention—they must have noticed that not all the people at sf cons are male. That's a really male chauvinist attitude—I'm astonished anyone in fandom believes that sort of thing any longer. After all, aren't fans supposed to be more enlightened than other people?[96]

Both the influx of new fans thanks to the appeal of multimedia franchises like *Star Trek*[97] and *Star Wars*[98] and the noticeable effects of second-wave feminism on fandom were seen by many fans as threats to the unity of the community. The refusal to bring politics into fandom (already a driving force in the "Great Exclusion") became a common argument again in fandom's criticism of women who attempted to introduce feminism into science-fiction fandom. In reaction to what he perceived as a forced politicization of Iguanacon 1978, Matt Hickman wrote:

> This letter is to vent my spleen on the matter of Harlan Ellison's[99] attempt to politicize the Worldcon and the boycott being instituted by the pro ERA-groups against the individual States that have not ratified the "Equal Rights Amendment."[100]

Hickman made it clear that whatever his opinion of the issues at stake, he did not think the Worldcon should be a place for politics, and that the organizing committee did not have the right to decide otherwise: "The Worldcon is not the property of the Guest of Honor, nor of the Worldcon Committee, it belongs to the membership." This resistance in the fan community both against those with an interest in science-fiction/fantasy-themed cinema and television, and those concerned with women's rights ultimately led to the emergence of a new fan community.[101] The female-dominated "media fandom" combined the interest in television and movie franchises with an investment in inclusionary politics and thus offered an environment for those who felt alienated and excluded by the rigid borders of literary science-fiction fandom. The programmatic statement of the *Star Trek/Star Wars* media zine *Organia*, for example, names feminism as an explicit concern: "Feminism is a strong concern throughout the zine, not just in the short Feminist section. Much of the fiction and poetry in the zine focusses [*sic*] on women or is told through the eyes of women."[102]

The community of media fandom, which over the decades developed into what is now most often talked about as transformative online fandom, will be the focus of the following chapter. We will see that in splitting off from traditional, male-dominated literary science-fiction fandom, media fans did not simply reproduce the organizational structures, the discursive practices, nor the ideals of community that drove the science-fiction community over decades and in some ways are still driving it today. Transformative online fandom is dominated by a very different concept of community and public discourse, as well as a different notion regarding the relationship between community and individual. This shows that any general/universalizing theoretical approach to fan communities has its serious limitations, since there are significant differences between fan groups based on their historical and cultural contexts, demographic structure, and communal self-conception. While Calkins' statement about the literary science-fiction community was an accurate description of 1960s science-fiction fandom, it cannot be applied automatically to any fan organization: not every fan community considers itself an "entity, something to be cherished, protected and prolonged at all cost."

2

"For the first time, we got to do some shouting back"

RaceFail '09, or: Journal-Based Fandom as Alternative Public Sphere

Introduction

> Hell, I'm one of the _black_ people who thought at first that the Internet was proving to be a bad place for this discussion to happen. But I changed my mind. Having it via the Internet gave us (people of colour and allies in SF/F[1] community) gave us [sic] numbers. It let us see each other. For the first time in this community, we weren't isolated voices which could easily be shouted down. For the first time, we got to do some shouting back.—Nalo Hopkinson, January 21, 2010

This comment by Jamaican American science-fiction author Nalo Hopkinson was written in response to an opinion piece published by Black fantasy author N.K. Jemisin on her blog under the title "Why I Think Race-fail Was the Bestest Thing Evar for SFF."[2] Both Jemisin's blog post and Hopkinson's response refer to a debate which caused considerable uproar in a not-so-small corner of the internet in early 2009. The events surrounding RaceFail '09, as the debate was dubbed by participants and observers, involved professional and amateur creators, critics, and academics, but most importantly countless readers and fans of speculative fiction. The debates around RaceFail '09 played out along lines that put different groups in opposition to each other, although the demarcations between these groups were not always clear-cut. Most commonly, RaceFail '09 was framed as a controversy between (white) writers and fans (of color). But as the debate unfolded, a deep rift also opened between professional writers and their affirmative fans on one side, and amateur creators and transformative fans on the other.

Over the course of about five months, thousands of participants talked about the role of race and racism in science-fiction and fantasy literature, in fandom, and in the publishing industry. RaceFail '09 engaged with race on several discursive levels, including the representation of race and ethnicity in popular media, the global distribution of cultural capital, and the industrial structures of cultural production; but RaceFail '09 also sparked a heated discussion about access to the hegemonic public sphere and the rules of public discourse.

The large number of overviews, summaries, and link collections about RaceFail '09, many of which are still accessible online, bear witness to the efforts participants put into archiving and documenting the debate, and thus to the importance they attributed to the discussion. Since the debate progressed over several months, involved so many actors, and was conducted in countless blogs posts and comment threads that often cross-linked and referenced each other, it is almost impossible to trace this conversation in a clear linear order. Most participants attempting to provide a chronologically or thematically structured overview introduced it with a disclaimer or apology for inevitably failing to do justice to the complexity of the discussion: "RaceFail is a decentralized internet conflict, and thinking about it in terms of sides, timelines, or threads are all (sometimes necessary) simplifications."[3] The hypertextual complexity of RaceFail '09 is one important reason for the lack of a consistent linear chronology; another is the fact that the discussion occurred outside of the framework of established institutions that would have had the normative power to install a dominant narrative.

What made RaceFail '09 so significant was, first, that it was in all likelihood the first conversation on race in the field of cultural production that directly and immediately involved this many people from so many different backgrounds speaking to each other at the same time. Rukmini Pande suggests that the involvement of professional writers in particular was significant because "it marked the first time in online fandom's history when SF/F's racist and imperialist characterizations were debated in a forum where authors and editors of SF/F magazines and journals had to engage with those questions."[4]

Second, while RaceFail '09 certainly leaked into offline fannish spaces such as fan conventions, the conversation itself was led almost exclusively online, most prominently on the journal-based social networking platform LiveJournal. In this chapter, I argue that it was not simply *possible* to have this conversation on social networking platforms, but rather that it was precisely these platforms which made the discussion possible in the first place. More specifically, it was the intersection between the cultural practices of transformative fandom on the one hand, and the communication technology of journal-based platforms on the other that led to the emergence of an alternative public sphere which facilitated fans' engagement with political discourse. Furthermore, the distinct discursive practices within this alternative public also encouraged fans to question and critique the conditions and rules of said discourse by interrogating the binaries that stabilize dominant public spheres, such as the dichotomies of public/private or political/personal.

In Chapter 1, I showed how the literary science-fiction community emerged in the early 20th century as an affinity community whose communal practices involved not only the creation and consumption of speculative fiction, but also the production, circulation, and collection of fanzines and other fan-made written materials. This fan group was influenced by a communitarian ideal that prioritized the unity of fandom and consensus among the community over the interests of individual members.

In this chapter, I contrast the understanding of community that dominated early/mid–20th century science-fiction fandom with the self-conception of online journal-based transformative fandom in the first decade of the 21st century. This more recent fannish formation is a more or less direct successor of so-called media fandom—the fan community that developed out of, or rather split off from literary science-fiction fandom in the late 1960s/early 1970s.[5] Much of established literary science-fiction fandom at the time was suspicious of televisual and cinematic sci-fi–themed texts such as *Star Trek*, and many traditional science-fiction fans were similarly critical of a feminist tradition that was emerging within science fiction around the same time. Consequently, many fans of televisual, cinematic, and soft or feminist science fiction organized themselves in alternative fannish circles which quickly grew into the large network known as "media fandom," in reference to these fans' interest in "media" (aka television and film) as opposed to "literature." With the transition of media fandom to the internet in the 1980s/1990s, and the subsequent shift toward journal-based platforms, the term media fandom was increasingly replaced by other names such as "online fandom," "transformative fandom," or simply "fandom," terms which in practice were often used interchangeably.

As I argue in this chapter, transformative online fandom entertains an understanding of public discourse and community that is distinctly different from the community of literary science-fiction fandom in the mid–20th century. In contrast to the more stratified and rigidly organized structure of literary science-fiction fandom, and its emphasis on community consensus, transformative online fandom promoted the ideal of a non-hierarchical, inclusionary, unregulated alternative public sphere, in which the ethical principles of consensus-building have to be constantly renegotiated. With the increasing presence of political discourse in journal-based online fandom, fannish identity also became (re)conceptualized as a quasi-political identity, a distinct difference from traditional science-fiction/fantasy fandom's attempts at keeping "politics" out of fandom.

As in Chapter 1, the focus here is less on the relationship between fan and text (including the creative-transformative practices fans engage in) and instead directed at the discursive practices as well as the processes of community formation and consensus-building among fans. Rather than perpetuate the notion of transformative fandom as a cohesive community, I highlight the points of conflict and controversy that provide insight into the self-understanding of transformative fandom, and into the dominant notions of community that circulate in these fannish spaces. Race-Fail '09 was one such controversy that severely tested the ties holding the public of transformative fandom together. Pande points out that the issue of race in particular tends to cause conflicts and tensions within fan communities; not only because of the different actors and opinions involved, but also because many fans consider it a political topic that does not have a space within fannish discourse in the first place. Therefore, "any discussion of race becomes an exception, an interruption, and a bringer of fandom drama."[6]

I draw on the theoretical discourse around the concept of the public sphere, which experienced a revival in the 1990s when the internet became increasingly accessible to the general public, in order to make two arguments. First, I propose that transformative online fandom can and should be conceptualized as an alternative public sphere, and that an understanding of fandom as alternative public aligns with transformative fans' self-conception of their own community. I argue that fans' understanding of their fannish spaces as alternative public sets them apart from traditional science-fiction fandom and its self-identification as a unified community.

Second, I propose that while the alternative public sphere of transformative fandom demonstrates the potential to alleviate or even overcome some of the limitations of the Habermasian model of the liberal public sphere, conflicts such as RaceFail '09 also show that transformative fandom's inclusive potential remains an ideal which fandom aspires to without having been able to fully realize it.

The Internet and the Public Sphere

In his 1962 work *The Structural Transformation of the Public Sphere* (*Strukturwandel der Öffentlichkeit*, first transl. 1989),[7] Jürgen Habermas declared the death of the autonomous bourgeois public sphere as a result of the way public opinion had been increasingly co-opted and commercialized by mass media conglomerates throughout the 20th century. In the 1990s,[8] however, the concept of the public sphere experienced a renewed interest, in particular from scholars at the intersection of media studies and political theory.[9] The emergence of Usenet (1980) and the World Wide Web (1991) inspired both enthusiasm and fears regarding the new technology's implications for concepts such as citizenship, participatory democracy, and public discourse. Internet optimists saw the WWW as a medium that would not only make possible a rebirth of the autonomous public sphere, but would also be able to do away with some of the limitations of the 18th-century bourgeois public sphere that Habermas had described in his work.

Habermas' account of the bourgeois public had gained a far-reaching influence in various academic fields, but also inspired fundamental criticisms from different sides.[10] A major point of contention was Habermas' idealization of the bourgeois public sphere as an ideal model of communicative rationality and deliberative democracy, that is, an inclusive space that allowed all citizens to participate equally in the negotiation of public opinion. His critics suggested that by downplaying the categorical exclusion of several groups from the liberal public sphere (in particular the working classes, the poor, and women), Habermas obscured the fact that the bourgeois public defined the "universal" citizen as male, white, of age, and economically independent,[11] and thus was hegemonic rather than universal in nature. Indeed, the supposedly inclusive public sphere not only functioned as a tool of class, gender, and racial distinction, but actually *depended* on those mechanisms of exclusion in order to function.[12] The distinction between the spheres of "the public" and "the private" in particular was used to justify the structural exclusion of women because of their association with the (private) domestic sphere,[13] and the exclusion of workers because of their association with the (private) realm of labor.[14] Habermas' critics also pointed out that, contrary to his ideal of a nationwide homogenous public, disadvantaged groups often formed alternative publics throughout history, such as proletarian[15] and women's public spheres[16] as well as Black[17] or queer counterpublics.[18] Furthermore, Habermas' focus on rational, objective discourse as the language of the liberal public sphere not only privileges those with access to education but also frequently devalues the opinions of non-hegemonic groups: "[I]t is a strategy of distinction, profoundly linked to education and to dominant forms of masculinity."[19] Last but not least, his narrative of the public sphere's decline as a consequence of mass media can be understood as a dismissal of popular tastes and audiences that reflects the anxieties of a cultural elite concerned with their seeming loss of influence throughout the 20th century.

At least initially, the internet seemed to hold the promise of a democratic mass medium that would not only refute the cultural pessimism of the Frankfurt School regarding the alleged decline of the public sphere in the 20th century, but would also be able to overcome the limitations of the historical bourgeois public sphere. The low access barriers,[20] the increased possibilities for networking across distances, and the flat, non-hierarchical structure of online communication brought forth decentralized publication models, an increasingly blurry producer/consumer divide, and a proliferation of collective authorship. These changes in the fields of cultural production and interpersonal communication made the internet appear as a technology that facilitated equal participation in the public sphere, even beyond the borders of the nation state.[21]

At the same time, other scholars suggested that it was impossible to productively apply the Habermasian concept of the public sphere to online spaces because the historical, political, and technological conditions of publicity had changed too dramatically between the 18th and the late 20th century. Since Habermas' description of the 18th-century bourgeois public sphere was based on the assumption of a nation state with a (more or less) clearly defined constituency of citizens, they argued, his definitions of citizenship and publicity failed to adequately describe a contemporary political landscape shaped by globalization and hypercapitalism.[22] Still others focused on the difference between face-to-face conversations (as Habermas described them in his account of 18th-century European salons and coffeehouses) and the virtual nature of online communication. Some suggested that online communication was inferior to face-to-face interactions and therefore a hindrance to rational discourse and consensus-building[23]; while others felt that in fact it far surpassed the possibilities of traditional forms of communication and therefore required the introduction of new theoretical concepts and a new terminology.[24]

Looking back at this debate almost three decades later, a considerable weakness in both positions was the attempt to essentialize the internet as a cohesive entity that would either perfectly fulfill the requirements for an autonomous public sphere, or would have to abandon the concept of communicative consensus-building entirely. This tendency to conflate the distribution technology with the social structures that both emerge from and shape technological innovation hindered a productive analysis of actual communicative processes in online spaces.

Since the 1990s, the diversification and commercialization of the internet (with all its accompanying developments in interpersonal communication, publishing, data storage, state surveillance, commerce, finance, culture, sex work, gaming, and online activism) have made it more, rather than less problematic to think of the internet's function, its mechanisms, and effects as entirely homogenous. Therefore, any working concept of the internet needs to take into account its decentralized multiplicity. While the internet does not automatically constitute a public sphere in itself, there is no reason why it should not be possible for public spheres *to emerge in online spaces*. Of course, these publics cannot be simply reproductions of the Habermasian 18th-century bourgeois public sphere—and *should* not be, since Habermas' critics have shown that the liberal public sphere in its specific historical manifestation only left very limited room for resistant or emancipatory potential. Nancy Fraser insists that the notion of the public sphere as "a space for the communicative generation of public opinion" and "a vehicle for marshaling public opinion as a political force" still has validity in the context of global online networks,[25] but that it needs to take into account the "current flows of transnational publicity."[26] At a time in which markets, political alliances, and cultural traditions frequently cross national borders, transnational organizations and global corporations contest not only the nation state's political control over its citizens, but also its cultural influence.[27] Thomas Olesen similarly suggests that the dominance of the nation state as unifying concept is increasingly undermined by other loyalties and alliances, and proposes "that individuals and social movements are increasingly forging ties that cut across national civil societies and create new spaces of political activism."[28] This move away from national politics doesn't necessarily lead to a decline in political interest, as Donatella della Porta and Alice Mattoni suggest, but it does encourage alternative forms of political participation:

> Recent research on political participation noted that, while some more conventional forms of participation are declining, protest forms are instead increasingly used. Citizens vote less, but are not less interested or less knowledgeable about politics. And if some traditional types of associations are less and less popular, others (social movement organizations and/or civil society organizations) are growing in resources, legitimacy and members.[29]

If individuals' identification with national citizenship is replaced with or at least contested by an identification with other, non-institutionalized constituencies, this also does away with the assumption that individuals can only perform as citizens of one single constituency at a time. In fact, socialized human beings are always part of a multiplicity of intersecting communities of social and political alliance that speak to their self-conception in different ways. This means that Habermas' ideal of a homogenous, "universal" (aka nationwide) public sphere can be replaced with an interplay between different, sometimes overlapping publics, some of them hegemonic, some of them non-hegemonic. Since non-hegemonic publics have to rely on alternative media to generate and disseminate public discourse, they provide a counterweight not only to the dominant legislative powers, but also to the power exerted by the cultural hegemony of mainstream media. Transformative online fandom has emerged as just such a non-hegemonic alternative public that relies on independent, alternative communication media and distribution channels.

Transformative Fandom and Journal-Based Platforms

As supposedly loyal or even *obsessive* consumers, fans seem to be especially tightly entangled in the net of the culture industry that Adorno and Horkheimer described in their influential critique of popular culture in the mid–20th century.[30] Habermas, whose work was influenced by Adorno and Horkheimer's writings about the culture industry, blamed the disintegration of the liberal public sphere in the early 20th century on the rise of mass media and the entertainment industry, "a media power which was used manipulatively and robbed the principle of publicity of its innocence."[31] According to Habermas, this development led to the marginalization of educated consumers of high culture, who were replaced with the passive consumers of mass culture. From the perspective of Habermas' *The Structural Transformation of the Public Sphere*, then, it would have appeared counterintuitive to think of fans as active participants in an (alternative) public sphere.

However, by the time Habermas wrote a second introduction for the revised edition of his book in 1990, he had changed his position on this point:

> In short, my diagnosis of a linear development from politically active to private, from an audience that reflects on culture to an audience that consumes culture, is too simplistic. My assessment of the resistance and specifically the critical potential of a diverse, differentiated mass audience whose cultural habits transcend class differences was too pessimistic.[32]

And he was not alone. Throughout the 1980s and 1990s, scholars increasingly began to question the Frankfurt School's image of the passive, uncritical consumer of mass culture, pointing toward audiences' active engagement with (popular) texts. Janice Radway's work on female romance novel readers[33] showed that the act of cultural consumption itself can be a form of resistance for disadvantaged groups who have often been excluded from access to cultural goods. Scholars such as Stuart Hall and John Fiske demonstrated how underrepresented groups become accustomed, out of necessity, to reading hegemonic texts against the grain, thus generating meaning that differs from the dominant interpretations of mainstream texts.[34] Roberta Pearson, Alan McKee, and Matt Hills respectively have also pointed out that the distinction between the "fan" on the one hand, and the "aficionado" or "expert" on the other, is often not so much a qualitative difference but works as a class distinction that has been used to systematically discredit specific groups of recipients, particularly lower class audiences, women, and children.[35]

The transformative fan in particular moved to the forefront of scholarly interest in the early 1990s, and has often been described as the opposite of the passive consumer. Unlike fans in traditionally "affirmative" or "celebratory" fan groups,[36] the members of "transformative" or "fanworks" fandoms don't connect with each other only or even primarily via the object of their interest, but rather through their fannish practices. Transformative fans don't "merely" consume, they reappropriate the texts they engage with in a variety of ways. They rework, rewrite, and critique the products of popular culture by producing fanfiction, fanart, fan videos, drama, roleplay, cosplay,[37] crafts, and filk,[38] as well as critical and fan-scholarly writings.

Transformative fanworks undermine traditional concepts of authorship, originality, and intellectual property because they do not approach texts as autonomous, complete works, nor do they look at published authors as the definite masters of their creations. Abigail Derecho speaks of fanfiction as "archontic literature"[39] to describe fans' understanding of texts as open archives that can be extended infinitely, as raw material that can be endlessly remixed and reworked. In reference to Michel De Certeau, who first spoke of the consumption strategies of popular audiences as "poaching,"[40] Henry Jenkins calls transformative fans "textual poachers,"[41] because they "hunt" in popular texts for elements they can appropriate and rework as they please. Transformative fandom's particular affinity for TV shows, transmedia franchises, and comic book series is perhaps due to the fact that these serial, collaborative works themselves undermine the concept of the complete autonomous artwork. However, transformative fans also don't shy away from appropriating and rewriting canonical texts such as Shakespeare's *Hamlet*.

Transformative fandom has traditionally been and still is considered an overwhelmingly female and queer-leaning space. In a 2013 survey among 10,000 users of the multi-fandom fiction archive AO3, 80 percent of respondents identified as female (in comparison, 4 percent identified as male) and 71 percent identified as something other than heterosexual.[42] Results from several other smaller surveys among transformative fans between 2004 and 2008 showed between 83.5 and 96.5 percent of participants as female, and between 47 and 84.5 percent as non-heterosexual.[43] This distinct demographic make-up can be traced back to the emergence of media fandom in response to the rift that opened around 1965–1970 in the established science-fiction community, when controversies arose over the popularity of the TV show *Star Trek* as well as the increasing success of feminist science fiction.[44]

Due to its history and demographic structure, transformative fandom has generally been seen as a forum that allows underrepresented groups to rewrite dominant/hegemonic (patriarchal, heteronormative, ethnocentric) narratives from their own perspective. While not every transformative work should automatically be considered politically subversive, many fanworks indeed do rewrite the source material by breaking with the conventions and norms of mainstream culture:

> Fanworks can be an amazing space within which to negotiate these boundaries because the limits become permeable. Gender-bending, race-bending, age-bending, alternate universes—all of these provide the opportunity to engage with, challenge, reposition, or remove these ideologies as depicted in the original media.[45]

The production practices of transformative fandom are highly specialized and include writers, artists, filmmakers, craftswomen, performers, costume designers, photographers, editors, proofreaders, translators, programmers, moderators, organizers, and archivists, all of whom volunteer their labor without expectation of compensation. Fanworks are non-commercial and circulate in a form of gift exchange culture,[46] where works are shared freely within the community, in exchange only for the (equally voluntary) labor and the approval of others.[47] Occasional attempts to commercialize fanworks, for instance by the short-lived company FanLib in 2007/2008[48] and more recently by Amazon, have been met with forceful resistance from fans:

> I have been against the whole concept of FanLib from day one as it's just a prelude to The Man selling us back our *own work* at a profit, and I'm sick of a group of boys who can't even be bothered to punctuate claiming to be collecting "the best fanfiction out there" and trying to become the public face of our community.[49]

The gendered opposition set up in this statement highlights the connection between transformative fandom as gift exchange economy and transformative fandom as female-oriented space. Thriving on free labor, fanworks can be seen as part of a history of women's unpaid labor in the "private" domestic sphere.[50] However, by consciously investing labor for the sake of their own and each other's pleasure in a way that defies culturally dominant, socially acceptable norms, and by resisting the commercialization of said labor, these practices acquire a resistant potential.

The centuries-long exploitation of women's domestic work as free labor and the systemic exclusion of women from the field of technology has also made media fans and transformative fans sensitive to the importance of controlling their own means of (re)production in the form of media outlets and platforms. The history of transformative fandom therefore is closely entangled with the history of women's access to and control over emerging technology, from the first xeroxed *Star Trek* fanzines[51] to the appropriation of VCR technology,[52] Photoshop, and HTML in the service of fannish interests.

The shift to what is known as "journal-based fandom" around the turn to the 21st century was similarly tied to technological innovations such as the introduction of the WWW in 1991 and the phenomenon of personal blogs. Most importantly, it was directly dependent on the invention of Live-Journal (LJ). Based on an open-source code developed by Brad Fitzpatrick in 1999, LiveJournal was one of the first online social networking platforms, introduced years before the advent of Facebook, Twitter, and Tumblr.[53] LJ wasn't specifically designed as a fannish platform, but its launch led to an almost immediate mass migration of media fans to the site.[54] "Perhaps the single most significant fannish change in the last 10 years," Rebecca Busker notes in 2008, was "the move from mailing lists to LiveJournal."[55] The LJ code was unique because it combined blogging, discussion, and network-ing features in previously unknown ways. Unlike the early text-only news-groups and MOOs, LJ supported different file formats from the beginning, permitting users to post images, video clips, and audio files; in contrast to later microblogging sites like Facebook or Twitter, LJ also encouraged the publication of longer texts. The equally text- and image-friendly platform made it easy to distribute not only longer written texts (such as fanfiction and meta essays), but also (audio)visual materials, which up to that point had to be sent by mail or shared in person at fan conventions.

More importantly, the platform facilitated community-building across previously separate social groups and enabled the circulation of public dis-course within this broader networked community. In the mailing lists and newsgroups of the early days of internet fandom, discussion topics had been limited to one fannish interest at a time and were strictly regulated. The fanfiction newsgroup alt.startrek.creative, for instance, was accompa-nied by the subgroup alt.startrek.creative.erotica.moderated for those spe-cifically interested in erotic fiction.

> These lists were good for many things, but longer, detailed, carefully orga-
> nized essays were not among them. In addition, although lists to discuss issues
> and themes across multiple fandoms existed, they weren't always easy to find.
> Perhaps just as problematic was an implied and even overt hostility to critical
> discussion.[56]

In contrast, the LJ friendspage feed allowed users to follow any number of interest-specific communities as well as the blogs of individual users. The high character limit (65,000 characters) for LJ posts, combined with the lack of content restriction, led to the proliferation of "meta" as a distinct genre. Meta essays are long(ish) nonfictional texts with an analytical focus discussing the state of fandom, the relationship between fictional characters, or the political, social, or cultural influences of certain texts. The conversation could immediately be continued with other fans in the comment section, which thanks to the threaded comments feature could be used like a multi-thread discussion board.

Of course, an active discussion culture was not new for fandom. Both early science-fiction fandom since the 1920s and media fandom since the 1960s had developed a practice of engaging in conversations across spatial distance by making use of the letter sections in fanzines. Fans wrote to the editors of fanzines, the letters were printed, and then editors or contributors would respond in the next issue. Readers also talked to each other via letters in the same or even in different fanzines, and fanzine creators responded to articles published in other fanzines. However, since fanzines were printed in often irregular installments and distributed by mail, it was painstaking work to closely follow these conversations across different issues and fanzines. What had been a time- and labor-intensive practice in the era of printed fanzines could now be done with a simple mouse click on LJ.

Because crosslinking to other users' posts or comments was easy, conversations could also be led across different journals and comment threads. As trends and discussion topics crossed easily between journals, so they did between fan communities: LJ's network of communities and journals connected members from different corners of fandom who had previously not interacted much: "As a result, fans have an increased peripheral, and sometimes even very specific, knowledge of other fandoms."[57] Transformative fandom merged into an amalgamation of various intersecting subgroups, including but not limited to fans of TV shows and movie franchises, young adult literature, Japanese manga, superhero comics, hockey, figure skating, soccer, J-Pop and K-Pop, and American boybands. LJ made "polyfannish"[58] behavior easy, and the simultaneous engagement with different and ever-changing objects of fannish interest became the norm: "In our own LJs, no one is confined to one topic. I can jump from Buffy to West Wing to Smallville to meta to the New York football Giants and no one can smack me down for being off topic."[59]

Instead of a focus on individual objects, journal-based fandom now drew on a shared archive of texts, an alternative cultural canon. Fans did not so much identify as fans *of something*, but rather simply spoke of "being active in fandom": "The impact of this shift has been profound, and in many ways it has served to take the focus off the source and put it on the fan, and in turn, on fandom."[60]

As different communities grew closer together, they also grew rapidly in size. Pre-internet and Usenet fan communities had been relatively
tight-knit groups where most people knew each other in person, and mailing address lists with detailed contact information circulated freely among
fans. Now, instead of a few hundred fans per country, there were millions
worldwide. The stratified structure of pre-internet fandom, with its hierarchically organized clubs and edited fanzine publications, transformed
into an open, sprawling, decentralized network of participants. The use
of names and addresses was increasingly replaced by pseudonyms, but
instead of leading to emotional distance between fans, the pseudonymous
space was perceived as a safe environment that allowed fans to share not
only their fanworks, but also deeply personal information such as (mental) health issues. As a consequence of sheer numbers, not all fans on LJ
knew each other personally; and yet LJ communities, multi-fandom discussion spaces, and fiction exchanges led to the development of a network of
affective relations between fans across different fandoms. The fannish identity was not primarily conceived of as a relationship between fan and text
anymore, but rather as a *social* identity: "These users tend to think of Live-
Journal more as a neighborhood than as a social network, an emotional
affiliation built on trust that exists in both face-to-face and virtual relationships."[61] The notion of LJ fandom as a community was emphasized by many
fans: "Regardless of age, those who used Live Journal commented on its
centrality to […] community making."[62]

Transformative Fandom as Public Sphere

As I have shown in Chapter 1, the labor fans invest into establishing
affinity communities and the efforts they put into maintaining these invisible townships (or "neighborhoods," as Alice Marwick calls them in reference to LJ) lead them to think of their communities as constituencies,[63] as
quasi-political bodies that come with the necessity to negotiate and resolve
conflicts within the group. Meanwhile, the communication networks of
transformative fandom also allowed fans to envision themselves as participants in a public sphere. Furthermore, the *public* visibility of fan communities contributed to fans' perception of their networks as alternative publics.
In her work on silent movie fans, Miriam Hansen already described how
the public visibility of female fans in the early 20th century turned them
into public actors. As Hansen explains, the street riots that were caused
by fans of movie star Rudolph Valentino in the 1920s became a politically
charged form of publicness precisely because they were perceived as a
threat by the general public, or, more specifically, by men: "these events

appeared to have been staged by women, to the exclusion of men, more precisely, [...] the Valentino cult gave public expression to a force specific to relations *among* women."[64] In a different way but to a similar effect, transformative fandom began to self-identify as a *public* in the sense of a constituency around the same time as it began to become *public* in regard to outward visibility and influence.

Transformative fandom had, before the advent of the internet, been mostly "underground," a secretive subculture whose publications were only circulated among initiated members of the group: "Early printed fanzines carried a samizdat-like air as they were quietly sold or exchanged via mail or at conventions; ad listings made use of codes to describe their content."[65] This shadow existence was at least partly due to a fear of social stigma and legal prosecution. The uncertain legal status of their work made fans wary of copyright owners becoming aware of fannish transformative practices. The oftentimes erotic or emotional works media fans produced earned them the derision of members in the "traditional" literary science-fiction community, who considered fanworks to be indulgent and derivative. Media fans were also forced to hide their fannish identities from employers, colleagues, families and partners, who would not have approved of women creating erotic art and fiction for their own pleasure and entertainment.[66]

The transition into online spaces made transformative fan culture suddenly visible to the general public. Mainstream media reported with increasing frequency on transformative fans and online fandom,[67] in particular with regards to the veritable explosion of *Harry Potter* fandom-related activity around the turn of the millennium. The entertainment industry had up to that point regarded transformative fan practices with an attitude oscillating between gentle encouragement and purposeful ignorance: "The culture industries never really had to confront the existence of this alternative cultural economy because, for the most part, it existed behind closed doors and its products circulated only among a small circle of friends and neighbors."[68] Now production companies began to engage more actively with transformative fandom, and their strategies for dealing with fans began to change. Some producers saw fanworks as a threat equal to online piracy and tried to restrict any fannish appropriation of copyright-protected materials. Adult content in particular became a source of perpetual conflict between fandom and the industry. In the early 2000s, Warner Bros. and author J.K. Rowling started sending cease-and-desist letters to *Harry Potter* fanfiction sites[69]; and in 2010, fantasy writer Diana Gabaldon clashed dramatically with transformative fans when she stated that writing fanfiction about her works was akin to "break[ing] into somebody's house" and "trying to seduce my husband."[70]

Other producers tried to contain the perceived threat by co-opting fannish practices: they focused on improving their relationship with the fans by actively encouraging fan participation in order to increase word-of-mouth publicity, gain valuable feedback, ensure viewer loyalty, facilitate the production of user-generated content, or create new markets for merchandise:

> As we have moved from an era of broadcasting to one of narrowcasting, a process fueled by the deregulation of media markets and reflected in the rise of new media technologies, the fan as a specialized yet dedicated consumer has become a centerpiece of media industries' marketing strategies.[71]

With fandom's transformation from an underground subculture to a visible public, the rift between copyright owners and transformative fans became a tug-of-war over legal, intellectual and moral authority. Fans defended the legal fair-use status of transformative works and felt that the producers and writers who openly disapproved of fanworks demonstrated ungratefulness and disrespect toward their fanbase. Furthermore, the industry's attempts at appropriating fannish practices and spaces caused concern among transformative fans who were determined to maintain a certain independence in regard to their publication outlets. One reason why LJ was valued so highly by fans was that it was based on an open-source code developed by an independent fan-friendly company. As Della Portfa/Mattoni point out, alternative media are not "merely oriented towards the creation of content and infrastructures," but "inherently political. Indeed, these media create spaces that oppose the dominant cultures in a direct manner, and, hence, challenge mainstream and mass media power that have the monopoly over the naming of realities."[72] However, after Fitzpatrick sold LJ in 2005 to SixApart, which in turn sold the platform to the Russian company SUP in 2007, fans were outraged when the new owners purged hundreds of journals in 2007 without prior warning, an event that went down into fandom history as "strike-through" (in reference to how deleted LJ journals appear visually on the site). Around the same time, the aforementioned FanLib debacle inspired further anger among fans who increasingly (and not without justification) felt that the industry was trying to sell them out. These attempts at commercializing fanworks and controlling fannish content motivated fans to create their own alternative platforms that would guarantee their continued independence and protection from commercial interests:

> We need a central archive of our own, something like animemusicvideos.org. Something that would NOT hide from google or any public mention, and would clearly state our case for the legality of our hobby up front, while not trying to make a profit off other people's IP and instead only making it easier for us to celebrate it, together, and create a welcoming space for new fans that has a sense of our history and our community behind it.[73]

This statement in a LJ post that generated over 600 comments marked the beginning of a process that in 2007 led to the foundation of OTW,[74] a member-owned non-profit organization advocating for the legal fair-use status of fanworks. Aside from their legal advocacy work, OTW also maintains *fanlore* (a wiki for fandom historiography), the academic open-access fan studies journal *Transformative Works and Cultures,* as well as the fiction *Archive of Our Own* (AO3), which reached four million users in August 2021.[75] In 2008, the non-profit journaling platform Dreamwidth (DW) was developed on the basis of LJ's open-source code, with the explicit purpose of providing an alternative to LJ, whose environment was becoming increasingly hostile to fannish concerns.

The industry's increased interest in fan practices made many fans feel threatened; on the flipside, however, it also made them aware of the influence they could exert on the field of cultural production, which led to a sense of ownership in regard to the texts fans engaged with, and to a feeling of responsibility to protect the "spirit" of the texts they loved, even against copyright owners, producers, and creators themselves.

> The potential for alternative public politics in fandom is so great, I think, because of the immense interest that fans hold within particular cultural objects. This is interesting not just in the sense of curiosity and excitement, but more importantly in the political-economic sense of investment and ownership.[76]

This constellation situated transformative fandom at the border between the private and the public sphere. Online fandom was *public* in its engagement with the field of cultural production and its facilitation of public discourse, but the fans' affective attachment and sense of ownership also made it a *private* matter. The journal-based platforms with their ambiguous position between private journal and public website,[77] and the parallels between fannish production and private domestic labor further blurred the distinction between the public and the private realm.

For Habermas, the separation of public and private was a necessary precondition for communicative rationality in the public sphere. Feminist and queer theorists, however, have argued that the private is far from apolitical[78] but rather a highly contested arena that regulates issues of intimacy, sexuality, reproduction, and labor in the domestic sphere. In the case of transformative fandom, it appeared that it was precisely this tension between public and private which contributed to a heightened political consciousness: "a medium that by its nature mixes the personal with the fannish must contribute to increased awareness and discussion of the sociopolitical."[79]

In fact, the LJ fan community was from the very beginning invested especially in sociopolitical issues located at the intersection of public and private, including but not limited to topics such as cultural representation, or the distribution of capital in the culture industry:

> [T]he fan joining to follow discussions on critical feedback will also become aware of discussions about misogyny in fandom or depictions of religious issues in a source as well. [...] Much as fannish discussion has abstracted to meta themes, it has also dug down into underlying issues, including questions of race, gender, sexual orientation and identity, religion, class, and other sociopolitical issues, not only as they manifest in a given show or comic, but as they manifest in fandom itself.[80]

These debates and controversies occurred with enough regularity that communities like *meta-fandom* were created with the primary purpose of archiving links to meta essays, and projects like *fandom_wank* and the *FFA Wiki* were dedicated to documenting and archiving the often sprawling collections of links, posts and comments related to those debates. These archival projects do not only document fannish controversies, they also represent a manifestation of fandom's self-conception as a space of public discourse. The fannish term "wank,"[81] which is commonly used to describe the heated drawn-out arguments erupting among fans, is somewhat misleading in its implication of self-absorbed irrelevance. While seemingly superfluous discussions about minor issues certainly occur, many of these debates are anything but irrelevant, both in regard to the questions they touch on as well as in their function of sustaining a fannish discussion culture. Anne Jamison suggests that even the discussions that appear unimportant at first glance are often symptomatic for more serious issues: "What sometimes seems like squabbling over petty issues is almost always a proxy for large, unresolved, and perhaps unresolvable concerns."[82]

Pseudonymity, Inclusivity and Race

Fan communities dedicated to speculative fiction, comics, anime, and television have always been connected through a transnational network of individuals and organizations. Fans from North America, Europe, Asia and Australia have been in touch in one way or another throughout most of the 20th century.[83] But attending transcontinental conventions in person could be difficult in particular for disabled or low-income fans, and thus this form of fannish engagement certainly privileged those who traveled easily. In addition, the organization of fan clubs and amateur presses mirrored in many ways the access barriers and hierarchical structures of official civic institutions and the publishing industry. In consequence, Western SF/F fandom in the pre-internet era appeared, at least on the surface, as rather homogeneously male, white, educated, and lower- to upper-middle class. However, to a certain degree this commonly accepted image of science-fiction and fantasy fandom is a myth, or at least a generalization, that emerged in fans' self-descriptive narratives and was perpetuated by later generations of fan studies scholars. Even a cursory look at fanzines from the first half of the 20th century, for example, makes it clear that women were an important part of science-fiction fandom from the very beginning. The Futurians (discussed in detail in Chapter 1) had a significant number of female members such as Virginia Kidd, Leslie Perri (aka Doris Marie Claire Baumgardt), Elsie Wollheim, Rosalind Cohen, and Mary Byers. As was typical for the era, many of these women were indeed married or otherwise related to male science-fiction fans, who had often introduced them to fandom in the first place. However, this doesn't negate the fact that they were active fandom participants who went to conventions and wrote for fanzines.

Both amateur and scholarly historiographies of fandom have more readily acknowledged the presence of female fans and writers for the era after the emergence of feminist science fiction and media fandom in the 1960s.[84] Yet the fact that even in the 1960s/1970s, Alice B. Sheldon still published under the male pseudonym James Tiptree Jr. was a symptom of the male-oriented dominant discourse in science-fiction fandom. Likewise, Joanna Russ's history as a writer of *Star Trek* fan fiction was at least partly due to the fact that the community of media fandom was more receptive to the type of science fiction she was interested in than the traditional literary science-fiction community.[85]

The absence and/or erasure of non-white fans from the history of science-fiction fandom has been even more systemic. It is quite telling that the Carl Brandon Society, which was founded in 1997 with the intent to promote racially diverse representation in science fiction and foster conversations about race, is named after a Black fan who never actually existed. During the 1950s/1960s, Terry Carr and Pete Graham, two white writers and fans, published satirical science-fiction stories in fanzines under the name "Carl Brandon," the persona of a Black science-fiction fan. It is likely that this hoax happened only because there was no significant presence of Black science-fiction fans within the community. However, it would be a mistake to assume that fans of color simply didn't exist. André M. Carrington, for example, points out that in 1929–1930, Jack Fitzgerald, a Black man, served as president of the first New York–based science-fiction club in Harlem.[86] Carrington does suggest that Fitzgerald remained an absolute exception within U.S. science-fiction fandom for several decades. But even if this aligns with most historiographic accounts of the fandom, from today's perspective the veracity of this assumption is somewhat difficult to assess, especially since, as Carrington himself argues, fanzine-based fandom's reliance on "written correspondence kept questions of sexuality, gender, and racial identification at a comfortable distance."[87] Thus, the Carl Brandon hoax says as much about the construction of narratives about the community as it does about the actual racial make-up of science-fiction fandom at the time.

The non-hierarchical decentralized structure of journal-based online fandom in the 21st century was supposed to do away with many of the barriers that prevented members of previously underrepresented groups from participating equally in fandom. Access to journal-based fandom did not come with formal restrictions: basic user accounts were free of cost, and it was not even necessary to have an account if fans only wanted to read other users' posts and leave anonymous comments. Theoretically, the space of LJ-centric fandom appeared to be open to anyone who had access to the internet (which of course presented in itself a barrier). Unlike the coffeehouses of the 18th century and the fan clubs of the science-fiction community in the early 20th century, online fandom seemed to provide the conditions for a more radically democratic alternative public sphere.

But formal restrictions and explicit exclusion are not the only way to regulate access to public discourse. Critics of Habermas' public sphere model did not only point out that access to the historical bourgeois public sphere was limited to financially independent white men of age, which made the 18th-century public sphere far from "universal." Habermas was also criticized for his suggestion that within the discursive space of the public sphere, existing social differences could and should be bracketed for the sake and duration of the conversation, so that the negotiation of public opinion could take place between truly equal participants. Critics such as Nancy Fraser and Michael Warner expressed their doubts about the ability of discussion participants to simply tune out or forget the various power imbalances between members. As Fraser argues, pretending to ignore inequalities does not make those differences disappear but in fact usually leads to their cementation: "[S]uch bracketing usually works to the advantage of dominant groups in society and to the disadvantage of subordinates."[88]

The convention of pseudonymity, which quickly became the norm in journal-based fandom and other online spaces, was thought to provide an at least partial solution to this problem. Unlike anonymity, the pseudonym allows participants to create and maintain a recognizable identity, but also leaves them in control over the amount of personal information they want to reveal. Factors that commonly influence offline interpersonal relationships, including gender, sexuality, race, age, class, education, (dis)ability, accent, or physical appearance, are often consciously left unmentioned. Critics of pseudonymity see this ability to omit identifying information as evidence for the inferiority of virtual communication, which they perceive as "less real" than face-to-face interactions. Only a strictly enforced real-name policy, they argue, can prevent uncivil behavior and online harassment, as it forces participants to assume responsibility for their actions. Amitai Etzioni, for example, considers the disclosure of participants' identity a precondition for the formation of functional online communities.[89] Sarah Banet-Weiser, who takes a much more ambivalent position toward online spaces than Etzioni's critical stance, still argues that sexist harassment by men's rights activists and other garden-variety misogynists is "bolstered through anonymity online, where rape and death threats become routine."[90]

Google+'s implementation of a real-name policy in 2011 became one precedent for the enforcement of real-name policies on social networking platforms, which was even more impactful because the policy change was combined with the automatic synching of users' G+, YouTube, and Gmail accounts. In 2014, Google abandoned its real-name policy for G+ again after vehement criticism from users.[91] Opponents of real-name policies argue that these practices don't actually prevent harassment, because trolls and harassers are often members of overrepresented groups who feel entitled to their behavior and don't require anonymity to hide behind.[92] Thus, harassment and discrimination of underrepresented groups continue to prevail in real-name online spaces as much as in face-to-face interactions. Fans in journal-based fandom have voiced similar criticism regarding the assumed superiority of face-to-face conversations:

> As a woman in male-dominated academic settings for most of my life, let me tell you, I don't think, gee all the face/face talks I have when I'm one of the few white women in the room with mostly white men (and maybe one POC) are all sparkles and butterflies! [...] So—why do *some* people want to claim the idea of face/face as somehow always inherently/essentially better than/superior to online? To say people will always be kinder? Is it because they have more control over their physical surroundings and who they spend time with and how much they can control who says what?[93]

As this fan points out succinctly, contributions made by those in dominant positions will often be perceived as more legitimate. Thus, individuals in positions of power are also the users to most likely benefit from real-name policies on social media.

Members of underrepresented communities have long been aware of this fact, as demonstrated for example by the centuries-old tradition of female writers using pen names or initials to publish their work. For them, pseudonymity can offer protection from harassment and allows them to participate in online spaces with a lower risk of facing discrimination or dismissal. The practice of "doxing" an individual by publicly exposing their offline identity is considered a form of harassment and a serious violation of privacy: "Revealing someone's 'real life' identity and location quickly came to be understood as a sin of great magnitude, whereas in the days of zines, such information was commonly shared."[94]

Thus, proponents of pseudonymity have embraced the practice as a way to level the slanted playing field of public discourse, and to protect its most vulnerable participants—not only because it prevents online harassment from spilling into "RL" spaces, but also because it allows participants to control how much information about their identity they want to share. As Benjamin Woo states,

> a great deal of fan activity has always been mediated by technologies that enable "disembodied" discourse (from the letter column, fanzine, and amateur press association to the bulletin board, the Internet Relay Chat channel or discussion forum) and, thus, tend to reinforce the Cartesian split between mind and body.[95]

At first glance, then, pseudonymity seems to allow for exactly the "bracketing of differences" Habermas thought of as a precondition for a functioning public sphere.

However, this does not mean that the notion of the "body" (in its gendered, sexed, racialized form) is completely absent from online communication, even if the bodies represented may not be precisely the same as the ones operating the keyboards. Lisa Nakamura explains how users *perform* embodiment in online spaces:

> Users of the Internet represent themselves within it solely through the medium of keystrokes and mouse-clicks, and through this medium they can describe themselves and their physical bodies any way they like; they perform their bodies as text. On the Internet, nobody knows that you're a dog; it is possible to "computer crossdress" (Stone, 1991) and represent yourself as a different gender, age, race, etc.[96]

This tension between the disembodiment of pseudonymity on the one hand and the constant performance of embodiment in online discourse on the other can create problems for internet users from underrepresented groups. When racial identity in online spaces is conceived of merely as performance, race is easily treated as a sort of imaginary category, a fantasy. Nakamura's work on MOO player behavior shows that white participants did not hesitate to appropriate race as an element of their own fictionalized online personas, for example by taking on an Asian-coded user name and description in a form of virtual yellowface: "The appropriation of racial identity becomes a form of recreation, a vacation from fixed identities and locales."[97]

In contrast, she argues, the invocation of *actual* race and ethnicity is unwelcome because it destroys the illusion of race as a fictional element in virtual worlds. In fact, the possibility to refrain from disclosing certain identity categories in online spaces has led to the general expectation that it's not only possible to hide one's racial or ethnic identity, but also that it's bad manners *not* to do so.

> Players who elect to describe themselves in racial terms, as Asian, African American, Latino, or other members of oppressed and marginalized minorities, are often seen as engaging in a form of hostile performance, since they introduce what many consider a real life "divisive issue" into the phantasmatic world of cybernetic textual interaction.[98]

Users who disclose their racial or ethnic identity are often met with aggression and accused of calling this hostile treatment upon themselves. Mimi Nguyen describes how the disclosure of her Asian American identity in online spaces frequently seemed to be interpreted as an invitation for racialized sexual harassment:

> Still, my body is invoked. That is, everyone brings it up, even in its conspicuous (visual) absence, or perhaps because of it. [...] That is, my body can probably be envisioned/pieced together easily enough: a digitized Frankenstein amalgamation of parts seen on All Asian Action or Hot Oriental Babes. The invocation of my body serves a purpose, then, something about keeping me in line; there are the threats of sexual violence, thinly veiled suggestions that they might enjoy the scene of my particular body in pain.[99]

It is understandable, then, why fans of color might choose to retreat behind the cover of pseudonymity and "pass" as white in online spaces in order to avoid similarly hostile reactions. However, not only does this practice require fans to omit a significant part of their lives and identities from their interactions with other fans; it also reinforces the normative image of online fandom as an almost exclusively white and English-language space. While the majority of transformative fans may in fact be white native speakers of English, Woo refers to data suggesting that "somewhere between 10% and 33% of fans [...] belong to visible-minority groups," even though "you'd never know it from reading many accounts of fan communities."[100]

Pseudonymity then, adds another layer of complexity to the tension between the public and the private in transformative fandom. On the one hand, it permits participants from underrepresented groups to hide their identities in order to avoid harassment and discrimination—in other words, their identity is kept private *because* it is considered *political*. On the other hand, the purposeful omission of cultural identity markers from online spaces leads to the perception that the public sphere of transformative fandom is far more homogenous in its demographic make-up than it really is. RaceFail '09 was one of the conflicts that brought attention to these different competing conceptions of the "public" and "private" in the fight over access to the public sphere.

RaceFail '09

The point of departure for the controversy around RaceFail '09 was a LJ post by science-fiction author Elizabeth Bear about the literary representation of foreign cultures, or as she titled it, "Writing The Other without being a dick."[101] In her essay, she advises writers on how to relate to characters that are different from them: "For one thing, stop thinking about this person you're writing as The Other. Think of them as human, an individual. Not A Man. Not A Woman. Not A Chinese Person or A Handicapped Person or A Person With Cancer or a Queer Person. A person."[102] Bear's original essay appeared on the surface as a well-meaning attempt to reflect on how to better write characters from underrepresented groups. However, fans of color responded critically to her post in several influential meta essays. They called out Bear for her ethnocentric way of presenting her own identity as the default and "othering" everyone else. Furthermore, some fans accused her of hypocrisy by pointing out that her own novels seemed to fall into the same trap she advised others to avoid. Bear and her fans reacted defensively to the criticism, and from there on the conversation escalated rapidly.

In the exchange that followed, Western and non–Western non-white fans came forward to describe how their cultural memory, their imagination, and therefore their creative output were impacted by the legacy of colonialism: "I grew up with half a tongue," Indian fan Deepa D. stated in her now famous essay "I Didn't Dream of Dragons," and went on to explain how her access to cultural capital was determined by the global dominance of Euro-American culture. Despite the transnational scope of transformative fandom, these fans were conscious of the fact that their fannish textual archive was dominated by a very limited number of languages and cultures, with the vast majority of sources coming from the USA and the UK and much fewer other contributions from countries such as Japan (manga, anime, and pop music), South Korea (TV shows and pop music), India (Bollywood cinema), or Germany (soccer and soap operas).

> I am lucky in that Indian culture is more widely represented in Western media than other colonised regions—when I talk about Bollywood in the yuletide chat room, there are people who have an idea about what I might be referring to [...]. Yet still, my ability to connect fannishly with people from different parts of the world is mediated through the coloniser's language and representation. Enid

Blyton, with her hideous caricatures of African tribal boys helping the intrepid British children is read from Johannesburg to Jaipur—Iktomi stories are not.[103]

Deepa D. and other fans criticized the perpetual under- and misrepresentation of non–Western characters or cultures in dominant Western narratives: the lack of protagonists of color, the stereotyping of non-white characters and the recurrence of racially charged narrative tropes, as well as the common problematic casting practice of "whitewashing."[104] In their meta essays, they didn't hesitate to directly call out the work of science-fiction and fantasy authors who were participants in the discussion. Bear herself, for instance, was taken to task for her portrayal of non-white characters in regard to her novel *Blood and Iron*[105]:

> It's about the fact that you and writers like you *don't have to think about this stuff*. That you have the ready made excuse that it all *"serves the story"* and that said character was written intelligently and as a well rounded individual with wants and needs of his own; with plots even. It's about the fact that I couldn't finish reading your book because I threw it across the room in disgust.[106]

The defensive response from Bear and several of her colleagues set the stage for the further development of RaceFail '09, although the conflict was not a clear-cut opposition between professional writers and fans. Several professionals (mostly writers of color) sided with the fans and embraced the emergence of a serious discussion about race; there were also participants who had both a name in professional publishing and in transformative fandom and had to navigate their investment in both communities at the same time.

Still, RaceFail '09 drew attention to the power imbalance between professional creators and their fans, revealed the conflicting perspectives on authorship and criticism that divided professional writers and affirmative fans on the one hand and transformative fan-creators on the other, and exposed the discursive norms that restrict access to the hegemonic public sphere. A transformative fan elaborated on this tension in one of her posts:

> I keep seeing the same thing happening this year: over and over again, in all of my fandoms, there have been battles between creators (backed up by their affirmational fanbase) and their transformational fanbase. The subjects are different (although RaceFail '09 "wins" in that respect for being the biggest, the most vociferous, and regarding the most serious, real-life-impacting subject matter) but the pattern is incredibly similar: the creators have a run-in with fans from the transformational side of fandom; the creators do not feel properly respected; the creators attempt to, well, beat the recalcitrant fans into submission.[107]

At that point, the discussion had already developed into multiple, frequently intersecting lines of discussion in various journals, posts, and comment threads. However, several argumentative threads revolving around the inclusivity of public discourse emerged as focal points in the conversations and were repeatedly cross-linked and referenced.

(1) Invisibility and exclusion: Professional writers such as speculative fiction writer Lois McMaster Bujold tried to explain the lack of a discourse on race in speculative fiction by suggesting that there simply hadn't been enough readers of color to warrant such a discussion: "never before have so many Readers of Color existed to *have* the conversation." A fan replied to Bujold directly in the following comment:

> I don't understand why you are laboring under the impression that sci-fans of color didn't exist simply because they avoided attending cons. [...] We were reading and discussing all along, we just weren't doing it in front of white people. Looking at Racefail ... is it any wonder why?[108]

Another fan took this exchange as inspiration for a roll-call under the title "Wild Unicorn Herd Check In"[109] in a post that gained 1070 comments from fans of color describing their history and experience as readers of speculative fiction. This discussion about the invisibility of fans of color in fannish spaces also drew attention to one of the more problematic consequences of pseudonymity: the fact that it led to a presumed "default identity" of whiteness. Fans explained that as long as they didn't explicitly identify themselves as persons of color, they were often automatically assumed to be white: "The extent to which the 'race-free' theory of the early Internet is related to white people's failure to 'see' people of color in online spaces, such as fandom, is exemplified by the surprise Bujold expressed."[110] In fact, some authors went as far as to question fans' identities even after they disclosed their ethnic or racial background, and accused them of merely pretending to be fans of color, thus discrediting their arguments by accusing them of being trolls in digital black/brown/yellowface.

(2) The normative function of rational discourse: Over the course of the RaceFail '09 debate, (white) professional writers repeatedly questioned fans' analytical reading skills and accused them of a lack of objectivity. In other words, they evoked the notion of "rational discourse" to deflect criticism and discredit their critics. After fans complained about the depiction of non-white characters in Bear's novel *Blood and Iron*, fantasy author Sarah Monette commented: "I think it's more accurate to say that [professional writers] are trying to talk about the book on a literary/analytic level whereas you got short-circuited before you could reach that kind of discussion by a personal/political reaction."[111] Transformative fans called Monette out for using the "tone argument," a common derailment strategy used to devalue marginalized participants in public discourse by dismissing their contributions as too emotional or subjective: "I am astounded that so many people wanking about their precious academic credentials

are completely ignorant of how goddamn OFTEN PoC have seen these same generalized dismissals. Too emotional, too loud, too angry, too uneducated, TOO FUCKING COLOURED."[112] Fans' anger at being tone-policed in the RaceFail '09 debate is an example for the way in which the idea of "rationality" in the public sphere functions not so much as an objective category but rather as a means of gender/class/racial distinction. Fans very succinctly pointed out that emotional distance from a discussion topic, which requires a clear separation of the personal and the political, is a privilege only open to those who will not be directly and negatively affected by the outcome of the debate. Those with the highest stakes in the discussion—the marginalized and underrepresented participants—will have the hardest time being "objective" or "rational." Professional creators also used the tone argument in a way that conflated race with gender, thus further discrediting both groups by associating them with irrationality. Fans who spoke up against racism and ethnocentrism in the science-fiction/fantasy community were dismissed not only because of their racial/ethnic identity but also because of their gender, as one fan remarks in a retrospective analysis of the controversy:

> That was part of the miasma around the RaceFail debate: the old boys' club of SFF book fandom that led to the dismissal not only of people of color but also of LiveJournal. They had the idea that LJ is full of hysteria and shrieking, and they asked, "Where are the rational people in this discussion?" That's very gendered.[113]

(3) The separation of public and private: The RaceFail '09 debate was shaped by a constant struggle over the border between the public and the private. Proponents of real-name policies, in particular among the professional writers, discredited fans' practice of pseudonymity as insincere. They accused fans of hiding behind their pseudonymous identities, suspected them of "passing" under a racial identity not their own, and even doxed a fan in the process, an action that was met with consternation from transformative fans and interpreted as "the old-guard power-structure reasserting its control."[114] And yet, some of the professional authors voiced their concerns when they felt that the public debate around RaceFail '09 was beginning to interfere with their own private lives. In March 2009, three months into the discussion, Bear called for a "cease fire." She argued that the discussion had gotten out of hand and complained that "it keeps following me home."[115] In response, fans of color pointed out that the ability to separate public discourse and private life was a privilege members of many disadvantaged groups did not enjoy. One fan of color put her own experience of the rather porous wall between public and private sphere into words:

> You see, I couldn't just decide not to have a conversation about race anymore, because it follows me home. My race issues ARE my home. Other people can

pick them up when they want to look at something shiny, something exotic tasty foreign bright colourful strange exciting; they toss them around, try them on. Start to explain them to me and find different names for them, like *classism* and *learning experience*.[116]

In Bear's request for a cease fire as well as in the critical responses she faced, the border between public and private kept being invoked as a line of defense. In particular, white participants in the discussion—professionals but also fans—expressed shock over how much the "private" realm of their personal lives and their emotional wellbeing were affected by the sometimes brutally honest exchanges that happened as part of the RaceFail '09 debate. At the same time, some professional writers didn't hesitate to purposefully violate the line between public and private by exposing personally identifying information about at least one fan to the public at large, thus making this fan vulnerable to attacks in her home. People of color in turn pointed out that the idea of a public sphere as a space free of private interests and emotional language was a privileged perspective. These fans argued that they themselves did not have the ability to retreat into the private sphere yet were simultaneously accused of invading the private lives of their white fellow LJ users when they said things that the other side experienced as hurtful.

(4) Free labor and the work of translation: One of the most common reactions among white authors in response to the critique from transformative fans of color was the request for guidelines on "how to do better." This turned out to be a deeply divisive point between fans/writers of color and white fans/writers. Fans of color in particular strongly resented the suggestion that they should take on the responsibility for explaining and educating other participants in the debate: "*I don't do Anti-Racism 101,*" one fan wrote in response to one of these inquiries. "It's extremely exhausting to do someone else's homework for them, especially when that someone is often tens of various white people wanting me to explain and/or award points (every. flipping. day)."[117] These complaints were usually not meant to reject the possibility of dialogue. Rather, they responded to the widespread expectation that marginalized groups should not only adopt the accepted language of the dominant discourse (in this case, the discourse of "rational" academic literary studies), but also translate their own language back to those in the dominant group. This double burden can be understood as a form of free labor, which plays a significant role in transformative fandom. Female-identifying transformative fans who willingly invest free labor in fannish activities do in some ways subvert the exploitation of free (domestic) labor that women have historically been expected to provide. Fans of color were equally conscious of the fact that for centuries, colonialism and slavery have allowed for the exploitation of non-white/non–Western

peoples and their forced free labor. Fans' readiness to invest free labor into the creation of fanworks, while refusing to provide free labor in the form of education for the sake of the hegemonic majority, also needs to be understood as a form of resistance that fans of color exercised consciously during the RaceFail '09 debate.

There was yet another way in which questions of labor played into the RaceFail '09 controversy. While lines were drawn, generally speaking, between amateur writers and fans on the one hand and professional authors on the other, it is worth keeping in mind that the professional writers willing to engage in this immediate exchange of opinions with fans were for the most part not dominant players in the entertainment industry, but rather independent authors, many of them not always able to make a living from their writing alone. Thus, it would be somewhat misleading to frame RaceFail '09 as a fight between consumers and the industry, since these authors were certainly more receptive, but also more vulnerable to the critique of their readers[118] than the producers and directors of major Hollywood productions who may be accused of practices such as whitewashing but generally don't suffer financially as a result.

While several participants reported emotional exhaustion and burnout as a result of their engagement in RaceFail '09, many considered the debate necessary and ultimately productive (or, to revisit Jemisin's initial quote, the "Bestest Thing Evar for SFF"). The fact that the community of transformative LJ fandom had made the debate possible in the first place was celebrated by many fans:

> And yes thank you internet, and especially the danga[119] platform of LJ, DW, IJ, and JF for allowing a broader, yet still immediate conversation than could be had in limited face-to-face space and kept the voices of FOC from being isolated, and that also afforded a platform to any of us who are less empowered in the face-to-face space where these conversations happen.[120]

The non-hierarchic structure of journal-based fannish networks as well as the practice of pseudonymity provided a space for conversations to develop that did not automatically favor those with gender, racial, class, or educational privilege. This distinguished the discursive structure of transformative fandom both from the traditional bourgeois public sphere as well as from traditional pre-internet science-fiction fandom.

RaceFail '09 never came to an official conclusion, nor did it end with any kind of official proclamation. Yet while the heated debate on LJ and related blogs and platforms ebbed after about five months, many felt that the dialogue that had been started by RaceFail '09 was not over, but was merely the beginning of a continuing conversation that would slowly help change the face of popular culture and fandom alike: "I think that the conversations *RaceFail* started [...] were critical, not only in terms of what was being discussed but the fact that they became a way for fans of color to find each other and build communities as well."[121]

Beyond this heightened sense of consciousness regarding issues of race and racism among both fans and professionals, RaceFail '09 also had a number of tangible results: fiction anthologies like *Long Hidden* (2014) and *We See a Different Frontier* (2013)[122] were published in direct reaction to the online debate. Author Nalo Hopkinson discussed RaceFail '09 in her keynote speech at the academic International Conference on the Fantastic in the Arts 2010, and fan conventions increasingly made an effort to include panels on race and ethnicity. Within the fan community, there was a noticeable increase in projects focusing on PoC representation in popular culture and fandom, such as the awareness-raising grassroots organization *Racebending.com*, journal-based fiction communities like *Dark Agenda,* and the *Remyth Project*, which focused on "taking back" non–Western myths and stories that had been appropriated by Western culture. Some fans introduced the term "chromatic" as an alternative to "of color" into fannish spaces. While not resulting in quasi-legislative measures or any kind of "official" consensus, this public debate about race that transcended the border between the alternative public sphere of transformative fandom and the dominant sphere of genre publishing did in fact bring forth visible results and continues to do so.

While the events of RaceFail '09 served to demonstrate the discursive potential of journal-based transformative online fandom, the debate also revealed some of the limitations of this alternative public sphere. In particular, the Western-centric textual archive of transformative fandom and the pseudonymity of fannish spaces were shown to facilitate the erasure of heterogeneous voices and contributed to the establishment of a "default" fannish identity that was for the most part considered English-speaking and predominantly white.

This conception of fans as typically white not only influences fannish discourses but also leaks back into mainstream representations of fans, geeks, and nerds in popular culture, which in turn further cement assumptions about the inherent whiteness of fandom. In his analysis of online discourses regarding the recasting of Spider-Man with a non-white actor in 2010/2011, Albert Fu points out that for many fans, a Black Spider-Man was unimaginable in parts because Peter Parker (the face behind the superhero) is conceived of as a nerd, and the idea of a Black nerd or geek seemed inauthentic to these fans: "A popular argument against a black Peter Parker is that he could not be a nerd if black."[123] Recent popular characters such as Troy Barnes (Donald Glover) on the TV series *Community*[124] or Miles Morales (Shameik Moore), the hero of *Spider-Man: Into the Spider-Verse*,[125] are revolutionary precisely because they contribute to a shifting understanding of fans, geeks, and nerds as not automatically and inherently white.

Conclusion

The negotiation of a consensus in the form of public opinion, which can then put pressure on the legislative powers, has generally been considered one of the main functions of the autonomous public sphere, from Habermas' model of discursive rationality in the bourgeois public sphere to Fraser's notion of contemporary transnational publics which are still meant to translate into a democratic force that attributes political weight to the opinion of the public.

But despite the fact that controversies happened regularly in the alternative public sphere of transformative fandom, the community never implemented quasi-governmental structures to regulate communication and interaction between fans; in fact, transformative fans generally tended to be suspicious of the potentially oppressive goal of universal consensus. Consequently, RaceFail '09 did not conclude in a universal agreement among discussion participants, not even among transformative fans themselves. Nevertheless, fans considered the conversation to be productive and efficacious, in regard to the question of race in fandom as well as in the way it influenced and shaped the rules of fannish discourse. The thrust of the conversation was channeled into different forms of social activism, the publication of alternative media, and the critical interrogation of communal and discursive practices. Instead of focusing on the unachievable goal of a universal consensus, fans saw a potential for change precisely in the continued process of communication and dialogue, and in the participants' continued willingness to question and test the premises on which their communication was based.

The difficulty of establishing clear-cut distinctions between different constituencies and publics within the broader fan community is part of what keeps this critical potential alive. The productive labor that was done during RaceFail '09 depended at least in part on the fact that the public of transformative fandom and the public of the professional writing and publishing community were not completely separate but rather intertwined in complicated ways. In fact, it appears that especially those who navigated different communal spaces simultaneously, and thus contributed to the intersection of different communities, were able to help sustain this critical potential, because it prevented the respective communities from becoming fossilized and forced them to interrogate their own discursive practices over and over again.

Curiously, it was precisely transformative fandom's quest for their own independent platforms that eventually brought about the decline of LJ-centric fandom. In response to the corporate takeover of LiveJournal, several alternative LJ-code-based platforms sprang up, including Insanejournal, Journalfen, and Dreamwidth (the most prominent LJ successor). This led to a splintering of fannish discussion culture into different, formally similar platforms. In addition, the foundation of AO3 by the OTW in 2008 encouraged fanfiction writers to share and archive their fiction primarily on AO3, and fic exchanges were increasingly held on AO3—which meant that the publication of fanfiction became centralized to an unprecedented degree, but also that a significant amount of fan engagement was redirected from journal-based platforms to this multifandom archive.

Simultaneously, LJ-code based journals faced more and more competition from other types of social media platforms. Starting around 2010, Twitter and Tumblr were increasingly used for fandom-specific communication. In particular Tumblr is often considered to be the main successor of LiveJournal, and this move is generally seen as a generational shift, in the sense that Tumblr is associated with a younger generation of fans: "Together with the rise of new fandoms and a younger generation of fans who engaged comfortably with social media, Tumblr eventually supplanted LiveJournal as a, if not the, key hub of multimedia online fandom activity."[126]

Just as with the migration to LiveJournal, the specific features of the online platform very much determined the discursive practices of fans engaging in fannish conversations. Like other more recent social media platforms (such as Instagram, Snapchat, or TikTok), "Tumblr is predominantly a platform for sharing multimedia content. Based on a dataset of 586.4 million posts analyzed by Yahoo Labs (Chang et al., 2014), the most popular post type is photo (78.11%)."[127] This emphasis on images as opposed to text, along with the absence of the comment section and the implementation of the "reblog" function on Tumblr, were some of the differences that fans of the LJ era often bemoaned as contributing to the decline of a productive discussion culture in fandom. Indeed, the set-up of Tumblr discourages the kind of immediate, lengthy, in-depth conversation that LJ and similar platforms were famous for. This is not to say, however, that productive discourse is not taking place on Tumblr, only that it looks different than communication on LJ. Elli Bourlai, for example, has written about the significance of Tumblr tags as discursive practice.[128] Lori Morimoto and Louisa Stein have argued that the seemingly uncontrollable dissemination of bits and pieces of information on Tumblr has led to a "diversification of fandom participation" and a "greater visibility of peripheral fans and fan communities."[129] While many fans who joined fandom during the LJ era still mourn some of the practices that were lost with the shift to Tumblr, the new platform also opened up other possibilities and allowed fandom to develop in unexpected ways.[130] The point to be made here, to conclude this chapter, is not necessarily that one type of platform is inherently superior to the other, but that the specifics of the platform impact the discourses taking place among their users. The fact that RaceFail '09 happened during the LJ era was thus not a coincidence, but in many ways facilitated by the unique characteristics of journal-based platforms.

3

"Yep, the Hugo award might be RUINED!"

Geek Masculinity, Puppygate and the Reputation of the Hugo Awards

Introduction

In September 2019, Kevin Standlee, Chairman of the World Science Fiction Society (WSFS)'s Mark Protection Committee, was told by an AO3 user in an online comment that perhaps he might benefit from a "cross-cultural interpreter." Due to a "cultural gap of which you are unaware," the fan explained, "you've managed to deeply offend and put off a number of potential and current participants in Worldcon and the Hugos. [...] The bridge you meant to build is currently a smoldering wreck."[1]

The terse but seemingly sincere advice for Standlee was voiced in the face of a heated disagreement between two fannish fractions that had played out for the past month across different online platforms. The bone of contention was the Hugo, one of the most significant awards for English-language fantasy and science fiction; or more specifically, the Hugo Award for Best Related Work that had been given to the fanfiction archiving platform Archive of Our Own (AO3) at the 2019 Worldcon in Dublin. Affirmational fans in the literary SF/F community who saw themselves as representing the World Science Fiction Society (WSFS) on the one hand, and transformative fans associated with AO3 on the other argued about who should be allowed to lay claim to a Hugo Award, and how much respect the prestigious award was owed by its fans. Over the course of the controversy, several participants expressed the opinion that fundamental subcultural differences between the two fan groups were to blame for much of the disagreement that erupted in the wake of the Hugo Award ceremony.

The conflict around the nomination and victory of AO3 in the category Best Related Work was the second controversy surrounding the Hugo

Awards within a mere five years. Only a couple years prior, the efforts of fandom-adjacent right-wing groups to hijack the Hugo Award nominations had gone down into fandom history as "Puppygate." In both cases, the Hugo was more than merely a contested object; it became a symbol for the face and voice of contemporary fandom as a whole. Somewhat paradoxically, the World Science Fiction Society, in charge of presenting the Hugo Awards, found itself on different sides in the two conflicts. During Puppygate, the WSFS and the Hugos represented the increasing diversity and inclusivity of science fiction in the post–RaceFail era, values that had to be defended from right-wing influences trying to turn back time. In the controversy between WSFS and AO3, however, the Hugos stood for the conservative gatekeepers of traditional science-fiction fandom, concerned with preserving the traditional values of the fan community against the queer, female-dominated network of transformative fan creators.

In following the controversies around the Hugo Awards, this chapter brings the themes and conflicts described in the previous two chapters around full-circle, since the fannish arguments analyzed on the next pages appear in many ways simply as the most recent reiterations of the conflicts self-organized fandom has wrestled with since its birth in the early 20th century. Yet, the Hugo controversies are also a symptom for the shift in power dynamics between different fannish fractions that have slowly but surely changed the internal structure as well as the public face of fandom since the turn to the 21st century. The ideal of (white, straight, English-language) geek masculinity, historically framed as the "original" default fan identity, has never been as contested as it is in the contemporary fannish landscape, where it is competing with the increasingly public and self-confident network of transformative fans. At the same time, fannish controversies have become openly and directly entangled with national and global politics to a degree that is now impossible to ignore.

Ultimately, both controversies developed along two divisive axes that have been at the core of many major conflicts within fandom throughout the past century, often overlapping and intersecting in complex ways. The argument over AO3's Hugo win revolved primarily around the "subcultural differences" between affirmational and transformative fans. The tension between these two fan groups has perpetually flared up at different times ever since media fandom split off from affirmational literary SF/F fandom in the 1960s/1970s to provide a more welcoming environment for fans of audiovisual popular narratives, transformative fans, as well as female, queer, and non-white fans who didn't feel quite at home in the male-dominated, predominantly white, and hierarchically structured world of science-fiction fandom at the time. As described in Chapter 2, the differences between affirmative and transformative fan circles played a significant role for example in the conversations around RaceFail '09, the sprawling discussion about race and racism that divided the SF/F community in 2009.

Puppygate, on the other hand, seemed primarily influenced by another theme that has meandered as a continuing thread throughout the history of science-fiction, fantasy, comic, and video-game fandom: the expectation that fandom should remain entirely free from politics. Science-fiction fans in the 1920s and 1930s who were inspired by the Gernsbackian tradition celebrated a vision of scientific progress that they considered to be an objective, apolitical outlook on the world and the future. The group of socialist-leaning fans who were excluded from the first Worldcon in 1939[2] faced pushback specifically because they were invested in making fandom a more explicitly political space as a way to counter the rise of fascism in Europe. In the 1960s and 1970s, female writers exploring feminism in their work were similarly faced with the objection that their work was unnecessarily political when they began "telling established professional writers such as Poul Anderson and Philip K. Dick that they were not as enlightened as they thought they were."[3] Many of the professional writers and affirmative fans involved in RaceFail '09 defended their ideal of objective literary quality against what they saw as the politicization of fandom by fans who called out racist themes in works of science fiction and fantasy.[4] And in 2014, the instigators behind Gamergate, a rather violent attack on female gamers that shook the video-game fandom for months, were driven by the self-proclaimed goal of keeping their fan community free from politics.

As will become apparent throughout this chapter, the two axes of tension outlined above are not as distinct as it may appear at first glance. In fact, a closer look at these various conflicts makes it clear that they are inseparably intertwined. As it turns out, both oppositions ultimately play out as struggles over the concept of "geek masculinity" and its contested place as the presumed default fan identity.

The goal of an "apolitical" fandom, for example, has never been determined by objective criteria, but has generally been derived from the normative ideal of what fandom should be like. Because the history of fan communities that tend to uphold the notion of a politics-free fannish sphere has been shaped by predominantly male voices, the ethnocentric masculinist "Gernsbackian ideology"[5] with its belief in modernity, technology, scientific progress, and free markets has become the model on which most concepts of an apolitical fannish environment are based. By framing any divergence from the fannish norm as an attempt to drag politics into fandom, the representatives of Gernsbeckian thought (and later, geek masculinity) have been successful in obscuring the political foundations of their own ideals. In the past, this mostly meant that female fans, queer fans, or fans of color interested in bringing their own experiences and per-spectives into fannish spaces were accused of wanting to make fandom "too political." Even academic analyses of these conflicts have at times perpet-uated the normative myth of "apolitical" science fiction. In an attempt to redeem the Sad Puppies and their concerns, Stevens/van der Merwe argue that the "Puppies seem to argue for awards consideration for SF narratives built more explicitly for entertainment (such as military science fiction),"[6] thus obscuring the fact that military science fiction is anything but apo-litical and certainly not merely "entertainment" but a subgenre saturated with ideological beliefs around imperialism, militarism, colonialism, and masculinity.

Meanwhile, the distinction between affirmational and transformative fans has historically also been heavily gendered. Because their fan efforts were more directly geared toward professionalization and more often encouraged by the industry, the practices associated with male-dominated fan spaces have traditionally been valued higher than the transformative practices of "fangirls," which have tended to be dismissed as derivative and illegitimate. "For example," Ashley Hinck elaborates, "material productiv-ity that is gendered feminine, like cosplay, is sometimes undervalued, while memorizing quotes, issues, and facts—gendered masculine—is praised as the demonstration of a 'true fan.'"[7] Thus, "geek masculinity," the normative default of affirmative fandom whose origins go back to the earliest days of science-fiction fans conversing in the letter sections of Hugo Gernsback's *Amazing Stories*, has consistently distanced itself both from a "politicized" fandom and from transformative fan practices, ostensibly with the goal to protect the integrity of its own fan communities.

Comic-Con, Twilight *and Masculine Bias in Fandom*

The by now (in)famous slogan "Twilight ruined Comic-Con" has gained the kind of notoriety that may seem disproportional when look-ing at the original incident that initially brought forth the catchphrase. The slogan's origins go back to 2009 San Diego Comic-Con (SDCC), where the crowds of fans showing up for the panel promoting *The Twilight Saga: New Moon*[8] inspired consternation and resentment among those who had no interest in the vampire romance. Comic-Con attendants wandered the halls of the convention center holding signs with the slogan "Twilight ruined Comic-Con" to protest the presence of the young adult fantasy franchise at the convention. "By Saturday," Suzanne Scott recounts, "the 'protestors' had multiplied and were ironically prompting the thousands of attendees standing on line to enter SDCC's annual Masquerade to 'Scream if you think *Twilight* ruined Comic-Con.'"[9]

That the anti–*Twilight* catchphrase is still cited a decade after its circulation at SDCC 2009 might have to do with the fact that it encompasses several of the interwoven conflicts and tensions affecting the fannish landscape throughout the past decade, from the anti–*Twilight* protests and RaceFail[10] in 2009 to the debate surrounding the 2019 Hugo Awards.

On the surface, the "Twilight ruined Comic-Con" complaints gave voice to the "ongoing frustration with the mainstreaming and co-opting of 'nerd culture,'"[11] in other words: to fans' discomfort with what they saw as Comic-Con "selling out." This doesn't seem like an entirely unjustified concern. Similar to the earliest Worldcons, which had brought together a mere handful of people, Comic-Con's beginnings had been rather modest. The first Comic-Con, which had taken place in 1970 under the name "Golden State Comic-Con," counted about 300 visitors. As the convention has passed its 50th anniversary however, its public face has become almost unrecognizable. SDCC visitors have been confronted with the increasing presence of multi-billion-dollar franchises at the convention, as well as a growing number of television series and movies that don't seem to have all that much in common with the world of science fiction, fantasy, and comic books, such as the Showtime family drama *Shameless* (2011–2021).[12] These brands came, almost by necessity, with an influx of new fans who were (at least supposedly) not like the usual Comic-Con veterans. Even though SDCC's contract with San Diego has been extended until 2024,[13] there have been signs that the San Diego Convention Center won't much longer be able to host the convention which has been suffering from overcrowding for years, with annual visitor numbers exceeding 130,000. The Covid pandemic of 2020/2021 radically and unexpectedly changed the conversation further when the decision was made to hold SDCC 2020 as a virtual event—how this will affect future considerations around convention spaces and organizing will remain to be seen.

Twilight thus functioned as a stand-in for all the additions contributing to the loss of intimacy and cult spirit that, at least in the minds of wistful Comic-Con regulars, had characterized SDCC in its earlier years. However, it is not a coincidence that SDCC's perceived decline was not primarily blamed on any of the other enormous transmedia franchises at the convention (such as the *Marvel Cinematic Universe*) but rather specifically attributed to *Twilight*,[14] the franchise based on a young adult fantasy romance novel with a female protagonist that targeted young female readers. As vastly successful as the teenage romance franchise was, within the broader fandom landscape *Twilight* also attracted an unusually high number of "anti-fans"[15]: fans passionate enough in their dislike of *Twilight* to invest time, energy, and sometimes money into actively discrediting the franchise, such as the members of the so-called Anti-Twilight Movement.[16]

Some of this intense dislike was directed at the texts themselves, that is, the *Twilight* movies and the novels they are based on. Anti-fans voicing their disapproval of the *Twilight* novels and films had the advantage of being able to justify their contempt by pointing toward the mainstream press, which had criticized the books for their "overearnest, amateurish writing"[17] and author Stephenie Meyer for the promotion of sexual abstinence as well as the romanticized representation of controlling intimate partner behavior. In particular the public disapproval of *Twilight*'s regressive, anti-feminist gender politics was often framed as coming from a place of concern for the texts' recipients, such as in a review by David Cox, who warned that the "spell that Twilight casts over Twihard poppets and even their full-grown Twimoms cannot be assumed to be entirely benign."[18] Behind this concern stood the implication that female teenage readers (and, apparently, their mothers) are not capable of distinguishing between reality and fiction and thus fall prey to the false promises of popular culture more easily than other demographics: "If these readers accept Bella as a role model to be emulated," Ashley Renfro cautioned, "society will be looking at a generation that perceives the aforementioned stereotypes as an acceptable, or even positive, way to view women."[19]

The media response to *Twilight* exemplifies how notions of aesthetic quality are linked to assumptions about audiences. In his famous 1979 study *Distinction*, French sociologist Pierre Bourdieu demonstrated how cultural taste functions as a means of class distinction: the upper classes distance themselves from the middle and lower classes through their exclusive and expensive tastes.[20] Taste as a means of class distinction became increasingly relevant in the 18th century with the simultaneous rise of mass culture and democracy in the Western world. As nobility started to see their political power decline, taste allowed them to set themselves apart from the rising middle classes; and in turn taste also let the middle classes establish their cultural and moral superiority over the working class.

Yet from the beginning these judgments of taste were rooted not only in class consciousness but also in gender distinctions. In fact, discourses of taste often conflated categories of class and gender. For nobility in 18th-century England, mass culture was "vile, effeminate consumption," and "middle-class tastes [...] were the work of weak, unregulated passions, womanly cravings after fripperies, fancies and all manner of Chinese trash."[21] This association of bad taste with femininity continued into the 20th century. When Siegfried Kracauer titled his seminal essay on early 20th-century movie culture "Little Shopgirls Go to the Movies," he too envisioned working-class film audiences as female, naïve, and too easily influenced by the love stories they saw play out on screen: "The little shop-girls learn to understand that their brilliant boss is made of gold on the inside as well; they await the day when they can revive a young Berliner with their silly little hearts."[22]

The association of bad taste with female audiences is especially prevalent in the context of popular culture. The upper classes can define their (expensive) tastes as superior to those of the middle and lower classes by labeling the latter as childish and unrefined; since the lower classes don't have the possibility of positive class distinction, men can at least position their tastes as superior to those of women and children who share their status. A similar logic can be observed within fan culture. As Andrea Braithwaite explains, "geek masculinity is relational: it is understood relative to forms of femininity as well as to hegemonic masculinity."[23] Historically, male-dominated fan communities have seen themselves as ridiculed by mainstream society because of their intense dedication to objects of popular culture. This perception of their low position in the cultural hierarchy has led male fans to understand their own masculinity as "shaped by historical injury."[24] In turn, they themselves have appropriated existing cultural value systems in order to position, within the geek hierarchy, their own tastes and practices as superior to the interests of female fans, or "fangirls."

And indeed, negative stereotypes about female fans have been perpetuated for at least a century, even since before Kracauer wrote his essay about movie-addicted working-class girls. In her work on the fans of silent movie star Rudolph Valentino in the 1920s, Miriam Hansen argued that the public discourse about the fan community was "strongly marked by the terms of gender and sexuality."[25] She showed how mass media at the time dismissed female fans and discredited Valentino's masculinity in the same breath, thus putting both female fans' "inappropriate" behavior and their taste in men into question. In the 1952 musical film classic *Singin' in the Rain*,[26] the female-dominated star fandom of the silent film era is mocked with nostalgic fondness: Kathy Selden (Debbie Reynolds) shamefully admits that she reads all the fan mags, and pretentious diva Lina Lamont (Jean Hagen) puts so much trust in the fan magazines that she starts to believe what the journalists write about her own life.

In the 1960s, female Beatles fans were still portrayed by the media with descriptors that strongly resembled the representation of movie star fans 40 years prior. According to the media, "Beatlemania was an affliction, an 'epidemic,'" Barbara Ehrenreich et al. write. "There appeared to be no cure except for age, and the media pundits were fond of reassuring adults that the girls who had screamed for Frank Sinatra had grown up to be responsible, settled housewives."[27]

Another four decades later, these century-old tropes made yet another appearance. *Twilight* fans' fannish behavior was often described as an obsession and likened to mental illness. Melissa Click reports that "the media have belittled the reactions girls and women have had to the *Twilight* series and the actors who play their favorite characters, frequently using Victorian era gendered words like 'fever,' 'madness,' 'hysteria,' and 'obsession' to describe Twilighters and Twi-hards."[28] The Screen Junkies' "Honest Trailers" parody of *Twilight* introduced the first film adaptation in the following way: "Based on the terrible books from one of the shittiest authors of all time comes a movie adaptation for teenage girls who aren't smart enough for *The Hunger Games*."[29] The fake trailer introduces *Twilight* fans as female, young, and lacking in intelligence, thus combining gender, age, and educational capital as the identifiers that have historically been used to determine "bad taste." The trailer's comparison with *The Hunger Games* is significant as well. *The Hunger Games*[30] are brought up as another franchise for teenage girls, but with their boyish female protagonist and action-heavy plot they are, in the eyes of the Screen Junkies team, far superior to the romance-heavy *Twilight*. In other words, *The Hunger Games* are better because they are less exclusively focused on a stereotypically female experience. "The refusal of Twilight to meet the needs of a masculine audience" is precisely what makes it, as Salter/Blodgett suggest, "one of the most mocked and attacked franchises on the web."[31]

The curious story of the *My Little Pony* series reboot (2010–2019)[32] makes apparent just how much the judgment of a text is often based on its consumer base. The animated series, commissioned by Hasbro to accompany their *My Little Pony* toy line, explicitly targets young girls who are also the main intended consumer group for the toy figurines. However, when *My Little Pony* unexpectedly started attracting a dedicated fanbase of adult men, these so-called "Bronies"[33] did not face public derision for enjoying a female-oriented youth-centric text; instead the male fans made it possible for *My Little Pony* to be elevated to the status of a cult text: "Bronies are the defining face of *My Little Pony* fandom, taking what would have been a 'pink ghetto' show and making it both masculine and cool."[34]

The different narratives around *Twilight* and *My Little Pony* thus perpetuate the dichotomy between the "fangirl," the young, naïve, hysterical female fan, and the "fanboy," the nerdy but knowledgeable male connoisseur of cult media. The public celebration of male *My Little Pony* fans affirmed the status of fanboys as the real fans or "trufen": "The resulting message is clear: it takes a real man (geek) to appreciate *My Little Pony*."[35] Meanwhile, fangirls are always under suspicion of being too emotional about their fannish interests, which they don't approach with the appropriate level of academic rigor: "Twilight fangirls fail to be good fans, and thus embarrass other fans, by liking the wrong things and liming [*sic*] them in the wrong ways."[36] Not only do fangirls (and other fans from underrepresented groups) face dismissal and ridicule for their "childish" or "unsophisticated" interests; their fan practices and activities are frequently perceived as an intrusion or disruption, prompting exclusionary measures from the larger fan community.

One such complaint was voiced in 2012 by fan and cosplayer Joe Peacock, who published a lament on the CNN blog *Geek Out!* about the presence of "pretty girls pretending to be geeks for attention"[37] at San Diego Comic-Con. Peacock hurried to explain that not every woman attending fan conventions qualifies as a fake geek girl: "I am good friends with several stunningly beautiful women who cosplay as stunningly beautiful characters from comics, sci-fi, fantasy and other genres of fandom. They are, each of them, bone fide geeks." What *was* a crime, in his eyes, was the infiltration of fannish spaces by women who, presumably, had failed to pursue successful "real-life" modeling careers and instead taken advantage of the women shortage in fandom to increase their erotic capital. "They're poachers. They're a pox on our culture. As a guy, I find it repugnant that, due to my interests in comic books, sci-fi, fantasy and role playing games, video games and toys, I am supposed to feel honored that a pretty girl is in my presence."

Interestingly, Peacock describes, perhaps unknowingly, these female fans with the same term ("poachers") that fan studies scholar Henry Jenkins borrowed in the 1990s from Michel de Certeau to describe the female-dominated practice of fanfiction writing.[38] Both Jenkins and Peacock purposefully use the term "poaching" to allude to the typically gendered nature of fannish practices. Where fanboys lean on average toward affirmative fan practices that treat the canon as a sacred text and are "more likely to collect (trivia and merchandise) than create,"[39] fangirls are "poachers" because they have "historically been more invested in subtext rather than text, and more attached to the 'fanon' (texts produced by other fans) than the producer's construction of the canon"[40]—a consequence of working with an archive of texts that for the most part don't take them into account as an audience. Yet, where Jenkins celebrated fannish poaching as a creative and resistant transformative practice, Peacock as a self-proclaimed defender of geek masculinity considered poaching a violation of fannish norms. He explicitly linked female-connoted fan practices to the image of the fake geek girl, which has become a common reference point as perceived threat in male-dominated fan spaces.

The "Idiot Nerd Girl" is a viral online meme/image macro series that originated in 2010, featuring the picture of a young white woman in glasses with the word "nerd" written on her hand. As the meme circulated online, the image was accompanied by different captions meant to illustrate the Idiot Nerd Girl's ignorance regarding fannish topics, and to "expose" her as an imposter who merely claims to be a geek. "According to this meme, there is a plague of girls who perform geekiness as nothing more than an affectation."[41] One iteration of the meme read, for example: "My favorite superhero? Probably X-man—Hugh Jackman is sooooo hot."[42] This version of the meme makes fun of a hypothetical female fan both for revealing her ignorance regarding the fannish textual archive[43] and for her obsession with attractive male actors instead of a genuine interest in comic books. But the problem with the fake geek girl is not only her alleged ignorance of cult texts, but rather her perceived posturing as a real geek—her fakeness "implies deceit, infiltration, and performance, rendering it far more pernicious and effective as an anti-fan gatekeeping strategy."[44]

The sexy cosplayers at SDCC did receive support from another male member of the SF/F/C community. In response to Peacock's complaint, professional science-fiction author John Scalzi wrote an opinion piece on his personal blog with the title "Who Gets to Be a Geek? Anyone Who Wants to Be."[45] Scalzi's essay—which was already mentioned in the introduction to this volume—advocated for a tolerant fan community with room for more than one type of fannish identity: "Geekdom is a nation with open borders. There are many affiliations and many doors into it."

His celebratory defense of multi-faceted geekdom inspired more than 700 overwhelmingly positive comments that praised him for capturing the beautiful spirit of what fandom is meant to be about. Yet while Scalzi declared himself to be an ally to fangirls and other "non-traditional" fans, he also positioned himself as an authority on the proper way of all things fandom by listing his own geek credentials (such as published works, award nominations, TV consulting work, committee work) and then stating triumphantly: "I outrank you as Speaker for the Geeks. You are *overruled.*"

His public display of allyship thus became an example of "white-knighting." "White knights, or men to the rescue, are a common form of advocate in both the media and geek communities,"[46] as Salter/ Blodgett explain. Using their social capital within the community to defend members from underrepresented groups, the interventions of white knights add weight to the plights of less influential community participants that might otherwise go unacknowledged. Yet by speaking on their behalf instead of giving them a voice of their own, white knights ultimately perpetuate the exclusion of those they set out to defend: "Although cast as being good in nature, the actions of the white knight serve to limit and bound the community of geeks by preventing women from being able to participate as real people."[47] The fact that Scalzi's list of credentials includes exclusively stereotypically male-connotated accomplishments made his intervention on behalf of fangirls more effective, yet simultaneously revalidated implicitly the norms of geek masculinity.

In addition, white knights often gain social capital through behavior that would be a reason for exclusion if done by other, less privileged members of the community. Even though his claim to be the "Speaker for the Geeks" was meant to be tongue-in-cheek, many of the commenters proceeded to affirm him in this position by addressing him as "O Speaker" and referring to him as "geek nobility."[48] By stepping up in defense of female cosplayers, Scalzi thus (intentionally or not) received validation for his own traditional geek credentials, a phenomenon that Rebecca Busker calls out when she writes that "the valorization that men like Scalzi and Jim Hines receive for speaking positively on women's issues does point to the way fandom still struggles with male privilege."[49]

However, the defenders of geek masculinity and their white knight opponents are not the only fans upholding masculine bias in fandom. Because the position of female fans in male-dominated fan communities is so precarious, and contingent on them complying with dominant norms, fangirls often find it necessary to set themselves apart from the "fake geek girls" in order to avoid being targeted themselves. Scott recognized this reflex even in her own reaction to the 2009 anti–*Twilight* protests:

> I did not actively participate in the Twihate protests at SDCC 2009, but I did occasionally resent the mass influx of Twi-hards at the convention. The root of my (comparably mild) annoyance didn't align with Twihate protesters complaints, and I found the misogyny simmering beneath the fan-on-fan protests both surprising and unsettling. My annoyance stemmed from being perpetually lumped into the most visible, vocal mass of female fans at the convention, based solely on my gender.[50]

In fact, *Twilight* was so well-suited to serve as the scapegoat for the decline of Comic-Con in parts because the franchise was highly controversial among female fans themselves, both within the broader SF/F community and in online transformative fandom. Many female fans who self-identified as feminists rejected the *Twilight* novels and movies primarily for their regressive gender politics, yet their objections nevertheless contributed to the ostracization of *Twilight* fangirls. Thus, they found themselves in a strange alliance with male fans suspecting a fake geek girl behind every female-presenting fan and implicitly ended up reaffirming the hierarchy of values that positions male-oriented texts as superior to works primarily addressing women. This appropriation of feminist *Twilight* critiques for the cause of an ultimately misogynist agenda is remarkable especially because female fans with an investment in feminist thought have historically been perceived to be as much of a threat to fandom as the "fake geek girls" ever since feminist science fiction gained a more visible and thus contested presence in the literary science-fiction community during the 1960s.

The Historical Erasure of Female Fans

The discourse surrounding *Twilight* evokes several other incidents from the history of Western self-organized fandom. When the original iteration of *Star Trek*[51] first aired on television in the late 1960s, it was met with a response that in some ways resembled fandom's reaction to *Twilight*.[52] The fans who were reluctant to embrace *Star Trek* saw it as a product of mass culture that didn't hold up to their qualitative standards of literary science fiction. *Star Trek* also managed to attract a large number of new fans, many of them female, who had not previously been involved in the sci-fi community. In 1988, Robert Runte lamented that the "mere size of the influx destroyed the close-knit intimacy of fandom […] Fans felt themselves a minority at their own celebrations (conventions)."[53]

Despite the fact that many long-term sci-fi fans were quite excited about *Star Trek*, and that by far not all *Star Trek* fans were female, the dominant narrative around the origins of *Star Trek* fandom was one of literary science-fiction fandom being overrun with crowds of young female fans who didn't know the last thing about science fiction. In other words, *Star Trek* too was once considered suspicious because the show was too mainstream and its fans too uninformed and too female.

This strategy of (re)framing female fans, queer fans, fans of color and their fan practices as new additions (or rather, intrusions) to fandom has been a common practice throughout the history of fan culture. There is more than sufficient evidence that women have from the earliest days been active participants in science-fiction fandom. Yet the fannish narrative that the "original" (and thus, most "authentic") science-fiction fans were white straight men has been so persuasive that even a female scholar such as Camille Bacon-Smith who specifically studied the role of female fans in science-fiction fandom didn't quite escape this discourse when she described the founders of science-fiction fandom as "young men, raised to expectations of employment and status that the worldwide Great Depression took away."[54] Similarly, female comic book readers have been erased from historiographies of comic fandom, despite the fact that they used to make up a large part of the readership, as Suzanne Scott points out:

> In comic books' Golden Age, at the height of its popularity as a mass media form in the 1940s, comics were equally popular with adolescent and preadolescent boys and girls […]. [T]he current discursive construction of women as a surplus audience obscures the fact that they were a preexisting segment of

comic books' audience at a time when comics consumption wasn't as stringently gendered.[55]

Fandom-adjacent tech culture is another community that has rewritten its own history to present computers and technology as traditionally male-dominated fields, producing a "distorted history of technological development that has rendered women's contributions invisible and promoted a diminished view of women's capabilities in this field."[56] In reality, "the job of programmer, perceived in recent years as masculine work, originated as feminized clerical labor."[57] When human computers were replaced by machines, those too were initially "manned" by women: computing, coding, programming were considered women's work all the way throughout the 1960s when the public prestige of computing began to increase and simultaneously women's participation in the field began to decline:

> During the 1980s, as computers and networked technology took centre stage as fulcrums of globalization and macro-economic change, the conflation of masculinity with computing was amplified. In advertising, in software design, in burgeoning fan cultures such as "hacking" and video gaming, in pop culture, in educational and training contexts and in computing-related professions, a singular message emanated: computers were for boys and men. Femininity and computing were positioned as antithetical to one another across multiple domains.[58]

Thus, while historical evidence clearly shows that women have been part of tech, geek, and fan culture throughout the entirety of the 20th century, the significant participation of female fans and tech geeks has been retroactively erased from most dominant narratives. In Chapter 2, I discussed how fandom's reliance on mediated communication (via fanzines and online platforms) and their preference for pen names and pseudonyms has actually facilitated this development because it allowed fans, scholars, and journalists to make often biased assumptions about the identities of the fans behind the pseudonyms. However, the retroactive erasure of women's roles in fan and tech communities was also supported by the (lack of) value that was attributed to their contributions at the time. For example, in the history of computing "the actual work performed by women contrasted with how employers categorized this work," leading to "the implicit assumption of computing historians that the low-status occupations of women meant that their work could not be innovative."[59] In male-dominated fannish spaces (that is, most prominent fan communities outside of star fandom, romance fandom, and transformative fandom), female fans were often thought of in their roles as the wives, girlfriends, or daughters of male fans, and their contributions were framed as supportive rather than creative or administrative. In general, women were tolerated in these communities, sometimes even welcomed, but only as long as they agreed to play by the same rules as their fellow male geeks and fans. As Scott worded it, "fangirls are welcome at SDCC, provided that they submit to the regulatory gaze of the panopti(comic)con."[60]

Over the past ten years however, fangirls, transformative fans, fans of color, and otherwise underrepresented groups of fans have increasingly refused to play by the rules of geek masculinity. The backlash these fans have faced in return should not be understood so much as a response to their mere presence in fandom—many representatives from all these groups had been part of various fan communities for decades. Yet when they started critiquing the status quo and voiced their expectation that they should be acknowledged as equals in male- and white-dominated fan spaces, they began to be labeled as fake geeks, poachers, intruders, and imposters.

Two interrelated developments within the recent broader fannish landscape are responsible for this noticeable shift of power dynamics in the geek hierarchy. On the one hand, the enormous growth of the sprawling network of communities that is known as transformative online fandom has significantly changed how these fans relate to each other, their fannish objects, and the world. In Chapter 2, I showed how the migration of media fandom to the internet in the 1980s/1990s, and subsequently to journal-based platforms around 2000 led to the reinvention of a fannish identity that was framed less as the secret member of an underground subculture and more as participant in a globally networked public sphere.

On the other hand, transformative fandom became increasingly public in the sense that it appeared more frequently on the radar of the general public, leading to a "mainstreaming of fannish behavior and increased attention to fans by media and show producers."[61] The higher publicness of fandom also meant that various fannish niches increasingly intersected with other, non-fannish alternative publics. This blurring of lines between fan communities and non-fannish movements and publics led, by necessity, to an increased awareness of the intersections between fandom and politics. This, in turn, contributed to a growing number of awareness-raising campaigns and social activism projects that will be described in detail in Chapter 4. It also led to conversations like RaceFail '09, which gave fans of color the chance to find a shared voice and demand to be heard by the wider fan community.[62] However, as will become apparent later in this chapter, this intersection of fan spaces with non-fannish political spaces also opened the door for the systemic infiltration of fan communities by right-wing groups, which further contributed to the overt politicization of the fandom landscape.

To summarize, transformative fandom in the years between 2005 and 2019 was shaped by the combination of

a. new generations of fans being socialized within widely connected, heavily female- and queer-dominated spaces,
b. fans taking control of digital communication and publication technologies through the foundation of independent media platforms such as Archive of Our Own and Dreamwidth in 2008,
c. fans experiencing a sense of empowerment through the participation in fan-organized social activism, and finally
d. transformative fan communities being increasingly acknowledged by mass media and creators as a cultural force in its own right.

The self-confidence fans gained as a consequence of these developments encouraged them to demand a voice in fannish spaces that had previously been designed to keep them out. While media fans in the 1960s had consciously retreated from male-dominated club- and convention-centric fan spaces to create their own fanzines and organize their own conventions, transformative fans in the 21st century set out to reclaim those same spaces without being willing to abandon or hide their cultural backgrounds and fannish origins. In the science-fiction and fantasy community, fans of color used some of the energy they had harnessed by joining forces in the Race-Fail '09 debate in order to push for more diverse and inclusive representation in genre fiction. Within comic book fandom, "[t]he years 2011 and 2012 were marked by increased attention to the place and perception of women within comic book culture."[63] At 2011 SDCC, for example, a female Batgirl cosplayer made her appearance as the "Batgirl of San Diego" who asked uncomfortable questions about female representation in comic books during various DC Comics panels.[64] A couple years later, the collective fanworks project *The Hawkeye Initiative* set out to critique the dominance of the male gaze in superhero comic art by replacing the hypersexualized female characters on comic book covers with the figure of Hawkeye, a male superhero owned by Marvel.[65]

Rather than the mere presence of women or fans of color in general, it was this unapologetic claiming of spaces and voices that was perceived as a threat to the ideal of geek masculinity by many fans in the still male-dominated communities of science-fiction and comic fandom as well as the hypermasculine gaming community. Fueled by a shift in the global political climate that led to the rise of populist right-wing movements and governments in a number of countries around the world, this perceived threat to the traditional fan identity led to a backlash that included, for example, the negative responses to *Twilight*'s presence at 2009 Comic-Con, and explains why the following decade was marked by a considerable number of publicly fought heated conflicts such as Gamergate,[66] the anti–*Ghostbusters*[67] campaign,[68] and the Fappening,[69] all of which were more or less explicitly driven by misogynist, racist, and homophobic sentiments. The two controversies around the Hugo Awards that will be discussed on the following pages were also both prompted by a backlash to the perceived politicization and diversification of fandom, although the Hugo Awards themselves ended up on different sides of the conflict in the respective debates.

Puppies Attack the Hugo Awards

Established in 1953, the Hugo Awards are among the oldest and best-known awards for English-language science fiction and fantasy.[70] They are named after Hugo Gernsbeck, founder of the science-fiction magazine *Amazing Stories*, which has often been credited with being the point of origin for self-organized science-fiction fandom. The Hugos are presented by the World Science Fiction Society but voted on by all current Worldcon members. Everyone who has paid the annual membership fee is permitted to nominate works of science fiction and fantasy that they consider worthy of an award under various categories. Shortlists are created based on these nominations, and Worldcon members cast advance votes so that the winners can be announced at the convention. Since the late 1950s, eligible voters have had the option to select "No Award" in any category if none of the nominees appeal to them. Since anyone able to pay the membership fee can become a temporary Worldcon member, the Hugo Awards have always been primarily an indicator for current popular trends and authors within the genre, rather than an impartial evaluation of literary "quality."

Although the strategy was considered to be in contradiction with the spirit of the Hugos, the official rules opened the elections up to the possibility of bloc voting. And indeed, Puppygate (as the event was titled by fantasy author G.R.R. Martin)[71] was not the first time bloc voting caused an uproar in the lead-up to a Worldcon. Jo Walton reports that during the 1989 nominations there was "a curious withdrawal—apparently P.J. Beese and Todd Cameron Hamilton's novel *The Guardian* [...] had enough votes for a nomination, but the administrators concluded that the votes were bloc votes and disqualified them."[72] The Noreascon[73] III organizing committee released a statement about the incident in June 1989:

> In counting the nominations, we observed a significant pattern of what appeared to us to be bloc voting, amounting to over 50 votes in some categories. The number of these votes was sufficient to place nominees on the final ballot in

the followin [sic] categories: Novel, Professional Artist, Fan Writer, Fan Artist and Campbell Award. More seriously, about half of these ballots were received with new Supporting Memberships, nearly all of which appeared to have been paid for by the same person or persons [...]. We were highly disturbed by this practice.[74]

While Walton accurately identified the contested title, her discussion of the situation is somewhat misleading insofar as the Worldcon committee did not directly disqualify any votes or nominees. Instead, they responded to the discovery by adding an additional (sixth) nominee to each affected shortlist, so that works which might have been pushed off the shortlist by the questionable ballots still had a chance. However, a number of fans read their statement as an accusation against the creators implicated in the scandal, which prompted Beese and Hamilton to withdraw their nominations after voicing their displeasure with the organizing committee.[75]

Ultimately the Noreascon III voting scandal revolved less around the strategy of bloc voting in itself, which most agreed was tasteless but within the rules of the game, but rather around the discovery that a handful of people had bought memberships (and thus votes) in other people's names. Still, it does indicate that longtime Worldcon members must have been well aware of this loophole in the Hugo nominations process, but did not see a need to revamp the voting process—not until Puppygate took bloc voting to an unprecedented scale in 2014.

Ironically, the same voting process that made bloc voting possible in the first place was one of the first things to be attacked by the Puppy Movement in their attempt to undermine the Hugo Awards. "The ugly truth is," self-proclaimed Puppy leader Larry Correia wrote in his critique of the nomination procedure,

that the most prestigious award in sci-fi/fantasy is basically just a popularity contest, where the people who are popular with a tiny little group of Worldcon voters get nominated and thousands of other works are ignored. Books that tickle them are declared good and anybody who publically deviates from groupthink is bad.[76]

Correia, a politically conservative fantasy author, had been using the phrase "sad puppy" as early as 2009 as a tag on his blog *Monster Hunter Nation*. Initially, the tag was mostly reserved for critiques of liberalism and the Obama administration. In 2013, however, Correia added the tag to a post headed by a photo of a tiny sad-looking puppy. Setting the mood by referencing an ASPCA TV commercial "where they play the sad song and show injured puppies and dying kitties,"[77] Correia outright asked his readers to nominate him for a Hugo Award. Despite his readers' assurances in the comment section, Correia did not end up taking home a nomination that year; but he gave himself credit for the success of other authors he had promoted on his blog and took this as motivation to repeat (and double) his efforts the following year. In his renewed appeal, he was far more outspoken about his beef with the Hugo Awards and vowed to expose the "popularity contest" that determined the Hugos: "I'm going to prove it is just a popularity contest by getting a nomination by being more popular."[78] He also complained that the current Hugo fashion seemed to favor "screeds about corporate greed, global warming, dying polar bears, or whatever the left wing cause of the day is."[79] Too many works, he argued, were nominated solely because of their emphasis on social justice rather than their literary quality or entertainment factor, and he called on his fans "to nominate some works that are actually entertaining."

Finally, in 2015 the Puppy movement managed to dominate the list of nominated works and drew significant media attention. Science-fiction author Brad Torgersen, to whom Correira had passed the torch, launched "Sad Puppies 3" with a call for action that sounded much like a political pamphlet. Torgersen lamented that "we've seen the Hugo voting skew ideological, as Worldcon and fandom alike have tended to use the Hugos as an affirmative action award."[80] He invited his readers to contribute suggestions for a slate of works that had been "unjustly" overlooked because they didn't comply with the current taste for social justice. As Jim Hines has pointed out, barely any of Torgersen's readers' suggestions made it onto the final slate, indicating that the released list of works was less a group effort and more based on Correia and Torgersen's personal preferences.[81] Theodore Beale/Vox Day, one of their nominees, jumped onto the bandwagon to start his own campaign, the Rabid Puppies: an angrier, more aggressive and overtly political version of Correia's Sad Puppies.

The impact on the 2015 Hugo nominations was significant. The Puppies made no real attempt to hide their efforts, but since they operated technically within the rules of the game, the WSFS seemed to feel powerless to intervene. Between the Sad and the Rabid Puppies, the final shortlists were heavily dominated by Puppy-approved authors. Fifty-one out of 60 Sad Puppy recommendations and 58 out of 67 Rabid Puppy slate titles made it onto the shortlists. Even though a handful of these authors withdrew their nominations, not wanting to be associated with the Puppies' agenda, the nomination and voting process was still overshadowed to a degree that prompted G.R.R. Martin to announce: "I think the Sad Puppies have broken the Hugo Awards, and I am not sure they can ever be repaired."[82] Martin's fatalistic response and countless other opinion pieces that circulated online in the following months made it clear that the Worldcon community was highly unsettled by these developments.

In response, science-fiction fans chose to beat the Puppies with their own weapons: by utilizing the existing WSFS voting rules to their advantage. In both 2014 and 2015, Worldcon membership numbers increased rather dramatically, only to drop off again in 2016.[83] In particular the supporting (non-attending) memberships spiked: in 2015, the total membership was more than twice the number of Worldcon attendees (10,350 vs. 4,644), indicating that many people bought memberships specifically to be able to vote either in favor of, or against the authors on the Puppy slates. This was confirmed by the unusually high number of final votes, which showed an increase from 3,587 in 2014 to almost 6,000 the following year.[84]

In the end, "Hugo voters turned out in inflated numbers to reject the Puppy candidates."[85] In most categories, non–Puppy authors were selected. In categories where the shortlist was entirely comprised of Puppy slate candidates, many voters selected "No Award," leading to the unusual outcome of several categories being left without a winner on the night of the award ceremony, a result that the Worldcon crowd chose to interpret as a victory over the Puppy invasion. When N.K. Jemisin, Black fantasy author, active RaceFail '09 participant, and one of Vox Day's nemeses, became the first Black writer to take home a Hugo for Best Novel in 2016, many in the science-fiction community saw her success as a sign that the Puppies' reign of terror had come to an end.[86]

However, Tasha Robinson argued that even though they failed in their attempt to take the 2015 Hugos in storm, ultimately the Sad and Rabid Puppies

> did win the day. The group successfully prevented a wide variety of other content from making it to the finalist list. […] And the Puppies didn't just dominate the finalist slate, they dominated the conversation for the entire convention. They forced everyone at Worldcon to acknowledge them and their agenda, and to take sides in the conflict or work around them.[87]

Getting particular authors elected had always been only one of the Puppy leaders' goals. From the beginning, Correira had made it clear that he was also trying to troll the Hugo voting process. "Much like the Joker," Buckels et al. explain, "trolls operate as agents of chaos on the Internet, exploiting 'hot-button issues' to make users appear overly emotional or foolish in some manner."[88] The Puppies took advantage of the WSFS's faith in their own rules and their reluctance to break protocol, by exploiting a well-known but rarely used loophole. And they very much succeeded in what they set out to do, considering that their actions plunged the Worldcon community into uproar for more than two years, and prompted the WSFS to implement changes to their nomination rules[89] in 2017 that would make bloc voting strategies less effective.

To acknowledge that one of the Puppies' explicit goals was to troll the

WSFS does not diminish their agenda's dangerous potential. In fact, even though trolling is often dismissed as childish, quasi-anarchist behavior, it can become immensely effective precisely because it claims to be devoid of a particular (political) purpose. According to Megan Condis, trolling is a practice steeped in masculinity, "a game in which one improves one's own standing both by enacting masculine performances of dominance and self-mastery, and by successfully baiting others into losing status by letting their mask of masculinity slip."[90] Her argument is supported by Buckels etc.'s findings that male users are more likely than women to engage in trolling behavior.

In the past decade, trolling has been frequently employed as a derailment strategy by right-wing groups and individuals to undermine social justice-related conversations or activism in various online controversies. In both its practice and in its general rhetoric, Puppygate resembled a number of other online controversies, from Gamergate with its vicious attacks on female gamers, game designers, and journalists in 2014, to the angry protests of male cult fans against the female-led *Ghostbusters* reboot in 2016. In all these conflicts, predominantly male conservative fans expressed their anger at the notion that concern for "quality" in science-fiction, fantasy, comic books, or gaming was replaced by a preoccupation with diversity and inclusivity. The main culprits, in their eyes, were fans that acted as so-called Social Justice Warriors, an insult for "a person who expresses or promotes socially progressive views" that became "a popular shorthand way to discredit and dismiss anyone who presented views that contradicted the straight white male majority."[91]

Stevens/van der Merwe have suggested that the Sad Puppies' arguments should be taken as serious concerns responding to shifts in the fiction publishing landscape, and that the Puppies' culture war rhetoric hides an otherwise valid critique: "it is the anti-feminist and anti-social justice rhetoric that understandably commands the attention of their opponents (both within the fan community and in media coverage), making productive communicative exchange difficult."[92] Yet this kind of argument obscures the immediate connections both between the Puppies' strategies and toxic geek masculinity, and between Puppygate and other right-wing groups. First, it is not a coincidence that it has been, as Suzanne Scott points out, primarily "white, cishet men who tend to decry the loss of fandom's subcultural authenticity, even as they reap the demographic, industrial, authorial, and representational benefits of this loss."[93] It is also, second, crucial to interpret Puppygate not only within the framework of fandom history, but also in the context of these other controversies playing out in different but connected corners of the internet, as well as against the backdrop of the alt-right ideology that fueled these debates. Despite their similarities, these various events have been, as Sarah Banet-Weiser argues, "routinely dismissed as an outlier, an anomaly, a technological 'glitch.'"[94] In both fannish and public discourse, the controversies are framed as isolated events instigated by "bad apples" who cause much trouble to their respective communities but don't reflect back on the group as a whole. This narrative allows fan communities to maintain their ideal of a unified, tight-knit community under threat from the outside[95] and to obscure the existence of structural inequalities by blaming racism, homophobia, and misogyny on a few misguided individuals. In contrast, Banet-Weiser emphasizes the importance of understanding these phenomena as the visible markers of "a broad networked structure, not as distinct expressions or outbursts."[96]

A closer look reveals quickly that the similarities in rhetoric and approach are not coincidental: several leading figures were involved in more than one of the above-mentioned campaigns. Theodore Beale/Vox Day, for example, had already gained notoriety in the science-fiction community prior to his involvement in Puppygate for being expelled from the Science Fiction and Fantasy Writers of America (SWFA). In her Guest of Honor speech at 2013 Continuum in Australia, N.K. Jemisin briefly referred to Beale's previous unsuccessful candidacy for the SWFA presidency, describing him as racist, homophobic, and anti–Semitic. This in turn prompted Vox Day to insult Jemisin on his blog by calling her, among other things, a "half-savage." When he linked his comments about Jemisin on the SFWA official Twitter account, the SWFA responded by retracting his membership.

At the time of the Puppies' attack on the Hugo Awards, Vox Day was also involved in Gamergate, which allowed him to rally support for the Puppy movement from Gamergate participants. Among them was alt-right celebrity and Gamergate figurehead Milo Yiannopoulos, who happened to be also one of the instigators behind the anti–Ghostbusters campaign: Yiannopoulos ended up being banned from Twitter permanently in response to his racist, misogynist, and transphobic tweets directed at Black Ghostbusters actress Leslie Jones.[97] The Puppies found further support in Yiannopoulos' employer Breitbart, the right-wing news platform run by executive chair Steve Bannon, who had previously been involved with the Hong-Kong-based company Internet Gaming Entertainment (IGE). IGE became known for using cheap labor in China to accrue virtual gold within the online game World of Warcraft[98] (WOW) and sell it to other players at game world market prices. His experience with WOW likely tipped Bannon off to the gaming community's aggressively conservative political potential: "It was Bannon who hired Milo Yiannopoulos, recognizing him as someone who could whip up disaffected gamers"[99] in the lead-up to the

2016 presidential election to garner support for Donald Trump's campaign, whose chief strategist Bannon would become.

Tracing the personal connections between various fannish circles, controversies, and national politics makes apparent that Puppygate, Gamergate, and the *Ghostbusters* controversy were all part of a networked movement closely linked to the rise of the alt-right: "Geek themes have been opportunistically integrated into white supremacist recruitment strategies, while the Gamergate rhetoric of 'social justice warriors' is now a regular part of the vocabulary of right-wing politicians and pundits."[100] During the summer of 2020, even male *My Little Pony* fans have come under critique for sharing blatantly racist fanart on the *My Little Pony* platform Derpibooru, eventually forcing the platform moderators to adjust their hands-off anti-censorship stance and announce that they would ban racist fanworks from the site.[101]

This entanglement of fandom with national politics highlights the irony that these campaigns were allegedly led in the name of keeping fandom free from politics. The fans who were swept up by Puppygate claimed to care only about quality literature and good entertainment, and expressed their frustration with what they saw as a politicization of fandom by those who kept writing about and nominating works with diverse protagonists or social justice-related messages. The viral meme "Actually it's about ethics in gaming journalism"[102] gets to the core of this paradox: the meme mocked Gamergaters who claimed that they were merely defending responsible journalistic practices in video game journalism even as they viciously attacked female gamers, designers, and writers. Banet-Weiser agrees

> that the gaming industry sees itself as "depoliticized." A common refrain from game developers is "We're just making a game, we're not sending a message." Any game that diverges from the standard fodder of games—sports, violence, war—is seen as "political," which is why [...] Zoe Quinn's *Depression Quest* was seen as an affront to the entire industry, and why adding gay romances to *Dragon Age* was considered such a threat.[103]

This argument, perpetuated by Puppies and Gamergaters alike, retains an echo of several earlier fannish conflicts throughout the 20th century—such as the First Great Exclusion of 1939 (discussed in Chapter 1), during which socialist fans were excluded from Worldcon because they tried to bring politics into fandom while fans from the centrist-conservative Gernsbackian wing of fandom perceived themselves as apolitical. Thus, the controversy behind Puppygate was not entirely new, but it was also not merely a reiteration of previous arguments. The strategic capitalization on existing fannish resentment in the gaming, science-fiction, and cult film communities by political figures in order to win a national election had previously been

unheard of. That the infiltration of fan culture by the alt-right was so effective had much to do with the agents' intimate knowledge of fandom—they
spoke the language of the community, played into existing tensions, and
thus succeeded in what was ultimately a weaponization of geek masculinity.

AO3 and the Reputation of the Hugo Awards

In 2019, the Hugo Awards once again became the scene of a heated
fannish controversy, yet this time the roles were differently assigned. Nominated under the category "Best Related Work" was the fanfiction platform
Archive of Our Own, a site run by the Organization for Transformative
Works which had been established in 2007 to give fanfiction writers access
to an independently owned publication platform without fear of legal
repercussions or attempts at commercialization.[104]

The nomination in itself was quite unusual, even considering the category AO3 was nominated under, which has always been somewhat of an
odd reservoir for rather different types of creations. Its history goes back
to 1962, when a "Special Award" was given at Chicon 1962 to Fritz Leiber
and the Hoffman Electric Corp. "for the use of science fiction in advertisements." Hoffman Electronics, a private contractor for the Defense Department, had commissioned a number of short stories by acclaimed authors
such as Isaac Asimov and Robert A. Heinlein. "These stories appeared
throughout 1962 as part of advertisements for Hoffman which originally
appeared in the pages of *Scientific American* but were also reprinted in
other magazines (such as *Fortune*)."[105] Even though this special award was
given for a set of fictional stories, the circumstances of Leiber's advertising
campaign made it one of the "things for which the Hugos did not have categories at the time."[106]

In 1980, the official category "Best Non-Fiction Book" was implemented, which Jo Walton refers to as an "odd category,"[107] since it was used
as umbrella for a broad range of different works, including memoirs, restaurant guides, and how-to books. Yet even this category didn't seem sufficient
to capture any type of creation potentially worthy of a Hugo Award. Thus,
1988 saw the momentary appearance of a category called "Other Forms,"
before "Non-Fiction Book" was renamed "Related Book" in 1998 and eventually turned into "Related Work" in 2010, which opened the category up to
genre-related works that didn't come in book form.

AO3's nomination was unexpected not so much because it wasn't a
traditional book publication, not even because it was an online platform—
online fanzines had been nominated ever since the mailing list SF-Lovers
Digest received a special award in 1989 as "the first online anything to get an

award."[108] Rather, AO3's nomination stood out because it marked a moment in fannish history when the World Science Fiction Society, representing the wing of traditional literary science-fiction fandom, finally appeared to officially acknowledge and honor the community of transformative online fandom.

Literary science-fiction fandom has generally been defined and under-stood itself as an affirmational fandom—despite the fact that the sci-fi community has always included not only professional authors and their fans, but also a significant number of fan writers. In fact, because so many professional writers started their careers as fans and fan writers, the creator/fan distinction has always been blurrier than it might seem at first glance. Yet, the notion of literary originality continues to hold weight as a writerly aspiration in the community, professional authors are treated with rever-ence, and the transition to professional published writer is the goal most fan writers aspire to. As obsession-inc explains, in affirmational fandom "the creator holds the magic trump card of Because I'm The Only One Who Really Knows, That's Why, and that is accepted as a legitimate thing." Since these fans rarely question the author's intention or literary genius, they are typically "the *sanctioned* fans. [...] It's also worth noting that these fans congregate online largely on creator sites [...]. Due to being the *sanctioned* fanbase, pseudonyms are not seen as necessary."[109]

This doesn't mean that fans in literary science-fiction fandom never write fanfiction—as will become apparent in this chapter, quite the oppo-site is true. Yet, many writers would not readily admit to it if they had ambitions to go pro. "Until a decade or so ago," one AO3 user states, "pro SFF authors who wrote fanfic had to treat their fic like radioafctive [*sic*] waste."[110] Fanfiction writers, who are in the majority female, are generally considered "the *non-sanctioned* fans," because they refuse to accept the unquestioned authority of published authors and texts. Transformative fandom "is all about laying hands upon the source and twisting it to the fans' own purposes [...]; everyone has their own shot at declaring what the source material means, and at radically re-interpreting it. [...] Due to being unsanctioned 'wild west' fans, pseudonyms are the norm and understood as such."[111]

Paradoxically, the conflict between these two segments of fandom at the 2019 Hugos erupted over what initially appeared to be a step toward, if not the unification, then at least a reconciliation between the camps. The award ceremony itself drew attention to the fact that the two communities are not as clearly separated as fannish discourse often makes it seem. The acceptance speech, for example, was given by Naomi Novik, a published fantasy writer with four Hugo nominations under her belt. At the World-con in Dublin, however, she appeared on stage in her function as long-time fanfiction writer and co-founder of the Organization for Transformative Works. In her speech, she specifically called on Worldcon attendants who also felt like a part of the AO3 community to identify themselves: "This Hugo will be joining the traveling exhibition that goes to each Worldcon, because it belongs to all of us. I would like to ask that we raise the lights and for all of you who feel a part of our community stand up for a moment and share in this with us."[112] A photo of this moment shared on Twitter[113] showed a significant part of the crowd in the room standing in response to Novik's request, making it clear that the fanfiction writers and readers of AO3 were also heavily represented at Worldcon.

However, this conciliatory, celebratory moment of harmony between the different communities was not meant to last. In fact, even in the lead-up to the award ceremony, loyal WSFS fans had expressed their discontent about the nomination. One AO3 user reports that "[w]hen Ao3's nomination was announced, Hugo-centric spaces started wanking immediately about how it (a) did not deserve to be nominated period, (b) it didn't deserve to be nominated because that's not what the Best Related Work category was originally for."[114] In the comment sections of Mike Glyer's science-fiction fanzine *File 770*, fans took AO3's nomination as motivation to criticize the inadequacy of the "Related Works" Hugo category. "The problem is the category definition, IMO," one fan argued, adding that "the actual category suffers first for being a catch-all category with very blurred boundaries, and second for its meat-and-potatoes eligible items just not being very popular."[115] In the same thread, another fan suggested that AO3 simply should not have been eligible for a nomination at all: "Not everything needs to be eligible for a Hugo and not every concept has to have a category. Some concepts just don't fit the Hugos well, or are too niche to get a lot of interest."[116] More explicitly resentful were the fans who complained that AO3 fanfiction writers were celebrating the archive's nomination as their own achievement. One of them declared that they "had it up to here with all of the poseurs on Twitter who are still proclaiming themselves to be Hugo nominees. That's just so disrespectful and unfair to the real Hugo Award finalists."[117]

The already bubbling tension between AO3 users celebrating the archive's Hugo success on social media, and WSFS fans criticizing their behavior as disrespectful escalated further after AO3 was awarded the Hugo at Worldcon. The main argument revolved around the seemingly technical question of who should be allowed to call themselves a Hugo Award winner, but the disagreement quickly touched on the core differences between the two fannish camps.

In the aftermath of the award ceremony, a *The Mary Sue* contributor with ties to the fanfiction community published an article under the title "Everyone Who Contributed to Fanfiction Site 'Archive of Our Own'

Is Now a Hugo Award Winner," with a shout-out to other fans "excitedly texting each other that we plan to add 'Hugo Award Winner' to our bios."[118] Many fans affiliated with AO3 similarly expressed their excitement on social media by referring to themselves as Hugo Award-winning fanfiction writers in a more or less explicitly joking manner. And at least two independent online vendors offered products inspired by AO3's Hugo win: a fan artist sold buttons spelling out "Hugo Award Winner" in cross-stitch on Etsy,[119] and a Kickstarter campaign offered enamel pins with the phrase "Hugo Award Winning Fanfiction Author."[120]

Some fans who primarily identified with WSFS were deeply displeased with these responses, and eventually WSFS issued an official request asking the OTW admin team to stop these behaviors. The OTW administrators accommodated their request by making a public announcement on AO3 with the title "Hugo Award—What it Means."

> The World Science Fiction Society has asked us to help them get the word out about what the award represented—specifically, they want to make sure people know that the Hugo was awarded to the AO3, and not to any particular work(s) hosted on it. Therefore, while we can all be proud of the AO3's Hugo win and we can all be proud of what we contributed to making it possible, the award does not make any individual fanwork or creator "Hugo winners"—the WSFS awarded that distinction to the AO3 as a whole. In particular, the WSFS asked us to convey this reminder so that no one mistakenly describes themselves as having personally won a Hugo Award.[121]

The post quickly acquired more than 700 comments, an unusual number compared to the handful of comments official AO3 announcements usually generate. The conversation that developed in the comments also sparked further conversations on other platforms, such as the anonymous discussion platform *failfandomanon*, frequented primarily by transformative fans, and *File770*, where mostly traditional SF/F fans convene. However, for the duration of this particular discussion there was an unusual amount of cross-traffic between the platforms as fans from both camps followed the debate that unfolded across different sites.

WSFS members and defenders continuously voiced their disapproval of AO3 users celebrating the archive's Hugo win as their own. They took offense with what they saw as fanfiction writers claiming to have won a Hugo Award for their own fanfiction, an idea that loyal WSFS fans rejected as absurd. They insisted that the Hugo Award for Best Related Work had been awarded to AO3 for its code, its archival features, and its administrative leadership, not for the fanfiction it actually hosted. Their concerns were twofold: from a legal perspective, they suggested that the wave of fanfiction writers calling themselves Hugo winners represented a trademark violation that did damage to the prestigious award's reputation; on a more emotional level, they felt that AO3 users' response was a sign of disrespect toward the Hugos and a demonstration of ungratefulness toward the organization that had presented them with an award. On *File770*, one fan lamented that "[f]or months now, hundreds of AO3 members have been extremely disrespectful and contemptuous of the human beings behind the Hugo Awards."[122] Another agreed: "People who haven't written anything that won the award calling themselves 'Hugo Winners' is an insult to the award, and the people who work hard to maintain it."[123]

Some *File770* commenters went as far as to suggest that AO3's Hugo win presented a similar affront to the Hugos as the attack of the Sad Puppies a few years prior. One commenter argued that "this is just Sad Puppies and 20BooksTo50K[124] under a different name: a special-interest group who wants to snag the cachet of a Hugo Award nomination for themselves, while having very little respect for what the Hugo Awards are actually intended to be."[125] Another also drew parallels between the two incidents: "They're different from 'puppies' as they probably don't start with a political agenda but, unlike puppies who tried to build into numbers, they already have the numbers. [...] And it's a social group, already set up to broadcast to its members."[126]

AO3 users engaged in the conversation were univocally offended at the comparison with the alt-right-supported troll attack on the Hugo Awards led by the Sad and Rabid Puppies since 2013. Fanfiction writers were amazed that their half-joking celebration of AO3's Hugo win was misinterpreted as not only overly serious but also read as malicious if not illegal. Several fans involved in the conversation diagnosed a fundamental break in communication between the representatives of affirmational and transformative fandom, suggesting that the WSFS loyalists' outrage was based primarily in a failure to understand the discourses of transformative fandom and the organizational structure of AO3.

They pointed out the futility of WSFS' demand that the AO3 team should reign in the behavior of their users. "The WSFS dudes don't seem to grasp that AO3 is a hosting website, not a society," one fan commented, adding that AO3 has "no power or desire to control what their 'members' are doing beyond a basic set of rules for what's not allowed on the site."[127] Fans also rejected the notion that they had not contributed with their fanfiction to the platform's success at the Hugo Awards. AO3 users explained that the distinction WSFS loyalists were trying to make between the archive and the writers did simply not apply to AO3's unique social structure: "I think I see the problem," a fan wrote.

> You don't understand what AO3 is; you are thinking it of a traditional publication, that buys work from authors to publish in its pages, but is actually considered the work of the editors and publishers. AO3 is a *co-op*, it is owned by and

the work of ALL its contributors. Yes, we are as much "Hugo Award winners" as the editors of a Hugo-winning zine.[128]

Other fans elaborated further: "The writers of Ao3 are *also* the editorial staff and curators of the site," one explained.[129] "And the beta-readers," another added. "Really, AO3 is ALL of Us. That's what an Archive of Our Own means. The lurkers, the tag wranglers, the people that send in tickets when something doesn't work per the FAQ, the whole community was part of this marvelous creation that won."[130]

The conflict over the 2019 Hugo Awards also revived past conflicts and tensions between the fannish camps that explained why some fanfiction writers were not inclined to pay the respect to the institution of the Hugo Awards that WSFS loyalists considered appropriate. An AO3 user who identified herself also as "Hugo Award Winner" and "Time Person of the Year (twice)" suggested that perhaps the reputation of the Hugo Awards was at risk not so much because of AO3 users claiming the Hugo win for themselves, but because of Worldcon's history of awarding the Hugo to people with highly problematic backgrounds: "Yep, the Hugo award might be RUINED! Never mind that they gave one to noted child molester Marion Zimmer Bradley, noted racists and misogynists Niven, Pournelle, Heinlein, and Piers Anthony—what might ruin the Hugo is fanfic authors enjoying a joke to express their celebratory joy."[131] Another user chimed in: "They sure didn't care about 'sullying' the award by giving it posthumously to serial groper and child porn enthusiast Forrest J. Ackerman this year, either."[132]

Some AO3 users also pointed out that they were less than sympathetic to WSFS loyalists' complaints about their alleged disrespectful behaviors because their own fan identities and practices had been disrespected for decades by traditional literary science-fiction fandom. As one fan explained: "That's what being a transformative works creator has been like for the last 40 years actually. You're talking about a population of largely women, many of them queer, who have been systematically mocked, marginalised and pushed out by WSFA for decades."[133] This experience was responsible for many of the conflicting discourses and communication practices in the two communities, as one transformative fan explained to a representative of literary sci-fi fandom who had crossed over into the conversation on AO3: "Ok, I'm assuming you're a Hugo type from 770 because your using your real name in a place where no one does," they started and went on to ask:

> You know why no one uses their real name here? Why we long ago left that vestige of Con fandom? People were afraid, afraid of being persecuted in real life AND in Con fandom. So we took names we made for ourselves. WE CLAIMED OUR SAFE SPACE. This was the only place we'd be accepted because we were weird, or queer, or somehow NOT of the norm.[134]

Some of the transformative fans voiced their disappointment over the conflict, arguing that it was a missed opportunity to reconcile the two groups of fans. One transformative fan explained their initial excitement over the Hugo win: "Seeing the WSFA side of fandom saying, oh, hey, your voices are important too? THAT WAS AWESOME. […] It felt like the two sides could finally see each other."[135] Another called for a cease fire, suggesting that they were tired of seeing the same conflicts play out over and over again: "Honestly every time this particular fannish cultural clash comes up I end up just wanting to lie face down and cover my ears until it goes away. Maybe … maybe we could all give each other a bit of benefit of the doubt?"[136] And one AO3 user suggested that the WSFS ultimately only hurt itself with its attempts at gatekeeping:

> I'm just … these are the people who routinely worry about the Graying Of Fandom and how to get more people involved in fandom at the WSFS level but they piss on the elements of fandom that they have a chance to recruit. And, despite the arguments to the contrary being floated here, transformative fanworks NEVER get nominated for Hugos. Not fucking ever. Ao3 is genuinely unique in that and it could have created a legit outreach effort. I'm just shaking my head over here.[137]

Conclusion

The previous comment also aligned with the perspective of transformative fans who saw the conflict between affirmative and transformative fandom primarily as a conflict between generations. They suggested that the WSFS loyalists who so adamantly opposed AO3's Hugo win were the surviving gatekeepers of an older generation of fans that was, sooner or later, going to disappear. Graydon suggested that the outrage in response to AO3 users joking about being Hugo winners was mostly a generational issue: "That generation of fans comes from a social norm where you can expect to be taken seriously."[138] Another fan suggested that the generational divide wasn't so much one between WSFS members and AO3 users but rather one between older and younger Worldcon attendees: "Since the crossover between Hugo voters under 50 and AO3 fans is really, really high, this is in some ways a changing of the guard moment."[139]

Whether the predictions about the impending demise of traditional literary science-fiction fandom will come to pass or not, the perception of the generational shift points toward an underlying tension that fueled the fire on both sides of the debate: the fact that AO3 user numbers vastly exceed WSFS/Worldcon membership counts, and that many among the Worldcon crowd are already part of the AO3 community as well. Many of the arguments made in the controversy came down to the perception that literary science-fiction fandom—which had so long served as the default gatekeeping institution of how fandom was supposed to work—was now on the defensive in the face of a new generation of fans who not only had created their own fan communities but also claimed a space in the historically male-dominated fan spaces of Worldcon and Comic-Con—with increasing success, as AO3's Hugo win proved. Some of the responses from WSFS representatives like Kevin Standlee and the fans conversing in the *File770* comment sections reflected the unease of a fan community in the process of losing its privileged place in the geek hierarchy, the realization that the oldest fan-organized spaces were not strictly adhering to the ideal of geek masculinity anymore.

Thus, the World Science Fiction Society found itself in a strange position. The organization had seen a shift toward increasing diversity in the years since RaceFail, and had fought hard to defend its emphasis on diversity and inclusivity against the onslaught of toxic masculinity in the shape of the Sad and Rabid Puppies. Yet, faced with the increasing visibility and influence of transformative fandom, their representatives suddenly found themselves in the position of conservative gatekeepers trying to fend off what they saw as an attempted take-over from the queer female community around AO3.

Fiction and Reality
*Between Transmedia Marketing
and Social Critique*

4

"A Loser Like Me"

A Community of Outsiders, Fan Activism and Transmedia Marketing in Glee Fandom

The Box Scene: A Beginning

The setting: a high school hallway. The characters: two teenage boys in skinny pants. The prop: a jewelry box. The dialogue:

> BLAINE: I think this year we should be thankful for the things we do have, not for the things we don't have. Which is why … I know that our relationship has reached a new level this year …
> KURT: If that's an engagement ring, my answer is yes.
> BLAINE: Kurt … just open the box.

This interaction between Kurt Hummel (Chris Colfer) and Blaine Anderson (Darren Criss), on-screen boyfriends in the high school musical dramedy *Glee* (FOX 2009–2015), took place during a scene that was shot for "Extraordinary Merry Christmas," the Christmas episode of Season 3.[1] The episode as a whole revolved around the fairly obvious conflict between the students' desire for a cheerful, present-laden holiday and their awareness of, and fight against, social inequality. Thus, Blaine's choice of presenting Kurt with a gift of low financial value, but high sentimental value—a promise ring made from gum wrappers—seemed to fit in nicely with the overarching theme of the episode.

When "Extraordinary Merry Christmas" aired, however, fans were disappointed to notice that the actual scene had been cut from the episode, even though promotional pictures of the scene had been circulating online and fueled the rumor mill. The announcement that the scene would be included in the Season 3 DVD box did little to appease them, but the story of the "Box Scene" did not end with what *Glee* fans criticized harshly as a tepid compromise.

In May 2012, Project Angel Food, a Los Angeles–based non-profit organization dedicated to providing meals for people with HIV/Aids, auctioned off the original script of "Extraordinary Merry Christmas" to raise money for their organization. When they found out about the auction, two *Glee* fans started a fundraiser called "The Box Scene Project," with the goal to raise enough money to bid on the script. In a joint effort, 113 fans managed to win the auction, with over $1,000 to spare—money that they chose to donate to Project Angel Food as well. The original script itself went to the individual who had given the highest amount, but not before it was scanned and distributed among the fans, thus being made accessible to everyone involved in the effort. Furthermore, their success inspired the organizers to turn The Box Scene Project into an ongoing non-profit initiative. The organization (which is still active today under its new name Represent: Because Representation Matters) pursued a twofold agenda: raising money for charities concerned with LGBTQ rights, and raising awareness for the representation of LGBTQ people in the media. "It is our sincere hope and belief," the organizers wrote in their mission statement,

> that by allying with other fans and groups, the money we raise and donate will help others continue to do good in our world while simultaneously increasing visibility and representation of LGBT characters and couples in popular media, and thereby helping to create a more equal and just world.[2]

In this chapter, I take on *Glee* fandom and The Box Scene Project to discuss how the ethics that fans perceive to be at the heart of a fictional text inspire them to social activism. In Chapter 2, I suggested that the increasing concern with sociopolitical issues within online transformative fandom in the last decade can be seen as a consequence of the changes transformative media fandom underwent after the migration to journal-based fandom in the early 2000s. I explained how the move toward journal-based fandom led to a merging of different communities into a loosely connected globalized network of fans with shared interests and practices. The shift from subcultural fringe phenomenon to alternative online public prompted the renegotiation and redefinition of the ethical guidelines within this broader community, which led to an increasingly politicized self-conception among fans. I argued that the self-awareness transformative fans in journal-based fandom developed as community and as actors in the political landscape led to an increased interest in various political and social issues with an outreach beyond the limits of their fan community.

This chapter, then, discusses how this heightened political awareness translated into action by focusing on *Glee* fans and their engagement in support of LGBTQ rights. The Box Scene Project demonstrates how the distinct ethical foundation that drew fans to the TV series *Glee* was also what inspired their civic engagement, and shows that the emotional attachment to the text, and the emotional investment in certain political issues are, for many fans, inseparable. In this context, I also analyze *Glee*'s rather ingenious transmedia marketing concept to show how it has both facilitated and complicated fans' *Glee*-inspired social engagement. I argue that the marketing campaign intentionally blurred the line between fiction and (mediated) reality with the purpose of increasing fan loyalty, and in so doing also facilitated the fan community's reach beyond of the sphere of fandom and thus the translation of fan activism into social activism. Yet the same communal structures that the show's transmedia marketing supported with the goal of ensuring viewer loyalty also led to the emergence of a practice of media criticism that did not shy away from targeting the creators themselves whenever they violated what fans perceived to be the show's ethical foundations. Therefore, while the activism emerging from *Glee* fandom cannot be seen as independent from the show's transmedia strategies, it also was never fully contained by the efforts of industry-driven fan management.

Before delving more deeply into the topic at hand, it seems necessary to acknowledge that the public perception of *Glee* has changed significantly in the years since the days of the Box Scene Project. The initial overwhelming enthusiasm for the show waned during the later seasons as fans became disillusioned with showrunner Ryan Murphy's creative decisions—some accusing him of listening too much to the demands of particularly vocal fans, some blaming him for not listening enough. Perhaps even more damaging to *Glee*'s reputation however were the real-life scandals and tragedies that surrounded some of the series' most prominent actors. Cory Monteith, who played bumbling handsome quarterback Finn Hudson, died in July 2013 at the age of 32, presumably as a result of the simultaneous consumption of alcohol and heroin. His death affected not only the cast and crew (he was dating co-star Lea Michele at the time) and the fan community, but also threw a wrench in the subsequent development of important storylines on the show. In January 2018, Monteith's co-star Mark Salling (on screen in the role of bad boy Noah Puckerman) died at his own hand in the midst of a court trial over child pornography charges, which came after a sexual battery charge in 2013. And Naya Rivera, famous for her role of Latina cheerleader Santana Lopez, tragically died in a swimming accident in July 2020. For many fans, these events have tainted their memories of the early days of *Glee* fandom. This chapter is not an attempt to obscure *Glee*'s complicated history from celebrated underdog to its fall from grace, but instead reconstructs the particular and quite unique atmosphere surrounding the TV series during its early seasons, while at the same time asking how fans navigate their disillusionment with creators or texts when those don't live up to the ethical or ideological standards fans have come to associate with them.

Fannish Solidarity: A History of Fan Activism

The Box Scene Project and its emergence from the interplay between fannish engagement and marketing interests is not the only, or first, case of fan-organized sociopolitical activism. In fact, the coinciding of fan activism (in this particular case, fueled by fans' interest in a particular episode of their favorite TV show) and sociopolitical activism (the fans' investment in social equality and media representation) was a prevalent phenomenon in different fan communities in the decade between 2005 and 2015.

Since 2006, the Can't Stop the Serenity project has organized screenings of *Serenity*, the 2005 movie sequel to the short-lived cult science-fiction show *Firefly* (FOX 2002–2003), every year on *Firefly* creator Joss Whedon's birthday, with the goal to raise money for Equality Now, a non-profit organization supporting gender equality.[3] The mid–2000s also saw a wave of fanwork auctions: fan-organized events in which fan creators could offer their own fanworks, from fanfiction over fanart to fanvids and fannish crafts, to be auctioned off to other fans willing to bid money on a fannish creation tailored to their personal preferences. The charity auction Sweet Charity ran bi-yearly from 2006 to 2010 and raised money for a number of causes, for example in support of sexual abuse victims. Other auctions like help_haiti on LiveJournal (2010) and subsequent events such as help_japan on LiveJournal/Dreamwidth (2011) were based on a similar model, but usually directed their efforts at supporting regions hit by natural disasters.[4]

The Harry Potter Alliance (HPA, now Fandom Forward),[5] founded by Andrew Slack, Seth Soulstein and Paul DeGeorge in 2005, was probably the most prominent example of fan activism–turned–social engagement and the one most often discussed in scholarship.[6] Within a few years, the HPA developed into a global organization with several hundred international chapters, distributed over all continents. HPA launched numerous campaigns for a variety of causes, ranging from the genocide in Darfur over child labor and analphabetism to marriage equality. For those campaigns, the organization employed various media strategies: in an early collaboration with the non-profit initiative Walmart Watch in 2006, for example, the HPA produced the fan video *Harry Potter and the Dark Lord Waldemart*,[7] in order to draw attention to Walmart's problematic labor practices. In 2014, visitors of the HPA website were temporarily stopped from accessing the site, a strategy meant to draw attention to the threatening loss of net neutrality.

This increase of fan-organized sociopolitical campaigns became noticeable enough that entire panels on fan activism were organized at LeakyCon[8] in 2013 ("Can Fandom Change the World?")[9] and 2014 ("How Fandom Is Changing the World"). The phenomenon also started to draw the attention of fan studies scholars.[10] The early scholarship on fan activism primarily focused on fans' personal transformation from fan to activist and on their engagement with fictional texts in order to answer the question "[w]hat causes the shift from save-my-favorite-show rallies to support-my-favorite-charity sociopolitical campaigns."[11] Most studies identified this kind of activism as a relatively recent development, although Kligler-Vilenchik et al. rightfully pointed out that a spirit of solidarity and the willingness to act on it has always been an important element of transformative fan communities:

> Fandoms have unquestionably always involved a significant component of helping others. Teaching other members about resources and tools, giving feedback on others' fan fiction, offering personal support and even charitable donations.[12]

This statement in itself already indicates the necessity to study fan-organized activism not only in its contemporary manifestations, but also in its historical dimension. A historical approach shows both that fans' awareness of and interest in sociopolitical issues is not as recent a development as it may first appear, and that there are, at the same time, distinct differences between, for example, the kinds of early community-oriented activism Kligler-Vilenchik et al. refer to, and more recent examples of fan-organized activism.

Typical for early forms of fan-organized activism are charity auctions that were held at fan conventions starting from the first days of media fandom. The organization of these early charity auctions was already closely tied to the participants' identity as fans, insofar as they expressed a sense of solidarity and community that was considered a characteristic trait of media fans. In 1994, Karen Ann Yost elaborated on this connection in a *Strange New Worlds* column: she discussed the different kinds of charity work media and science-fiction fans engaged in, from cash donations over blood drives to recycling programs, and stressed the significance of charity work for fannish identity. However, the connection between the benefiting cause and the fan community's object of interest was often relatively arbitrary in these early auctions, in the sense that it was often determined primarily by a popular star's personal connection to the respective charity. "Many fan clubs adopt a favorite charity of the actor they support," writes Yost, and continues:

> British actor Paul Darrow (Avon in *Blake's 7*) is a regular sponsor of charities in both England and the United States. One of his favorite organizations is Canine

Companions for Independence (CCI). [...] During one Christmas drive, the California-based Paul Darrow Appreciation Society raised $661 to donate to CCI in Mr. Darrow's name.[13]

Blake's 7 fans raised money for an assistance dog non-profit organization not necessarily because they had a special interest in the training of service dogs *per se*, but because an actor they admired was dedicated to the cause. Similarly, ZebraCon[14] attendants who participated in the auction on behalf of the Pediatric AIDS Foundation did so primarily because of *Starsky and Hutch* star Paul Michael Glaser, whose wife and two children had been infected with HIV after a blood transfusion during his wife's pregnancy. This incentive for social engagement, in which celebrities leverage their influence to inspire their fans, is still common today. In fact, as Lucy Bennett has shown in her discussion of star-inspired campaigns,[15] contemporary celebrities increasingly seem to realize that civic engagement can be used as a way to connect with their fans. In 2015, for example, actor Jared Padalecki (known for his roles on *Gilmore Girls* and *Supernatural*) started a campaign under the title *Always Keep Fighting* with the goal to raise money and awareness for people with mental health issues.[16] The same year, he revealed that he had been struggling for years with depression and anxiety himself. His honesty in regard to his own mental health struggles lent additional authenticity to his awareness-raising campaign, and at the same time made the actor more relatable to his fans who were dealing with similar issues. The parasocial relationship between actor and fans was thus channeled into a charitable cause that the celebrity was intimately connected to.

Starting around 2005, however, fan-organized initiatives also began to take other forms. On the one hand, the outreach of these campaigns increasingly extended beyond the sphere of the fan community. Kligler-Vilenchik et al. recognize this different trajectory when they remark that they

see a different discourse about helping others, one that is often expressed in terms of social justice or equality. The key difference in this discourse is its outward focus, its concern for those who aren't part of the narrowly defined community, as well as some participants' desire to create structural social change.[17]

On the other hand, while the trajectory of fan-organized initiatives now frequently extended beyond the realm of fandom, the connection between the cause and the fannish text/object tightened in comparison to earlier forms of fannish social engagement. Furthermore, the strategies employed in these campaigns relied more heavily on fandom-specific practices, thus establishing a closer connection between the participants' fannish identity and their fan-organized activism.

The fanworks auction, for example, could certainly be seen as a mere continuation of the tradition of fannish charity auctions, but the strategies used to raise money are actually rather different. Unlike earlier auctions at fan conventions, the fanworks auction relies primarily on fans providing labor in the form of fan-specific practices: writers, artists, and craftswomen in transformative fandom offer the kind of fiction, art, podfic, video, or craft they usually produce as part of their participation in fandom, and the bidders receive a piece of fanwork that complies with their personal wishes or preferences. Thus, the fanworks auction establishes a closer relationship between fan identity and social engagement because it is through common fannish practices that donations are raised. In the context of the auction, practicing fandom and being socially engaged become one and the same thing. This kind of auction also does not seem to break with the ethical principles of transformative fandom, according to which fans are expected to exchange creative works, services, advice and feedback freely and without monetary compensation[18]: the money raised in the auction is donated directly to charity (buyers are asked to provide evidence that they have donated to a specific organization), and writers and artists are not actually compensated for their work. Still, some fans have argued that these auctions do in fact somewhat complicate the system of fannish gift exchange culture since they attach a material value to fanworks.

By connecting fans from very different corners of transformative fandom, these multi-fandom events also affirm the ideal of a global transformative fan community that is held together through its practices rather than the investment in one specific text.[19] Consequently, the incentive for the participation in the fanworks auctions is not so much inspired by fans' attachment to a specific text, but rather by an identification with the practices and ethics of transformative fan culture.

More typical for the new wave of fan-organized activism, however, were initiatives that emerged directly from fans' engagement with specific texts. In those cases, identifying as fan of a particular text came with a personal investment in specific sociopolitical issues, and the fans saw their activism as "a way to bring into the real world the ethics of the imaginative texts they love."[20]

Rhonda Wilcox explains, for example, how fans of Joss Whedon's prematurely cancelled series *Firefly* (the "Browncoats," as some like to call themselves) developed a "meta-myth"[21] based on the characters and themes of the show, "the tale of a unified reality within and surrounding *Firefly/Serenity*"[22] that inspires their social practice. By raising money for charity through screenings of the *Firefly* movie sequel *Serenity*, these fans attempt to imitate the "Big Damn Heroes"[23] which make up the crew of the spacecraft Serenity: unlikely heroes who nevertheless always end up doing the right thing. These actions cannot be separated from the values the fans have come to associate with the show: "this activity is certainly an extension of the Browncoat narrative of resistance, independence, and chosen family/ caring."[24]

In Tanya Cochran's analysis of social engagement among Joss Whedon fans, she explores the reasons for why fans of Whedon's TV shows and feature films, in particular fans of the space western *Firefly* and the fantasy series *Buffy the Vampire Slayer* (WB/UPN 1997–2003),[25] became involved specifically with Equality Now, a non-profit organization that promotes gender equality and raises awareness of gendered violence.

One obvious reason is that Equality Now was backed by showrunner Joss Whedon himself, but Cochran shows that Whedon fans' involvement with Equality Now was not simply another example of fans investing in the same charity as a specific celebrity, even though Whedon's personal influence certainly played a not insignificant role in motivating fans. That he could function as a credible representative of and even inspiration for feminist activism, however, was due primarily to his reputation as the creator of complex strong female characters. In particular his early show *Buffy the Vampire Slayer* has been read as a feminist text by many fans, who also praised him for his credible female protagonists in other works, from *Firefly*'s Zoe Washburne (Gina Torres) and River Tam (Summer Glau), to *The Avengers'* Maria Hill (Cobie Smulders) and Natasha Romanov (Scarlett Johansson). Therefore, fans' motivation to actively support the women's rights organization Equality Now was rooted in their engagement with the texts (at least) as much as it was influenced by their attachment to Whedon himself. As Wilcox elaborates: "The fans have also folded into their meta-myth the creator, whom they see as one of them."[26]

How closely fans' readings of the texts were tied to Whedon's public persona became obvious when a public letter written by Whedon's ex-wife Kai Cole appeared in 2017.[27] In her piece for *The Wrap*, Cole revealed that Whedon had cheated on her and emotionally manipulated her for decades while publicly proclaiming his support of feminist ideals. Fans responded not only with disappointment about his personal failings, but also felt it necessary to reevaluate his work and ask whether his characters held up in the light of these recent revelations, or whether perhaps there had always been indications in his texts that he wasn't quite the feminist he proclaimed to be.[28]

And a lot of us trusted Whedon and his characters and, yes, even his performative feminism. His work has plenty of male gaze and women in refrigerators and some narratively pointless rape scenes—it's all right there, in hundreds of hours of television and films—but boy, it sure is a lot more comfortable to listen to a guy tell you he's a feminist than listen to a lot of women telling you he's not.[29]

In the work of the fan organization Harry Potter Alliance, social engagement and fans' emotional investment in the text were even more closely
intertwined. The fans involved with HPA explicitly saw themselves as car-
rying on the spirit of the books they had come to love. The mission statement on the HPA website proclaimed:

> The Harry Potter Alliance turns fans into heroes. We're changing the world
> by making activism accessible through the power of story. Since 2005, we've
> engaged millions of fans through our work for equality, human rights, and
> literacy.[30]

Similar to the "meta-myth" Wilcox identifies among *Firefly* fans, Ashley
Hinck has shown in detail how J.K. Rowling's *Harry Potter* novels served
as the "public engagement keystone" that anchored fans, allowing them to
identify as part of a community by providing an ethical foundation from
which a concept of social engagement could grow. Hinck explained how
the HPA used the philosophy underlying the fictional texts to inspire fans
to social activism. "The HPA's ethic of speaking out rejects apathy disguised
as neutrality,"[31] which correlates with the fictional characters in the novels who see it as their mission to stand up against oppression and injustice. However, while Hinck argues convincingly that the ethics of a fictional
text can be used to inspire activism, the opposite perspective needs to be
acknowledged as equally important: the fact that the text's ethical foundations may very well be the reason it appeals to certain fans in the first place.
Liesbet van Zoonen, whose remarks on fans in *Entertaining the Citizen*
have been repeatedly cited in scholarship on fan activism, argues that fan
groups, like political constituencies, "rest on emotional investments that
are intrinsically linked to rationality and lead to 'affective intelligence.'"[32]
Her emphasis on the significance of rationality and intelligence at the core
of fans' engagement suggests that fans' emotional investment in specific
sociopolitical issues might not be simply the result, but rather the cause for
their engagement with certain texts.

But regardless of whether audiences are drawn to the text because
of the message it conveys, or whether their engagement with the text first
encourages their interest in social issues, it is clear that the foundational
ethics of the text influence their decision to become active and the direction
their activism takes. As has already been hinted at in the discussion of fans'
disillusionment with Joss Whedon's presumed feminism, this affective connection can also motivate fans to turn *against* the producers of a text who
fail to comply with the ethics that initially appealed to them. In 2020, *Harry
Potter* fans had to grapple with similar questions as Joss Whedon fans a
few years prior when author J.K. Rowling made news with repeated public
transphobic statements, including an entire essay laying out the reasoning

behind her controversial position.[33] This was devastating to *Harry Potter* fans who had grounded their sociopolitical practice in the ethical philosophy of Rowling's fictional universe, but in particular for transgender and non-binary fans who had identified with the vision of tolerance they had found in the novels. To them, the "series no longer felt grounding and nostalgic, but stress inducing."[34] As with Joss Whedon, some fans also read her texts now in a new light and found that some of her more problematic positions had in fact already been hinted at in her work: "There are also several scenes that can be read as transphobic, including more than a few in which a male character wearing a dress is played for laughs."[35] *Harry Potter* fans responded in different ways to these developments: some chose to abandon a fandom that had been a significant part of their lives for years, while others only distanced themselves from the creator but—in true transformative fandom style—claimed ownership over the fictional universe, arguing that the characters and the world ultimately belonged to the fans. The Harry Potter Alliance changed its name to Fandom Forward in June 2021, and the fansite The Leaky Cauldron, for example, announced that they would no longer post information about or statements by J.K. Rowling, but also explained that they had "seen countless people use the Potter books and fanfic to explore their own identities while spreading love and acceptance. We know that this is still possible, and we know that we want to continue to be part of that movement."[36]

As will become clear over the following pages, many *Glee* fans were also attached more to the ethical beliefs that had made *Glee* attractive to them than the show itself. The example of *Glee* and The Box Scene Project in particular show that many fans did not only get involved with social issues such as LGBTQ representation and bullying because they love *Glee*; rather, they loved *Glee* precisely because the show focused on issues they were already invested in. Here, the love for the text and the dedication to the cause became inseparably intertwined.

Glee's Success: Identification with the Misfit

Glee, the show about a group of social outcasts in a high school glee club, started as a small teenage-oriented dramedy on FOX in 2009, but became one of the most talked-about TV shows of the decade (and eventually ended after six seasons in 2015). For many *Glee* fans, their emotional connection to the show was linked to its representation of minority students, in particular LGBTQ characters and same-sex couples, as Marwick et al. confirm in their empirical study of teenage *Glee* fans:

> [W]e consistently found that our young participants used Glee to appreciate and navigate their own sexualities and experiences. Both our participants and

many of the Twitter accounts we observed seemed to have strong emotional ties to the program and its characters. To young people, the continued representation of minority characters in media is extremely important, not only to validate their own existences but also to open them to the experiences of others.[37]

Characters from different underrepresented groups are in the majority among the protagonists of Glee, most of whom are continuously harassed by fellow students and even the teachers for being different. Soprano Kurt Hummel is repeatedly abused emotionally and physically for being an effeminate gay boy, Artie Abrams's (Kevin McHale) wheelchair makes him vulnerable to the ableist attacks of fellow students, and even popular cheerleader Quinn Fabray (Dianna Agron) becomes the victim of harassment as a result of her teenage pregnancy. All of them are also mocked simply for being part of the show choir: "Stop it right there, Mercedes," Kurt tells his friend who admits that she wishes for a boyfriend. "We are in glee club. That means we are at the bottom of the social heap."[38]

Two rituals of humiliation in particular are suffered so frequently by those at the bottom of the social hacking order at McKinley High that they gain symbolic significance over the course of the show. The most popular way of demonstrating someone's unpopularity is to "slushie" them by throwing a frozen drink at their face. Slushieing scenes on Glee are often staged as dramatic (and traumatic) experiences: in the episode "Mash-up,"[39] for example, quarterback Finn Hudson (Cory Monteith) is pressured by his football teammates into slushieing fellow student Kurt Hummel to reaffirm his heterosexuality, but Kurt takes the higher moral ground by sparing Finn the decision and pouring the slushie over himself. The other frequently repeated ritual is the practice of throwing unpopular students into the dumpster in the school parking lot. For Kurt, this seems to be an almost daily ritual at the beginning of the show. Both practices are portrayed as forms of cruel violence that are particularly stigmatizing because the bullied student has to wear the visible traces of his/her humiliation for the rest of the day. The sympathies of the show, and therefore the audience, are clearly with those suffering this degrading treatment from their fellow students.

Very quickly, the series attracted a strong fanbase of people who identified with the show in a very personal way. In her online manifesto "In Defense of Gleeks," a fan who called themselves a "NYC-Dwelling, twenty-something aspiring actor and singer who makes lattes for a living," explains what drew them to the show:

> I often say that folks who condemn Glee don't "get it." This has absolutely nothing to do with IQ. This is not about intellectual understanding, it's about an emotional connection. I was, without a doubt, one of these kids in high school. [...] I remember being that kid, feeling hopelessly awkward and going through

all the worst parts of puberty, all while being a shy introvert to boot. I had very few friends freshman and sophomore year, and if my one lunchtime companion was absent that day, I would eat alone in the hallway outside the cafeteria. It wasn't until I found the drama club: a band of other misfits like myself—the bad kids, the stoners, the sexually confused, the prissy christian choir girls, the D&D nerds, the band geeks—that I finally felt like I'd found a home; A group of people who understood what so many others didn't about me.[40]

For this fan, *Glee* is a show in which they find themselves, because the show about social outcasts reminds them of their own time in high school. They also suggest that those who haven't gone through the same experience might not be able to fully understand what the show means to them, or as they say: they "don't get it." *Glee* fan Josey, who appears in the 2011 *Glee the 3D Concert Movie*, seems to contradict her at first glance when she defines the appeal of *Glee* for herself and others: "Everybody watches Glee. It doesn't matter what race, gender, what your sexuality is—anybody can be a Glee fan."[41] However, it was precisely between these two poles that the self-conception of the *Glee* fan community took shape: between the inclusiveness of "anybody can be a Glee fan" and the assumption that to understand the show, one needs to be familiar with the social and emotional cost of being an outsider.

Glee's focus on the suffering of social misfits clearly hit a nerve with teenagers: "*Glee* started at a really good time for me, because I was starting my new school, and I was getting bullied for being a bit of a loser," a girl explains in her video message directed at the *Glee* cast, which was featured in the British television documentary *I Heart Glee* (2013).[42] With *Glee*'s rise to popularity, the issue of peer-on-peer bullying in high schools also moved to the forefront of the American consciousness. During the 2000s, an anti-bullying movement had already begun to develop in the English-speaking world and brought forth initiatives like the National Bullying Prevention Month, founded in 2006 by PACER's National Center for Bullying Prevention. But shortly after the premiere of *Glee* on U.S. television, violence and harassment among teenagers in schools and colleges began to draw increasing attention. It is impossible to say whether the heightened attention toward bullying should be attributed primarily to *Glee*'s popularity, or whether it was in fact *Glee* that jumped on the already moving bandwagon, but it is clear that initiatives to prevent and stop bullying kept popping up in the wake of *Glee*'s TV premiere. In September 2010, columnist Dan Savage started the It Gets Better[43] project, in which celebrities (and others) recorded inspirational video messages for LGBTQ teenagers experiencing discrimination. In 2011, Lee Hirsch's documentary *Bully* came to the theaters, accompanied by the awareness-raising campaign The Bully Project.[44] In March 2011, the then presidential couple Barack and

Michelle Obama hosted a White House Conference on bullying prevention and launched the U.S. Federal Government's website StopBullying.gov.[45]

These initiatives were accompanied by a slew of media reports about bullying incidents in American high schools and their sometimes-fatal consequences. In October 2010, for example, the *Huffington Post* published an article about a high school in Mentor, Ohio, where four students had killed themselves over the course of only two years after being bullied by their classmates. "One was bullied for being gay, another for having a learning disability, another for being a boy who happened to like wearing pink." The fourth left a suicide note that "told of her daily torment at Mentor High School, where students mocked her accent, taunted her with insults like 'Slutty Jana' and threw food at her."[46]

Coincidentally or not, *Glee*'s version of Mentor High, the fictional McKinley High School, was located not even 200 miles away from Mentor in Lima, Ohio. The significance of location as a sacred place for fans of cult texts has been discussed by several scholars[47]; but while Lima, Ohio, plays an important role for fans of *Glee*, it carries a different meaning than New Jersey did for fans of *The Sopranos* (HBO 1999–2007) or Albuquerque for *Breaking Bad* (AMC 2008–2013) fans. For one thing, *Glee* was for the most part not actually shot in Lima, but in Los Angeles, California. Although a town of that name does in fact exist in Ohio, *Glee*'s Lima does not so much reference a specific extra-diegetic location, and *Glee* fans don't generally feel the need to travel to Lima. There is no need for a pilgrimage because the show suggests that even if the spectators don't know Lima, they know places just like it. With settings including a generic shopping mall, the auto repair shop "Hummel's Tires and Lube," a coffee shop called "Lima Bean," and the mediocre Italian restaurant "Breadstix," *Glee*'s Lima is purposefully interchangeable, a nondescript representation of Midwestern small-town America that stands in for any other place in the United States where high school is a mostly miserable experience. When head cheerleader Quinn Fabray finds out she is pregnant on the show, she laments: "I really thought I had a chance of getting out of here!"[48] For Quinn and her fellow glee club members, leaving Lima after graduation is the light at the end of the tunnel, and there is nothing worse for them than the prospect of being a "Lima Loser"—that is, not being able to escape and getting stuck for the rest of their lives in a place where being different is not an acceptable option. "We live in Ohio, not New York ... or some other city where people eat vegetables that aren't fried," popular quarterback Finn reminds his stepbrother Kurt in the episode *Theatricality*,[49] when he reprimands him for being too flamboyant and demonstrative about his homosexuality.

The allegorical significance of *Glee*'s Lima can be illustrated quite effectively with the shout-out to *Glee* in an episode of the not-at-all related cop show *Hawaii Five-O* (CBS 2010–2020) about the murder of a sex worker. The victim's last client turns out to be a high school teacher from Lima, who has to explain to the investigators why he paid a sex worker for her services. "Have you ever been to Lima, Ohio?" the suspect asks during the interrogation. "I mean, come on. This is Hawaii, I just wanted to have fun."[50] This blink-and-you-will-miss-it, tongue-in-cheek reference is so effective precisely because Lima, as portrayed on *Glee*, represents the exact opposite of Hawaii; that is, the opposite of fun and freedom. Unlike locations in other cult TV shows, the fictionalized town of Lima, Ohio, is not a place viewers want to escape to from their own lives: quite the contrary, Lima is the place everyone wants to escape *from*.

On *Glee* itself, it is not Hawaii, but rather New York City that is usually pitched against Lima as a quasi-utopian place. Rachel Berry (Lea Michele) and Kurt Hummel, the most ambitious members of the glee club, are convinced that New York is their destiny, both as the place that will make them famous and the place where people will accept them for who they are. Kurt's father Burt (Mike O'Malley) agrees with that notion when eventually he sends his son off to New York after his high school graduation:

> BURT HUMMEL: New York is going to be a breeze, compared to Lima. Think about all the crap you've been putting up with the last couple years. You know the difference between this place and New York?
> KURT HUMMEL: Decent bagels?
> BURT HUMMEL: New York is filled with people like you. People who aren't afraid to be different. You can feel at home there.[51]

The physical transition from small town Lima to the metropolis New York goes along with the symbolic transition from teenager to adult, but more importantly, from being an outsider to a place of belonging. In the show, this transition does not begin only when the high school graduates finally move to New York after the show's third season. In fact, their transition process begins in the same moment the students first join their school's glee club. Within the city limits of Lima, glee club fulfills the function of a symbolic New York, and even for those who will never make it out of Lima, it is the place where they can feel at home.

The Glee Cast: Losers Like Us?

The fans' strong investment in this utopian fantasy was supported by the public narrative surrounding *Glee*'s production history, which highlighted parallels between the intra- and the extra-diegetic levels of the show. The mediated narrative about the show's creation and the actors' personal backgrounds was presented in a way that mirrored the premise of the show. On *Glee*, McKinley High's glee club "New Directions" is consistently portrayed as the "underdog" in high school competitions because their group works without a budget, without the streamlined performances of competing glee clubs, but also because their group lacks the physical homogeneity of other choirs, as the coach of a more successful glee club points out to McKinley's glee club teacher:

> SCHUESTER: I love my kids.
> GOOLSBY: What? No you don't. They're hideous. My kids are at least attractive. Yours look like they haven't been baked properly.[52]

Glee's perceived credibility as the voice of the unappreciated was supported by the fact that the show itself was initially presented in the media as the underdog in the 2009 TV season. "I never thought the show would even last. [...] I just didn't think people would get it," creator Ryan Murphy is quoted by *Entertainment Weekly* in 2010.[53] Similarly, the younger members of the cast were introduced as newcomers for whom the show finally indicated a break. Publicity during the first season took care to point out that while some cast members had prior acting experience, many were new to the show business. Amber Riley, the actress playing Black diva Mercedes Jones, had previously auditioned for *American Idol* and been rejected, a fact that was highlighted rather than glossed over in the publicity for the show. Cory Monteith, who starred on *Glee* as quarterback-turned-glee club leader Finn Hudson, talked in interviews about his past struggles with drugs and alcohol and his difficulties of finding work as an actor before he was cast on *Glee*.

Chris Colfer in particular lent himself to this kind of parallel between the characters on the show and the actors playing them. The role of gay soprano Kurt Hummel was his first real acting gig, and the story of his audition, told and retold in countless interviews, became part of the myth surrounding the series. When he auditioned for *Glee*, showrunner Ryan Murphy liked him so much that he created the role of Kurt specifically for him, or so the story went:

> As soon as I walked in the door, Ryan Murphy looked at me and asked: "Why do I have a feeling you've been in *The Sound of Music*?" And I said, well, I was Kurt in *The Sound of Music* when I was fourteen. And then lo and behold, when I went to the next audition, they were replacing Rashish, an Indian student, with this new character named Kurt, and I thought, *interesting*, and I was the only one there auditioning for Kurt, and I thought, *interesting*, again ... and the rest is history.[54]

In interviews during the first two seasons of *Glee*, Chris Colfer was also repeatedly asked to speak about his own high school experience in his hometown of Clovis, California. In his responses to this question, he always confirmed that he had suffered abuse at the hands of his peers in middle and high school himself: "I actually was bullied so much in middle school that my parents homeschooled me for 7th grade," he said at the New Yorker Festival in October 2011. "I kept getting shoved into lockers, because I was very tiny." Colfer's public confession that he was a victim of bullying further underscored the similarities between the actor and his character, and highlighted the parallels between Clovis, Mentor, and Lima, the actual and fictional places where peer-on-peer abuse takes place. Just like the students in Glee want to get away from Lima, Colfer talked about his hope for a similar escape: "I would always go to these auditions thinking: 'This is my way to escape. This is my way to get out.'"[55] This media narrative suggested that for Colfer, being cast on Glee was as significant as joining glee club was for his character Kurt. Repeatedly he stressed that he had had very few friends before being cast on the show, and that on the set of Glee, he had for the first time found friendship and acceptance: "We're a big family behind the scenes. They're the best friends I've ever had, besides the CEHS Kitchen staff."[56] This recurrent evocation of the ideal of family by cast members is also mirrored by Glee characters on the show, who often speak of their glee club as a family, as cheerleader Brittany S. Pearce (Heather Morris) does in the episode "New York": "Well, family is a place where everybody loves you no matter what. And they accept you for who you are. […] I love them, I love everyone in glee club and I get to spend another year with the people I love. So, I'm good."[57]

But there was another experience that actor Chris Colfer and his character Kurt had in common: both came out as gay during Glee's first season in 2009. In a storyline that turned out to be one of the most popular and iconic stories Glee ever told, the fourth episode showed Kurt joining the high school football team as kicker in order to impress his all–American mechanic father, only to come out to him as queer later in the episode.[58] Somewhat less theatrically, Colfer officially came out on the talk show Chelsea Lately in December 2009.[59] Even though fans rumored that the network had wanted him to keep quiet about his sexuality, his coming-out clearly did not hurt FOX, or his own reputation, in the slightest. Cast in an odd twist of events for a part that had to be written into the script for him, he had originally no more than a supporting role, but over the course of Seasons 1 and 2, Chris Colfer/Kurt Hummel became one of the biggest successes of Glee. As a result of the character's popularity, his part continued to be expanded until he was without doubt one of the show's main protagonists. Colfer himself did not only win a Golden Globe for the role in 2011, but was also named one of "the most influential people in the world" on the 2011 TIME 100 list.[60] Over the course of little more than a year, Colfer had somehow been turned by the media into the spokesperson of queer

American teenagers. The audience's positive reaction to Kurt also opened the door for the introduction of other LGBTQ characters on the show. Cheerleaders Brittany and Santana (Naya Rivera), originally depicted as sexually adventurous but heterosexual BFFs, eventually came out as bisexual and lesbian respectively and in fact became one of the show's most beloved couples. Season 2 introduced Kurt's future boyfriend (and eventual husband) Blaine; in a twist of bittersweet irony, Kurt's most cruel bully Dave Karofsky (Max Adler) was revealed to be a tormented closeted boy; and at the end of Season 3, the show introduced transgender student Unique (Alex Newell).

Despite a comparably large number of LGBTQ characters, in particular later seasons of *Glee* have been criticized for the heteronormativity of their plotlines. As both Frederik Dhaenens and Lynne Joyrich[61] have discussed, the show's integration of same-sex couples into the heteronormative structures of monogamous relationships and marriages, its romanticized image of nuclear family models and traditional concepts of masculinity, and its reluctance to treat bisexuality seriously did not seem geared toward radically challenging public perceptions about gender, sexuality, and family. However, this certainly justified criticism did not change the fact that many viewers considered *Glee*'s representation of LGBTQ teenagers on American broadcast television revolutionary. As problematic as the notion of empowerment through mere visibility and representation may be, for many of the teenagers watching *Glee*, representation meant everything:

> Me frantically trying to MacGyver my computer into a DVR to capture that first Brittana kiss is an example of why positive representation for minorities is so important on TV. That was the first time I had ever seen a lesbian couple on TV, and they looked so happy; a possibility I had given up on for myself. Fiction or not, Brittany and Santana's story felt like part of what my story could be, and that changed things in a big way.[62]

Similarly, in the caption to a YouTube fan video "How Klaine Changed the World," the creator wrote about Kurt and his boyfriend Blaine: "This is not just a ship.[63] This is a positive step forward in changing the way people view others in society."[64] And another fan explained: "People ask me all the time, 'Why do you love this show so much?' or 'Why is this show any different from other shows on TV?' My answer is always the same: 'Glee is changing the world.' You may not realize it. But it is."[65]

It is not a coincidence that the notion of change, of transformation, features prominently in all these statements. The belief in *Glee*'s potential for progress and social change played a significant role in fans' relationship with the show. *Glee*'s transmedia marketing further supported this connection by consistently blurring the lines between fiction, mediated reality, and the fans' own lives. Aside from the publicity campaign's efforts to highlight the parallels between actors and fictional characters, *Glee* also promised fans the possibility of change in their own lives in two regards, both of which intersected in the institution of the glee club: the desire to be part of a community and the dream of becoming a star.

Glee fans, or "Gleeks,"[66] as they called themselves, felt that the show allowed them to experience the transition from being an outsider to becoming part of a community[67]: "I think that we are the majority. We are the quirky, weird kids. We don't all look the same way," explains a girl who is interviewed for *Glee The 3D Concert Movie*,[68] once again giving expression to the oscillation of *Glee* fans' self-conception between inclusivity ("the majority") and exclusion ("quirky, weird"). However, the "we" in her statement does not only refer to fans, but also to the fictional characters, as well as the actors playing them, who all became part of *Glee*'s community of outsiders. Not only did fans recognize themselves in the characters and identify with their goals and dreams, they also drew parallels between the fictional characters on *Glee* and the actors' personal lives. Especially in regard to Chris Colfer/Kurt Hummel, fans were able to follow the story from tormented outsider to an accepted member of the group not just on the fictional level of the show, but also in their mediated experience of Colfer's own life. Colfer's success story provided the real-life legitimation for Kurt's story and lent it additional credibility.

Both the marketing campaign for the show and the showrunner/writers tapped into this sense of community and referenced it frequently. One symbol for the connection between fans, characters, and actors became the Loser-L hand gesture that had appeared early on as part of the marketing campaign. It was soon reclaimed by fans as a gesture of belonging—and ultimately made its way back into the show, where the characters used it in a public performance at a glee club competition, thus closing the circle between fictional narrative, marketing, and fandom.

Glee The 3D Concert Movie similarly promoted the idea of the *Glee* community as one big family that accepts everyone for who they are, no matter how different. In parts, the movie was a recording of the 2010 *Glee Live! In Concert!* Tour, a series of live performances during which the actors appeared on stage exclusively in character—that is, they starred not as Lea Michele or Chris Colfer, but as Rachel Berry and Kurt Hummel, thus creating the illusion that fans could actually meet the fictional characters in real life. At the same time, *Glee The 3D Concert Movie* was also a documentary about *Glee* fans and contained extensive footage of fans at the concerts, as well as segments featuring individual fans who got to tell their personal story and what *Glee* meant to them: including a young woman with

Asperger's who talked about making friends in the *Glee* fan community, a young man of color recounting his coming-out story, and a teenage little person who was elected prom princess at her high school. By never quite breaking the illusion of fictional characters performing live, not even in the backstage interviews with the cast, and by mixing these segments with features about fans, the film quite effectively blurred the line between fiction and extra-diegetic mediated reality.

"In relation to cult geography," Matt Hills writes, "we are all 'outsiders' in a sense since the notion of the 'inside' is displaced here into a mediated point which, by definition, cannot arrive: [...] we cannot ever get 'inside' the originating text."[69] *Glee*, however, suggested that such a transcendence of mediated reality was in fact possible. By giving fans the chance to see their favorite characters perform live on stage, by highlighting the parallels between the *Glee* actors and the fans' personal lives, and by suggesting that fans could actually become a part of this phenomenon, *Glee* created a sense of community that extended across the different spheres.

You Can Be a Star: Transmedia Marketing Around Glee

While *Glee The 3D Concert Movie* focused on the concept of *Glee* as family, the casting show *The Glee Project* and the Give a Note charity campaign primarily promoted the idea that everybody could become a star. The Glee Give a Note campaign was a music competition that took place in the fall of 2011 and was organized by the National Association for Music Education, the Give A Note Foundation and FOX/*Glee*. High school glee clubs were invited to submit short videos explaining why the music program at their school was in need of financial aid, and the awarded grants were financed from the proceeds of the *Glee* Season 2 DVD. Thus, the campaign confirmed the competitiveness of the musical theater world, all the while providing publicity for the show's producers, highlighting their concern for art programs in high schools and boosting the show's reputation as socially conscious programming. At the same time, the campaign did directly benefit high school art programs and was focused on the idea of the show choir as a team, thus stopping short of promoting the idea of individual students becoming stars.

The promise of stardom that was perpetually invoked in the marketing and publicity around *Glee* was made much more explicit with *The Glee Project*, a spin-off casting show that premiered on *Oxygen* in 2011. The show served as a public audition platform for *Glee*, and the winners of the competition were promised a minor role on the show. The casting call promo for Season 2 highlighted the idea that *The Glee Project* gave everyone a chance to be part of *Glee*. Two winners from Season 1 appear in the promo, exclaiming: "We auditioned online. And now you can do it too!"[70] Over the course of two seasons, six candidates (winners and runners-up) were cast for roles on *Glee* and actually appeared on the show. But while their success seemingly fulfilled *The Glee Project's* promise of stardom for everyone, Matthias Stork points out that participants of the casting show were in fact carefully selected for their compatibility with *Glee's* conceptual vision.[71]

Furthermore, despite the fact that six of the finalists actually appeared on *Glee*, most of them did not have a significant presence on the show, nor were they particularly well received by the audience. This was in parts due to the fact that most of their plotlines were barely more than forced add-ons, and their appearances simply too brief to leave a lasting impression. Probably the most successful addition to the *Glee* cast via *The Glee Project* was Alex Newell, a queer Black young man who was cast in the role of trans girl Unique Adams and thus represented one of the very few transgender characters on television at the time.

The casting show *The Glee Project*, along with the fact that *Glee's* fourth season was scheduled for the time slot after the talent shows *The X Factor* and *American Idol*, were part of a marketing strategy promising fans that they could be just as successful as the stars of *Glee*. And in fact, the early *Glee* boom in particular contributed to an increased interest in high school and college show choirs in Canada and the USA in 2010 and 2011.[72] *Jazz Times* published a survey among show choir directors showing that

> forty-three percent noted a sharp rise in student interest and enrollment, plus a huge number of requests from choir members that songs from the show be added to their repertoire. At the University of North Texas in Denton, Joe Coira announced the creation of a new vocal group the day after *Glee's* first season finale, and was shocked when more than 100 students showed up to audition.[73]

This development seems to indicate that the message sent by *Glee's* transmedia marketing campaign was taken, at least to some extent, at face value, and that not all Gleeks were content to simply watch the fictional characters move from small-town Lima to New York City, or follow the actors' careers from unknown bullied high school students to celebrated television stars, but wished to experience the rise to stardom themselves.

Stork has rightfully criticized *Glee's* transmedia marketing for this attempt to reach fans through the promise of individual success. He traces the development of *Glee* from surprise TV hit into a distinct brand crossing a variety of media platforms, including a line of soundtrack albums and hit singles, a concert tour, and a feature-length movie, and points out how *Glee's* transmedia marketing strategy promotes viewer loyalty by implying that the fans could be as successful as the actors.[74] But while Stork is certainly right in assuming that a career in musical theater was important to many fans of the show, I am more reluctant to agree with his assessment that *Glee* fandom exhausted itself in the fans' aspiration to achieve individual professional success. Instead, I argue that for many fans, *Glee*'s promise of stardom was associated more with a fantasy of achieving acceptance and possibly revenge rather than the mere ambition of monetary and professional success. More importantly, *Glee*'s transmedia marketing with its message of "You can do it, too!" was successful also in a likely unintended way: while it gave fans the confidence that encouraged them to become active beyond the limits of their fan community, many of them did not (only) channel their passion into their possible but ultimately unlikely future careers as superstars, but rather into attempts at recreating the social utopia they saw represented by the show.

Labor of Passion: Glee's Utopian Vision

For the most ambitious characters on *Glee*, the dream of becoming a star is what keeps them going, even in the face of perpetual harassment and disappointment. Rachel and Kurt dream of Broadway, Mercedes wants to be the new Whitney Houston, Mike (Harry Shum Jr.) aspires to become a dancer, Artie plans to go to film school. But throughout the first three seasons, the show does not actually portray their dream of reaching stardom as a realistic career goal; instead, it functions as escapist utopia and equally as a revenge fantasy. The original song "A Loser Like Me,"[75] which the glee club performs at a regional competition in Season 2, explores the outsiders' fantasy of finally getting to prove that they are so much better than their tormenters. While fans easily and readily identified with the dream of the outsider finally achieving well-deserved fame and respect, actual stardom appeared to be something that was more difficult to relate to. In fact, *Glee*'s ratings started to drop at precisely the moment when the dream of success in the show business actually started to become reality for some of the *Glee* characters in Season 4. Similarly, the low acceptance of *The Glee Project*, which was canceled after only two seasons, indicated that fans had been much more invested in the show's initial message of community and solidarity than in the marketing's promise of stardom.

Naomi Lesley points out that even on the show itself, the concept of success is not tied primarily to the idea of material or professional achievements but is measured first and foremost in terms of character growth, passion and belonging. *Glee*, she suggests, "contrasts the corrupted pursuits of upward mobility, prestige, and material acquisition with the pursuit of happiness, and the ugly world of monetary and political calculation with the pure exchange of love."[76] In her analysis of the show, she teases out the message's double-edged nature: she, too, acknowledges that this philosophy with its focus on individuality and its promotion of free labor in the name of passion has the potential to be exploited by a neoliberal agenda, but suggests that it also opens up space for utopian thought:

> In the educational world of *Glee*, both utopia and activism are set into motion through musical performances that train the students for a life of emotional investment and passion. [...] The energy and hope Will produces may make the students available for co-optation and exploitation; however, they are also the only sources of power available for imagining social transformations.[77]

That this fantasy resonated in particular with *Glee* fans in the community of transformative fandom is not surprising, given the fact that an essential aspect of transformative fandom is the belief in a gift exchange culture that aims to interrupt the circulation of capital.[78] Fans provide free labor—the labor of passion—in the form of fiction, art, mentoring, technological and organizational skills, among others, and in exchange benefit from other fans' works and their feedback, encouragement, and praise. In fact, the gift economy of transformative fandom has much in common with the ideal of solidarity and community in *Glee*'s show choir—both are meant to invoke a utopian space outside of commodification and capitalism. In "Opening Night," Rachel is experiencing stage fright on the night before her Broadway debut after reading too many negative reviews online, but her friend Kurt reassures her:

> Give me your phone. You're being unplugged until after your opening night. No going on the Internet for anything. [...] Okay? We are going to hermetically seal this loft into a big love bubble and fill it with positive affirmations and validations from people who know you and love you and have no doubt that you're going to be amazing. If you need your cup filled, we'll fill it right here.[79]

By taking away her smartphone, he literally cuts her off from an outside world running on competition and evaluation, instead sheltering her in the safe space of her community where friends are responsible for giving her what she needs: love and appreciation, without expecting anything in return.

Just like the students on *Glee* channel the passion of song into resistance against the status quo, fans appropriated the participatory potential of *Glee*'s transmedia marketing by setting aside the promise of professional success in favor of their belief in a social utopia. *Glee* fans' investment in the idea of social change found expression in the repeated vocalization of their wish to change things, and in their frequent references to the utopian space that the show had opened up for them: "I've found, thanks to *Glee*, that hope is the idea that can make the most difference," writes one *Glee* fan.

> Think about it. Hope for a better day tomorrow. Hope that you know one day you'll get out of the school where kids are bullying you. Hope that you'll find what gets you excited, and makes you want to *do* something. Hope that *YOU* can make a difference.[80]

For another fan, blogging is her way of making a difference:

> Here's my confession, I guess: A bunch of fictional TV characters turned this grown person into a slightly crazy, but more hopeful, human being determined to make sure other people get the same opportunity in any way possible. All of this talk about social media and TV shows and finding ways to use the fandom is my way of trying to accomplish that.[81]

These statements capture the moment where the self-understanding of being a fan merges with fans' social conscience into the conviction that being a Gleek and fighting for change belong together. The ethical foundation of *Glee*-inspired activism was the set of beliefs that drew fans to the show in the first place (the idea that everyone is worth getting a chance, that being part of a community provides strength, that intolerance and harassment should not be tolerated), whereas the marketing promise of individual agency facilitated their decision to take action. The perpetual convergence of fiction and reality in the show's marketing strategy made the possibility of actual change seem realistic and thus provided *Glee* fans with the sense of agency necessary to inspire action.

In some cases, this convergence of fannish and political engagement was put into practice on a micro-level that could be read more easily as a form of self-expression rather than social activism, for example in fans' reactions to "Born This Way."[82] The episode focused on the characters' struggles with their self-image, with body image issues and internalized homophobia. For the final musical number, Lady Gaga's hit "Born This Way,"[83] the members of the glee club wear T-shirts naming a physical or character trait they are ashamed of (ranging from "Nose" over "OCD" to "Can't Sing") as a demonstration of self-acceptance and provocation alike. Kurt's shirt announces "Likes Boys," whereas lesbian student Santana's shirt reads "Lebanese" (thanks to Brittany's imperfect spelling). Reproductions of these T-shirts were later sold as merchandise, and during the *Glee* concert tour, many fans in the audience wore various versions of the shirt. However, not all of them wore the official merchandise; in fact, instead of buying the official product, many fans felt inspired to create their own shirts that better reflected their personal circumstances. On the one hand, these T-shirts (both the merchandise and the handmade versions) functioned as a means to connect with the fictional characters on the show as well as other *Glee* fans, and thus supported community-building in a mostly affirmative way. However, while fellow *Glee* fans were instantly able to recognize the T-shirts as a reference to the show, outsiders most likely did not perceive in particular the self-made shirts as fan articles and thus were bound to read them as a personal and potentially even politically charged statements.

Changing Things: The Move to Fan-Organized Activism

While wearing a "Born this Way" T-shirt might seem insignificant compared to initiatives like the Box Scene Project, which more explicitly crossed the border from personal statement to organized activism, they all had in common that they were grounded in what fans perceived to be the spirit of *Glee,* and motivated by the belief that actual change was possible. In the case of the Box Scene Project, the organizers felt encouraged by the realization that a group of fans could actually make an impact after they were able to acquire an episode script, and later, indirectly, succeeded in getting the actual scene released.[84] They continued their efforts to create change by raising money for organizations supporting disadvantaged youth and LGBTQ people such as Project Angel Food, Young Storytellers Foundation and Baycat; by organizing a panel discussion on media representation; and by financing scholarships and grants for students and young independents in the media arts. Another success was the acquisition of the script for the episode "The First Time,"[85] which featured four students venturing to a gay bar, and Kurt and Blaine's first time having sex. This script, too, was distributed among fans, to make the LGBTQ–themed storylines accessible to others in the fan community. After the cancellation of *Glee,* The Box Scene Project changed its name to Represent: Because Representation Matters and continued its advocacy work to promote "equal media representation in film, television, and theater for the LGBT community, women, people of color, folks with disabilities, and all who live at the intersection of these identities."[86]

Since all these projects relate to the issues that fans perceive to be at the heart of what constitutes *Glee*—diverse representation, LGBTQ rights and support for struggling youth—, this form of fan-organized activism can be understood as affirmative: it is ultimately inspired by and carried out in the spirit of the show. Even if unintended, this kind of initiative cannot be unwelcome to producers. Since the fans' efforts also draw attention to the text that inspired them, *Glee*-inspired activism also automatically creates publicity for the TV show and therefore functions, in one way or another, as indirect advertising for the brand name *Glee*.

However, creators run the risk of finding out that fans' loyalty to the ethical principles that initially attracted them runs deeper than their attachment to the text itself. Therefore, fan-organized activism can just as easily turn into a critique of the text and its creators if they violate the same ethical code they originally put in place. The initial campaign behind The Box Scene Project combined both aspects of fan-organized activism, the affirmative and the resistant side. Originally, the organizers' activism was inspired by the omission of a particular scene from the show: a romantic scene between *Glee*'s (at the time) only gay couple that treated Kurt and Blaine as "just another love story" and showed the deep affection between the boyfriends. For fans whose emotional attachment to *Glee* was linked closely to its treatment of LGBTQ characters and same-sex relationships, this scene was charged with as much symbolic value as the promise ring featuring in the clip. The omission of the scene from the episode, then, appeared to these fans as a slap in the face, in particular since the episode focused heavily on the heterosexual lead couple Rachel and Finn.[87] Fans felt strongly that Kurt and Blaine's sexuality had played a role in the producers' decision to cut the Box Scene from the Christmas episode.

Early scholarship on fan activism tended to define it in a way that was clearly distinct from political forms of activism: fan activism was used most commonly as a term for fan-organized campaigns against decisions by writers or producers that fans were unhappy about, such as the cancellation of a show or the departure of a beloved actor. This type of fan activism was considered resistant mostly in the sense that it encouraged fans to actively use their influence as consumers in order to push back against the authority of creators and producers. But fan activism is not always just a demand for more of the same (more episodes, more appearances by an actor/actress), it can also be the promotion of an agenda driven by sociopolitical concerns. This is especially prevalent when it comes to issues of representation in popular culture, where the fans' interest in the text and their investment in issues of societal significance begin to merge.

LGBTQ and female fans, especially those with an interest in genres predominantly written for straight male audiences such as science-fiction or crime, have long been used to not seeing themselves represented, or not represented adequately, by the texts they consume. For them (as for members of other underrepresented groups), subversive or resistant readings of popular texts have been one of the few strategies that allowed them to take pleasure from texts not specifically created for them. But faced with an increasing social acceptance of alternative sexualities and gender expressions on the one hand, and an entertainment industry that is paying closer attention to the practices and interests of fans on the other, at some point this simply didn't seem enough anymore. As Henry Jenkins and John Tulloch have pointed out, "resistant reading is not necessarily a sufficient response to dissatisfaction with the images currently in circulation. [...] It is [...] no substitute for other forms of media criticism and activism."[88] Jenkins and Tulloch made this statement as early as 1995 in their study of the Gaylactic Network, an organization of queer science-fiction fans and an early example of fan activism motivated by sociopolitical concerns. For more than a decade, the Gaylactic Network fought to convince the producers of *Star Trek* to include an LGBTQ character into an episode of *Star Trek—The Next Generation*[89] (1987–1994). They argued that *Star Trek's* pluralistic vision itself seemed to demand the inclusion of queer characters and found it hard to imagine a 24th-century galaxy whose inhabitants were supposed to be exclusively heterosexual. Ultimately, their efforts were not successful, and the fans were left with a number of episodes that not so subtly touched on the issue of queerness in a merely metaphorical sense, and their own imagination that allowed them to read *Star Trek* against the grain.[90]

While *Glee* fans hardly had to fight the creators over the inclusion of a queer character, their critique of the show's treatment of LGBTQ characters came from a similar place. The Box Scene Project's initial campaign arose from the concern that *Glee* did not treat its same-sex couples the same way as its heterosexual romantic pairs. In this regard, fans' fight for the release of the Box Scene was directed against the show itself, which in their opinion had violated its own ethical code by cutting the scene between Kurt and Blaine.

Here, The Box Scene Project closed the gap between fan activism and media criticism. Media criticism has long been a significant aspect of the work and practices of transformative fans, to the point where the line between fannish discussion and media journalism is often blurry. Meta pieces in journal-based fandom[91] offer long, detailed, and insightful commentaries on various aspects of popular texts that often resemble academic research papers in regard to depth and reach, even as they consciously employ a different, more accessible tone. On the other side of the amateur/professional divide, professional publications like the media blog *The Mary Sue*[92] explicitly addresses a feminist fannish audience with its mixture of fannish "squee"[93] and serious media analysis.

The Box Scene Project likewise expanded its efforts to include media criticism with its awareness-raising campaign Fandom for Equality,[94] which was launched alongside the organization's fundraising campaigns. This blog project aimed to draw attention to the representation of women, LGBTQ people, people of color, and people with disabilities in mass media by offering think pieces and analyses focusing on the representation of underrepresented groups in contemporary popular culture.

Another media criticism project inspired by *Glee* was The Glee Equality Project,[95] a fan-organized campaign on Tumblr that, in contrast to Fandom for Equality, directed its focus exclusively toward the show itself. The Glee Equality Project was dedicated to evaluating the representation of LGBTQ characters and couples on *Glee*. Keeping a tally of all the public displays of affection shown on the series, the organizers called *Glee* out on its unequal treatment of straight and gay couples. In their mission statement, the organizers write:

> Glee's strength, the reason it has been celebrated and held up as an example, is its wealth of young characters who among them represent a spectrum of diversity and sexuality. Characters who've captured our hearts and imagination. [...] But [...] [t]here is a troubling double standard in how it has treated its young LGB characters and couples. Kurt and Blaine, Brittany and Santana have a lot of issues in common [...]: lack of discussion, lack of privacy, constant chaperonage, rationed displays of affection.

When the initiative went on an open-ended hiatus in February 2013, the project organizers stated that while *Glee* had indeed improved in regard to its LGBTQ representation, their work was not over: "we also said we would still be watching: that as long as Glee is in production there will be a need to watch and judge whether the show is meeting expectations."

While different in scope, both Fandom for Equality and the Glee Equality Project were ultimately inspired by the ethical foundations fans considered to be at the core of the television series *Glee*. But while fan-organized sociopolitical activism often seems to be inspired by the ethics of the texts fans are invested in, these ethical beliefs can turn out to be stronger than fans' loyalty to the text when they feel that the text or its creators betray their own standards. This indicates that even for dedicated fans, their loyalty to a text is far from absolute and rather depends on an unwritten contract between the text and its consumers: a contract that entails certain ethical principles that fans expect writers and producers to uphold. If this contract is violated, the utopian ideas fans associate with a text might become more important than their trust in the creators' authority. Consequently, these texts don't only inspire fan activism, but can also become the subject of fans' media criticism. Fans of Joss Whedon's female characters reevaluated their attachment to his work when information about his marriage and attitude toward female coworkers became known. *Harry Potter* fans, who had used the *Harry Potter* novels and movies as inspiration to work toward a more tolerant and just world distanced themselves from the creator of the fictional universe when J.K. Rowling drew public attention with her repeated transphobic statements in 2020. And *Glee* fans relied precisely on the sense of ownership and agency that *Glee's* transmedia marketing campaign had tried so hard to install in them in order to criticize the show when they felt that that *Glee* didn't live up to the standards it had set for itself.

Conclusion

The first part of this book showed that transformative fan communities are grounded in a sense of community and solidarity that facilitates fan-organized sociopolitical activism. In this chapter, it became clear how fans' affective attachment to a specific fandom can provide the emotional and ethical motivation for fans to reach out beyond the borders of their own community. In these cases, fan-organized social activism specifically draws on the ethics of the texts fans engage with. The text functions as the ethical codex of their constituency, which influences and inspires fans and directs their attention toward specific sociopolitical issues. Furthermore, the organizational and technical skills that fans acquire through their engagement within the fan community also provide them with the necessary tools to plan effective campaigns: they already know how to rally people and connect them, how to distribute work, how to moderate and organize.

The transmedia marketing strategies of the contemporary entertainment industry both facilitate and complicate fan-organized activism. One the one hand, transmedia marketing campaigns increasingly strive to appropriate fan platforms, practices, and interests in order to ensure fan loyalty. On the other hand, the heavy use of participatory elements in transmedia marketing, geared toward binding fans to the brand, can also inadvertently support civic participatory engagement by boosting the fans' sense of agency and ownership.

In the following and final chapter, I turn toward another example of the dynamics between transmedia franchises and fans' sociopolitical concerns. The analysis of *The Hunger Games* franchise and the discourses surrounding it further problematizes the relationship between audiences and transmedia marketing strategies I have begun to discuss in this chapter. In the case of *Glee*, it became apparent that the marketing and the publicity accompanying the show tapped into fans' emotional attachment to the text by developing a narrative of community that transcended the line between fiction and reality and included not only the fans, but also the fictional characters and the actors playing them. *The Hunger Games* franchise, however, employed a marketing campaign that seemed to categorically undermine the politically resistant message of the original texts and appeared to capitalize on values that the text itself criticized: the celebration of capitalism and the dismissal of social responsibility. On the one hand, fans with an emotional investment in the political message of the novels felt that they needed to "rescue" the source text from its appropriation by the marketing, which led to an increased effort by fan activists to draw attention to issues of social inequality, poverty, and media censorship. On the other hand, the final chapter will show that even texts which appear to extend an explicit invitation for political engagement can be read very differently by different parts of their audience. While *The Hunger Games* trilogy became a symbol of anti-capitalist, anti-government resistance for many activists around the globe, not all fans felt alienated by the marketing campaign accompanying the films and instead embraced its focus on hedonism and luxury.

5

"We Are the Districts"

Fans' Reactions to Lionsgate's Hunger Games
Transmedia Marketing Campaign

"Fire is catching": The Hunger Games *as Political Reference*

During the 2014 protests that took place in Ferguson, Missouri, in the wake of the trial over the killing of Michael Brown, a remarkable photograph circulated on the social networking platform Facebook. The photo showed a line of graffiti, hastily sprayed onto a monument in the city of St. Louis, Missouri: "If we burn, you burn with us."[1] The message was easily identifiable as a quote from *Mockingjay*, the third and final novel in Suzanne Collins' young adult fantasy trilogy *The Hunger Games* (2008–2010). In the novel, the impoverished and exploited Districts rise against the wealthy Capitol after decades of oppression, and the rebels invite others to join their cause with an illegal video message containing the slogan "If we burn, you burn with us."[2] Quoted by an anonymous graffiti artist in St. Louis, the phrase established a parallel between the rebellion in the fictional dystopian universe of *The Hunger Games* and the protests against systemic racism and police brutality in the United States.

Coincidentally or not, the distribution of the photographed graffiti via social media followed the very same media strategies that the rebels in *The Hunger Games* use to undermine the official propaganda of their totalitarian government. Headquartered in the Capitol, the dictatorial government of Panem uses censorship, state-controlled television, and media surveillance to keep its oppressed population under control. The Capitol is ultimately defeated when its own weapons are turned on it as the rebels begin to hack mass media to spread its messages of dissent. "By becoming adept at interpreting and using information and the media, [Katniss] not only survives, but also outwits the Gamemakers, undermines the power of the Capitol, and sparks a revolution."[3]

Those engaged in the anti-racism protests in the United States similarly used mass and social media to draw attention to their cause. The city of St. Louis covered the *Hunger Games*–themed graffiti up quickly[4] in an attempt to erase the revolutionary message, and thus only few could have seen the writing in person. Yet the photo of the graffiti, disseminated through social media, made the message ultimately impossible to contain.

The spray-painted slogan in St. Louis was neither the first nor last time *The Hunger Games* universe served as textual reference for a contemporary activist group or movement. In 2013, activists with the Great Plains Tar Sands Resistance unrolled banners featuring the Mockingjay symbol and *Hunger Games*–inspired slogans at the Devon Tower in Oklahoma City to protest against Devon Energy's fracking practices and their involvement in toxic tar sands extraction. It was a peaceful protest that nevertheless ended with arrests, earning the activists the threat of terrorism hoax charges.[5]

In the fall of 2014, U.S. Walmart employees and workers in the fast-food industry appropriated the fictional rebels' three-fingered salute[6] in their fight for fair wages during the Black Friday Protests and Fight for $15 demonstrations.[7] On the other side of the globe, the same gesture was also used by anti-government protesters in Thailand after the military coup in May 2014: a number of people were arrested for using the salute, and movie theaters canceled showings of *Hunger Games: Mockingjay I*[8] in response to the arrests.[9] In appropriating revolutionary symbols, gestures and slogans from the *Hunger Games* universe, these different protesters attempted to make their political agenda more relatable by drawing parallels to the oppressed population in a fictional text. This strategy was based on the assumption that others would be able to make the connection because they had read *The Hunger Games* and understood it in a similar way. In some respects, this seemed like a safe bet: Collins' extremely popular young adult trilogy develops a fairly nuanced ethical and political philosophy and draws obvious connections to real-life issues such as state surveillance,[10] environmental damage,[11] globalized markets, and social inequality: "Panem is a microcosm of the system whereby developed nations exercise their economic power over poor populations in exchange for food or material goods."[12] According to Brianna Burke, a major strength of the trilogy is also that it explicitly spells out these connections, thus making them understandable to young readers (or really, any readers with limited knowledge about the global economy of the early 21st century). Amber Simmons likewise commends *The Hunger Games* for making real-world issues relatable to young readers, and even suggests that the novels could be used in high schools to encourage social action among students: "By incorporating the Hunger Games trilogy into the classroom, teachers can encourage students to look at current issues of violence and domination in our world."[13]

The connection between the fictional text and real-life politics appeared to be firmly established in public U.S. discourse, judging by the way public media soon began to use *The Hunger Games* as a catchphrase to discuss issues of social inequality. When CNN refused to cut short their coverage of the White House Correspondents' Dinner so they might report on the breaking anti-racism protests in Baltimore in April 2015, *Daily Show* host Jon Stewart and his correspondent Jessica Williams (dressed up as *Hunger Games* character Effie Trinket, played by Elizabeth Banks) compared CNN's attitude to the Capitol's media censorship during the uprising in the *Hunger Games*.[14] And during the primaries for the 2016 U.S. presidential election, democratic candidate Bernie Sanders' official Twitter account shared the picture of a young Sanders supporter holding a sign that compared Sanders to the Mockingjay, accompanied by the caption: "Casey knows a political revolution when she sees one."[15] This message was especially salient, since Bernie Sanders' campaign was focused on enacting political change against what he saw as a corrupt state, and received significant support from younger generations.

Considering that the concern with social and environmental injustice has emerged as the apparently dominant reading of the *Hunger Games* trilogy, it was a surprise that these issues were never mentioned in the large-scale, elaborate marketing campaign to promote the release of the *Hunger Games* film adaptations in 2012. In fact, even the spectacle of the Hunger Games competition itself, which provides the title for the trilogy, was very much put on the backburner in the campaign launched by the production company Lionsgate in cooperation with the agency Ignition Creative. Unlike the activists using the text as political reference or the teachers working with the novels to encourage social consciousness, Lionsgate did not tap into the presumably dominant reading of the text, choosing instead to draw fans into the fictional universe by addressing them as inhabitants of the Capitol—as members of Panem's ruling class that oppress and exploit those living in the impoverished Districts. Collins' novels critically depict life in the Capitol as revolving around luxury goods and excessive consumerism (expensive food, luxurious living quarters, fashion, and body modification), and these elements that had been so critically called into question in the novels were precisely what the marketing campaign focused on.

In the previous chapter, I used the example of *Glee* fandom to show how transmedia marketing strategies employed to create consumer loyalty can actually inadvertently inspire fannish activism, but also encourage fans' critique of the text and its creators. In this chapter, I focus primarily on one element of Lionsgate's *Hunger Games* campaign: the website *Capitol Couture* and its related tie-in products. I discuss the seemingly contradictory relationship between Lionsgate's marketing campaign and the texts it promotes and analyze discussions on social media to study consumers' responses to the campaign. While many fans rejected the identificatory potential of *Capitol Couture*, approached it as an extra-diegetic corporate paratext and felt the need to protect the message of the fictional text from its appropriation through the film production company, others accepted Lionsgate's transmedia marketing as part of the *Hunger Games'* diegetic universe, readily identifying with the inhabitants of the Capitol, and even embracing the campaign as an absolution from social responsibility. I argue that these different reactions to Lionsgate's marketing are ultimately rooted in differing readings of the fictional text—readings that determine whether fans consider the campaign a commercial paratext or a form of transmedia storytelling. Ultimately, Lionsgate's marketing campaign and the responses it brought forth undermined common assumptions not only about the relationship between text and paratext, but also about the understanding of alternative readings as politically resistant.

Transmedia Marketing, Transmedia Storytelling

Lionsgate's big-scale, long-game combination of viral marketing and tie-in merchandising is a sophisticated example of a contemporary transmedia marketing campaign that relies on transmedia storytelling. This specific form of "commercial intertextuality"[16] has become an increasingly popular branding strategy employed by entertainment franchises in recent years to maximize profit and encourage consumer loyalty.[17]

The term "transmedia storytelling" was coined by Henry Jenkins in his 2006 *Convergence Culture*, where he applied it to the franchise surrounding the movie trilogy *The Matrix* (1999–2003).[18] Jenkins showed that *Matrix* fans were encouraged not only to watch the movies themselves but to follow the narrative arc across different media platforms:

> The filmmakers plant clues that won't make sense until we play the computer game. They draw on the back story revealed through a series of animated shorts, which need to be downloaded off the Web and watched off a separate DVD. Fans raced, dazed and confused, from the theaters to plug into Internet discussion lists, where every detail would be dissected and every possible interpretation debated.[19]

This kind of storytelling across different media requires audiences to trace various narrative threads on different platforms if they want to feel like they have all the relevant knowledge, and it rewards those who do so with the feeling of being part of an interpretative community of insiders. At the same time, transmedia storytelling facilitates brand loyalty, because it forces consumers to engage with or buy different products associated with the franchise.

In his discussion of *Torchwood* media tie-ins, Matt Hills modified and expanded on Jenkins' definition of transmedia storytelling by suggesting that transmedia franchises do not always use different platforms in order to tell one single coherent story as Jenkins proposes.[20] Instead, transmedia storytelling allows creators and companies to develop different partial versions of a story or universe that do not necessarily always add up to one cohesive image but may also present alternative versions of a character or event. In engaging with this kind of transmedia storytelling, audiences may choose which parts of the story or fictional universe they want to consume and include in their interpretation or reading of the text. In the case of the British TV show *Torchwood* (2006–2011) for example, it is certainly possible to watch only the television series without feeling left out of the loop; yet, the tie-in novels and audio plays may offer different interpretations of certain characters or events that will let fans see the TV show in a different light.

While Jenkins mostly embraces transmedia storytelling as a new form of narrativity in the age of media convergence, Hills is more critical of transmedia storytelling in its function as branding and fan-management strategy. He suggests that franchises use media tie-ins to react to audience criticism by offering alternative versions of the story/text without having to make them part of the "main" text, such as in *Torchwood*'s treatment of its most popular romantic couple Jack Harkness and Ianto Jones: the tie-in audio play

> *The House of the Dead* (Goss 2011a) not only enables Jack and Ianto to be reunited post–*Children of Earth*,[21] but also to proclaim their love for one another. This honours the Jack-Ianto relationship, providing fan service for loyal audiences who felt the pairing was poorly treated by the events of series 3.[22]

But while seemingly giving fans invested in the couple's relationship what they want, the reunion between the lovers in the audio play can also be seen as an attempt to manage and control unauthorized fan texts: by the time "The House of the Dead"[23] appeared, fans had already written hundreds of stories presenting their own version of what in fannish terminology is called a "fix-it."[24] By providing an "official fix-it" in the form of a radio episode, the creators implicitly invalidated fans' versions of the story, thus regulating their transformative reading practices.

The *Pottermore* website,[25] an online platform providing background information and insider knowledge about different characters and events in the *Harry Potter* universe, serves a similar purpose. As Cassie Brummitt explains, site content is sanctioned and authorized by *Harry Potter* creator J.K. Rowling, and the "emphasis on Rowling's creative intentions privileged her as an authority and underlined the canonicity of the new content [...]; the website, through direct connection with Rowling herself, could present itself as a viable extension to the books and an alternative text to the movies."[26] Bethan Jones points out that by using this authority to support and devalue certain fan theories, in particular in respect to romantic pairings, "Pottermore is indeed regulating participatory culture."[27]

Despite their different perspectives on transmedia storytelling, Jenkins, Hills, and Jones have in common that they consider the practice primarily within the context of fictional texts, and understand transmedia tie-ins as part of a diegetic universe that often tie into an overarching narrative. Despite the fact that they certainly acknowledge the strategic use of transmedia storytelling in order to bind consumers to a brand, they discuss it mainly as a narrative strategy in fictional texts. This treatment of "text" as a fragmented archive of potentially infinite alternative versions also correlates with the reading and writing practices of transformative fans. Similar to the practices of transmedia storytelling, transformative fanworks undermine the traditional understanding of the autonomous unity of the work of art and instead bring forth a kind of "archontic literature" (Derecho, "Archontic Literature"), a theoretically endless archive of variations and continuations. This means that transformative fans in particular possess the media literacy that allows them to engage fruitfully with transmedia narratives, because they are accustomed to working with texts in similar ways.

Brummitt, on the other hand, focuses much more on the potential of transmedia storytelling as a marketing strategy, when she discusses the 2015 relaunch of *Pottermore* in the context of an expanding *Harry Potter* franchise brand. In fact, in marketing and advertising literature, transmedia storytelling does not necessarily relate at all to a (fictional) narrative or diegetic universe. For marketing scholars and practitioners, the "story" can simply be the message told about a product meant to be sold. Jason Thibeault, for example, explains how transmedia storytelling can be used to sell shoes: in this case, neither the product nor the campaign surrounding it are narratives in the narrow sense, but the message that is conveyed across different media platforms is thought of as a story that is told to make sense of the product's selling points.[28] This broad understanding of "storytelling" in the context of marketing work is further complicated by the fact that social media like YouTube have made it possible for corporations to actually employ more conventional forms of storytelling to sell their products. As part of *Pereira & O'Dell's Crossroads* campaign for Coca-Cola in Latin-America, for example, renowned director Dustin Lance Black shot a short narrative film about the friendship between a gay teenage boy and his straight friend. *El SMS* (2015) was distributed via social media and could be consumed like any other LGBTQ–themed short film. The only indication that this was in fact a form of advertising were the Coke bottles that one of the boys fetches from the fridge toward the end of the film.[29]

In all the above-mentioned examples of "commercial intertextuality,"[30] the two definitions of transmedia storytelling (narrative form vs. marketing strategy) are not clearly separated. In fact, the existing literature on transmedia storytelling discusses almost exclusively examples from commercial contexts in which the two functions are generally intertwined.

However, I propose that it would be useful to introduce a terminology that distinguishes more clearly between transmedia storytelling as narrative form and transmedia storytelling as branding strategy. Therefore I use the terms "transmedia storytelling" and "transmedia marketing" not interchangeably, as has often been done, but rather to distinguish between the two different functions of transmedia narratives. I define transmedia storytelling specifically as a narrative strategy that could very well exist outside of a commercialized context (or as much as any fictional text can). In this vein, I understand transmedia storytelling (with Hills and Jenkins) as the practice of telling a (fictional) narrative across different media in various parts that either form one coherent storyline or contribute to the same diegetic universe. The term transmedia marketing, on the other hand, I use to describe the strategy of selling a product—whether it is a story or a shoe—through a campaign that distributes promotional messages across different media platforms and may potentially encourage consumer participation in the context of social media.

In order to illustrate the differences between the two terms and how they can be helpful in analyzing transmedia franchises, I want to return briefly to the marketing campaign around the brand name *Glee*, an example of a recent large-scale transmedia campaign that I described in detail in Chapter 4. The U.S. high-school musical TV show, which aired on FOX from 2010 to 2015, was accompanied (among other things) by a number of hit singles and soundtrack albums; a concert tour during which the actors performed in character on stage, thus creating the illusion that fans could actually meet the fictional characters; and a casting show that offered fans the chance to compete for a guest role on the show so that they could themselves become part of *Glee*. While all of these products were part of a transmedia marketing campaign attempting to tie *Glee* fans to the brand, only the concert tour was strictly speaking a form of transmedia storytelling, as it maintained the illusion of the diegetic space, suggesting that the characters themselves were touring the country. The casting show, on the other hand, was not a form of transmedia storytelling, since it did not present itself as part of the diegetic universe. However, it did employ another strategy that it shared with many transmedia marketing campaigns: by offering audiences a chance to become part of the fictional universe, it blurred the line between mediated reality and diegesis.

In the context of my argument, this distinction is relevant because of the way transmedia storytelling significantly complicates the relationship between "text" and "paratext." In his discussion of media paratexts, including promos, spoilers, and merchandise, Jonathan Gray shows that the function of the media paratext and its relationship to the text is a complex one. For Gray, paratexts are not independent extratextual entities; they cannot be completely separated from the text because they influence consumers' reception of the text itself: "rather than simply serve as *extensions* of a text, many of these items are filters through which we must pass on our way to the film or program, our first and formative encounters with the text."[31] However, transmedia storytelling poses yet another problem for the distinction between paratext and text, namely the fact that the text itself is not a unity confined to one medium anymore, but sprawls and extends across different media and platforms. Because consumers do not necessarily accept all offers for a further exploration of the text, depending on what fits into their interpretation of the text and what does not, a piece of narrative might be considered part of the text by some consumers, but seen as a form of marketing or promotion (and thus, a paratext) by others. For example, on the website *Pottermore, Harry Potter* author J.K. Rowling continues to publish tidbits of information about the seven *Harry Potter* novels, often concerning the background or the future development of certain characters. Depending on whether this information fits into fans' previous readings of the novels, fans will decide whether they consider these bits of transmedia storytelling part of the text,[32] or whether they see them as a form of retroactive author's statement, that is, a paratext that does not necessarily influence their reception of the text. In this complex network of textual elements, it is not only the paratext that influences audiences' interpretation of the text, as Gray suggests, in the sense that "frequently we may find that audience talk and reaction to a text may have originated with the paratext."[33] Rather, recipients' interpretation of the text will also affect their relationship to the paratext. In fact, their previous reading of the text may decide whether they will accept additional narrative fragments as part of the text or see them as extratextual paratexts.[34]

Capitol Couture: The Future of Fashion

The examples of transmedia marketing discussed in the previous section all have in common that their use of transmedia storytelling serves, in one way or another, to strengthen the consumer's emotional or intellectual attachment to the text, that is, it facilitates fans' identification with the characters, raises the stakes they have in the development of the storyline, or encourages their engagement with the (personal, ethical, political) values promoted by the text. In chapter 4, I demonstrated, for example, how the marketing campaign around *Glee* tapped into fans' emotional investment in the message of solidarity and tolerance that the show promoted.

It stands to reason that, had the *Hunger Games* marketing campaign followed these examples and taken a similar approach, it would have capitalized on the seemingly obvious potential for identification with the oppressed people in the districts, or the revolutionaries trying to overthrow the Capitol. This is after all what the political activists did who appropriated the *Hunger Games* as a reference in their respective causes, and this is, presumably, what teachers build on when they use the *Hunger Games* to speak about social responsibility in the classroom.

Lionsgate, however, chose a different route, addressing the fans not as potential rebels, but rather as proud citizens of Panem, the totalitarian state founded in economic exploitation. In a viral marketing campaign that included several Tumblr-based websites, a YouTube channel and other social media, *Hunger Games* fans were invited into the diegetic space of the fictional universe. However, unlike *Glee* or *Harry Potter* fans, they were not addressed as allies and friends of the fictional protagonists, but as their opponents.

At the center of the viral marketing campaign were two Tumblr-based websites, *The Capitol* and *Capitol Couture—The Future of Fashion*,[35] which complemented each other by touching on different aspects of the text. *The Capitol* was set up as the official website of Panem's government and was heavily dominated by the pseudo-fascist aesthetics and propagandist rhetoric that characterize the representation of the government in the *Hunger Games* movie adaptations.[36] This website explicitly addressed fans as citizens of Panem by asking them to register for an identification card that "officially" identified them as inhabitants of the fictional state. With the premiere of *Hunger Games: Mockingjay I* in 2014, this website got "hacked" by the revolutionaries. Although most of the propagandist content remained untouched, the homepage showed Katniss (Jennifer Lawrence) instead of President Snow (Donald Sutherland) on the throne in the picture, and a line of revolutionary graffiti was scribbled across the screen.

Capitol Couture, on the other hand, presented itself as a fashion and lifestyle magazine from the fictional Capitol that reflected the glamorous, frivolous surface of Panem's capital. The mission statement on the magazine's homepage announced that *Capitol Couture* wanted to "celebrate the incredible achievements coming out of the Capitol—the beating heart of Panem."[37]

Appearing as a magazine from Panem's capital, *Capitol Couture* was a piece of transmedia storytelling that also aimed at blurring the line between mediated reality and fiction. The online magazine was promoted by advertisements in other, actual magazines and by billboards in urban spaces like a regular fashion magazine. Neither ads and billboards nor the magazine itself ever explicitly promoted the *Hunger Games* movies, thus consistently maintaining the illusion of being part of the diegetic universe. The content of the magazine blended stories about fictional characters set within the diegetic storyworld with information about the contemporary fashion scene and references to actual fashion designers and real make-up brands. For example, the magazine included a cover story on the (fictional) *Hunger Games* character Johanna Mason (Jena Malone), with references to a number of actual designers in the description of Johanna's outfit. But the same issue also featured an article on the work of Annouk Wipprecht and Lauren Bowker, actual contemporary designers who work with the kind of futuristic materials one might expect from designers in the fictional word of *The Hunger Games*.

The interrelation between fiction and mediated reality was even further supported by art challenges in the magazine, which encouraged fans to directly insert themselves into the diegetic space by creating and submitting *Hunger Games* fan art to the website. Their submissions were published on *Capitol Couture* under a category called "Citizen Activity." This strategy once again reaffirmed fans' identity as citizens of Panem and turned them into actors within the fictional universe, while at the same time incorporating non-commercial transformative fanworks into a marketing campaign. By taking advantage of user-generated content,[38] the campaign was able to regulate and control fannish practices as well as, in Joe Tompkins' words, "get fans to enhance the value of the *THG* brand through their own participatory labor."[39]

Some of the articles in the magazine also functioned as set-up for product placement, as advertisement for tie-in products that resulted from collaborations between *Lionsgate* and different companies on occasion of the movie premiere of *Hunger Games—Catching Fire* in 2013. The promotion of the tie-ins was seamlessly incorporated into the mix of fiction and mediated reality that made up the content of the magazine, as if these products, too, were simply part of the diegetic universe. *The Capitol*, the website for Panem's fictional government, likewise included product placement into their content by presenting an actual Mazda commercial as part of their "Capitol TV" programming; unlike the car promoted in the Mazda commercial, however, the products advertised in *Capitol Couture* were specifically developed for the *Hunger Games* campaign.

For the luxury online fashion retailer Net-A-Porter, costume designer Trish Summerville developed the *Capitol Couture Collection*,[40] a women's clothing line inspired by the costume design of the *Hunger Games* movies, with prices ranging from between $75 for a T-shirt to about $1,000 for a dress.[41] After the nail lacquer company China Glaze had produced the nail polish line *Colours from the Capitol* in 2012, the make-up company Cover-Girl followed one year later with the release of *Capitol Beauty*, a make-up line with color schemes based on the 12 districts of Panem. Make-up for the Mining District, for example, included eyeshadow in the shades of "Turquoise, Silver Sky, Onyx Smoke" and nail polish in shades of "Bronze Beauty and Black Diamond." Last but not least, high-end chocolate manufacturer Vosges Haut-Chocolat offered a series of chocolate flavors under the headline *Capitol Confections*, which included a line of chocolate bars also named after the 12 Districts of Panem, as well as a number of confectionery boxes named after different characters from the *Hunger Games* universe.

From the perspective of a marketing department, there are straightforward reasons to explain why Lionsgate chose this particular approach to promote the *Hunger Games* movies. It was perhaps only to be expected that the marketing for a young adult franchise featuring a female protagonist would specifically target female audiences with stereotypically female-oriented products, considering the ongoing trend of gendered marketing for male- and female-oriented products. Following the enormous success of *Twilight*, franchises based on young adult novel series with female protagonists such as *The Hunger Games* or *Divergent* were primarily marketed to female audiences, while movies in the *Marvel Cinematic Universe* and the *Star Wars* universe have been criticized for targeting a primarily male audience, despite the fact that women make up a significant part of the science-fiction and comic community. This often includes the almost complete erasure of female protagonists from their merchandising, as scholars and critics such as Suzanne Scott and Richard Berrigan[42] have pointed out. Scott rightly argues that "paratexts function to codify gendered franchising discourses" by perpetuating the invisibility of important female characters such as Rey (*Star Wars*), The Black Widow (*The Avengers*), or Gamora (*Guardians of the Galaxy*) through their absence from merchandising products like t-shirts or action figures, despite the fact that (female) fans keep asking for them in online spaces with hashtags such as #wheresrey.[43]

It is also reasonable to assume that Lionsgate had an interest in developing high-price tie-ins with the potential to achieve a higher revenue than any products that might have been associated with the image of the impoverished districts. Unsurprisingly, marketing magazines univocally praised Lionsgate's campaign for its ingenious strategy, designed to both make profit and secure fan engagement. Sarah Luoma from *The Strategist* likened the *Hunger Games* campaign to Warner Bros.' marketing efforts surrounding the *Harry Potter* franchise, and commended Lionsgate's viral marketing for establishing "a deep emotional connection with the characters that drives brand loyalty."[44] This is a somewhat surprising statement, since a deep emotional connection to the main protagonists is most certainly not part of the *Hunger Games* marketing strategy, however successful it might have been in other ways. Seth Soulstein, co-founder of the fan organization Harry Potter Alliance, explains why Luoma's comparison of Lionsgate's viral marketing to the marketing around the *Harry Potter* movies also falls short. The strategy Lionsgate employed for *The Hunger Games*, he suggests, would not work in the context of the *Harry Potter* franchise at all: "It's as if, for the Harry Potter movies, it was all just Death Eater stuff—buy 'Down with Mudbloods' T-shirts and so on."[45]

Just as the *Harry Potter* series clearly condemns the fascist ideology of the villains rallying behind Lord Voldemort, the *Hunger Games* novels seem to be equally explicit in their critique of the Capitol—not necessarily of its individual inhabitants, but certainly of their consumer habits and the economic system that makes their lifestyle possible in the first place. However, the *Hunger Games*–themed websites as well as the tie-in products addressed fans as citizens of Panem and were clearly designed to invoke the image of the wealthy Capitol, the same political and economic force Katniss Everdeen and her allies are trying to bring down. The marketing campaign's apparent invitation to identify with the society in the Capitol seems to categorically contradict the novels' critique of the exploitative system that enables the Capitol's luxurious lifestyle.

Lionsgate's campaign for the *Hunger Games* films was not the first marketing strategy that put the audience in the position of the "bad guys" in a fictional text. Perhaps most prominently, *The Beast*, an Alternate Reality Game (ARG), was launched in 2001 as part of the marketing campaign for Steven Spielberg's movie *A.I.—Artificial Intelligence* (2001).[46] Today, *The Beast* is mostly discussed as one of the first ARGs,[47] but it was also an early example for a viral transmedia marketing campaign. In *The Beast*, players could become members of the so-called Anti-Robot Militia and participate in anti-robot protests. Only later, they would find out that the game they were playing was connected to the film *A.I.—Artificial Intelligence*, which tells the story of an android boy who sets off on an odyssey to become "a real boy." At some point during his adventures, the android boy and his robot friends are hunted, captured, and tortured by a rogue group which turns out to be the Anti-Robot Militia—the same group ARG players had participated in. Andrea Phillips describes her experience with *The Beast*:

A friend of mine sent me a link to this website for the Anti-Robot Militia. We had no idea what it was, but it was really weird. These people were talking about how robots aren't alive and have no right to exist. It was anti-robot hate speech. We were so baffled by this that we started looking around. My friend found more websites and then found a Yahoo group called Cloudmakers, which were people looking into this thing. It was amazing because we didn't quite know what these interrelated websites were. We called it "The Game," and we called ourselves Cloudmakers, but we didn't have any other language to describe it. […] There was an interesting tension in that whole experience that you don't see anymore because times have changed.

We didn't know who was behind it to begin with. We didn't know it was a movie tie-in. There were Anti-Robot Militia rallies that we went to. That was fun. I think somebody wound up searching for the wrapping of packages that had been sent to the venues to look at the return label [and found] they had been sent from Microsoft. And then because of the characters mentioned in the story and this idea of a little robot named David, we figured that it was going to be a tie-in to the film *A.I.* But there was no moment when we saw, "In theaters on such and such date…" within the context of the game.[48]

While it was obvious to its players that *The Beast* was a game set in a fictional world (since the anti-robot agenda was clearly not responding to any real-life situation), it is important to keep in mind that the participants were drawn into the narrative of the game without knowing that it was part of a larger storyworld and in fact a marketing strategy to promote Spielberg's movie. It is impossible to know if the reaction to the game would have been the same if participants had seen the movie first. However, Phillips' nostalgic reminiscence about supporting anti-robot hate-speech and protests raises the question whether players felt any guilt or responsibility over their participation in the game when they were eventually confronted with the Anti-Robot Militia's violent actions in the movie, and whether this was an effect the producers might have intended, or not.

An answer to this question may be found in fans' response to the "gameplay marketing"[49] campaign preceding the release of Christopher Nolan's *The Dark Knight* (2008).[50] The ARG allowed fans to work for the villainous characters The Joker (Heath Ledger) and Harvey Dent (Aaron Eckhart) in order to access additional information about the upcoming movie. The fans working the Dent front had to support Dent's (fictional) campaign to be elected for District Attorney, while the "Joker asked his henchmen to perform various activities in the physical world, from taking pictures of themselves as his henchmen at certain places in select cities to retrieving special cakes that contained cellphones for later instructions."[51] Unlike the anti-robot protests for *The Beast*, there was nothing morally ambiguous about the actual tasks performed by the Batman fans in this game, but the fans working the Dent and Joker fronts still actively chose to side with characters who were clearly framed as villains within the fictional storyworld.

"Is it totally ironic?" Fans' Readings of the Campaign

Neither *The Dark Knight* ARG nor *The Hunger Games* campaign could have recreated the experience of *The Beast* for their own audiences. By the time the marketing campaign for the first movie was launched, the *Hunger Games* book trilogy already had a significant international following made up mainly of digital natives who were bound to recognize *Capitol Couture*'s terminology, references and rhetoric as relating to the novels they had read and the movies they were waiting to see. So one can assume that most recipients of *Capitol Couture* understood that the website was part of *Lionsgate*'s efforts to promote the first installment of the *Hunger Games* film adaptations. What *Capitol Couture* had in common with *The Beast*, however, was that it seemed to offer very little guidance in regard to its intended reception, forcing fans to consider their stance toward the material. Consequently, the campaign became a major point of contention among *Hunger Games* fans, who argued on a number of online platforms about the right way to read the campaign.

"Is this irony? Hypocrisy? Bread and/or circuses?" one fan speculated in a comment on the feminist media blog *Jezebel*.[52] Their list of possible readings (irony, hypocrisy, entertainment) neatly summarizes the three major positions among fans regarding the campaign that emerged from an analysis of fan discussions on different English-language online platforms frequented by recipients and consumers of the *Hunger Games* novels, movies, and marketing campaigns. In order to compile relevant data, I ran several online searches over the course of six months (May–November 2015) to find the most prominent articles and blog posts about Lionsgate's online marketing on platforms frequented by fannish audiences and those interested in popular culture and/or fantasy literature. The majority of the relevant data is not comprised of the original articles, but rather the discussions that developed in the respective comment sections. In total, I took into account 15 articles/blog posts and 378 individual comments (see Table 1). The comments and opinions were not analyzed based on the demographics of the participants, and not only because pseudonyms make such information about the commenters' age, gender, or social status difficult to access. Rather, the focus of this analysis is on overarching trends as well as on the specific discourses on different public online platforms. The data reveals that the three dominant—and conflicting—positions regarding the *Hunger Games* campaign crystalized similarly across all online spaces, despite differences in the focus and target audiences of the respective websites. This seems to indicate that there were no obvious ideological lines between different demographic groups (for example in regard to age). A discussion on Tumblr, which is frequented by a dominantly young, often teenage audience, and a conversation on Tor.com, which targets the professional(ized) science-fiction community, produced very similar arguments.

Article/Post	Author	Date	Website	Comments
"You know what's ironic about the Hunger Games?"	Allinablur	1/11/2012	Tumblr[53]	1,340 notes, 108 answers/adds = comments
"Update: Lionsgate Still Trying To Make *The Hunger Games* Theme Park Happen"	Victoria McNally	8/20/2014	The Mary Sue[54]	20 comments
"District Fashions Are on Display In The Latest *Hunger Games* Couture Offerings"	Jill Pantozzi	6/19/2014	The Mary Sue	23 comments
"*Hunger Games* Clothing Line Is Available for Purchase Despite a Serious Lack of Butterfly Dresses"	Rebecca Pahle	12/31/2013	The Mary Sue	8 comments
"CoverGirl Emphasizes Capitol Decadence For Their Hunger Games Makeup Line"	Isabella Kapur	8/16/2013	The Mary Sue	9 comments
"The Internet Has Done It: We've Found the Dumbest *Hunger Games* Tie In"	Susana Polo	11/8/2013	The Mary Sue	28 comments
"Want to Dress Like You Live in Panem? Capitol Couture Is Here!"	Laura Beck	9/19/2013	Jezebel[55]	40 comments

Article/Post	Author	Date	Website	Comments
"Volunteering for the Hunger Games? Don't Forget the CoverGirl Lipgloss"	Dodai Stewart	5/17/2013	Jezebel	38 comments
"There Are McQueen Shoes On The *Hunger Games* Fashion Tumblr!"	Dodai Stewart	1/24/2012	Jezebel	54 comments
"Is the Capitol Couture Clothing Line Sending the Wrong Message to *Hunger Games* Fans?"	Emily Asher-Perrin	9/18/2013	Tor.com[56]	16 comments
"Crossing the (Fashion) Line"	The Girl with the Pearl	9/5/2013	Victor's Village[57]	17 comments
"You'll Have to Kill a Child but at Least You'll Look Good Doing It"	Lilinaz Evans, Georgia Luckhurst, and Melissa Campbell	11/20/2013	SPARK Movement[58]	17 comments
"Hunger Games Month: The brilliant irony of Lionsgate's marketing"	Ashley Leckwold	3/17/2012	The Diary of a Dimension Hopper[59]	Individual blog, no comments
"Capitol Couture: Innovation or Complete Contradiction?"	Stephen Riordan	9/23/2013	The Lone Wolf[60]	Individual blog, no comments
"You have to Love Lionsgate's Commitment to the Dark Side: Catching Fire's Misfired Marketing…"	Siobhan O'Flynn	8/30/2013	in medias unrest[61]	Individual blog, no comments

Table 1: Articles, blog posts, and comments about the *Hunger Games* marketing campaign.

Irony

Many fans who appreciate Lionsgate's marketing campaign chose to read the campaign as an ironic, self-reflexive strategy that forced fans to reflect on their own position within a global economy. In a discussion thread on *Jezebel*, one participant states: "[T]he marketing for Hunger Games has always felt kinda meta"; another *Jezebel* reader calls the campaign "kind of clever, actually, in a tongue-in-cheek way."[62] These recipients seem to understand *Capitol Couture* primarily as a form of satire breaking down the fourth wall to raise questions about the relationship between consumer and text, such as: Does buying a movie ticket to see *Hunger Games: Catching Fire* automatically puts the spectator in the same position as the members of the Capitol? That is, does watching the big-budget studio-produced film at a large chain-owned movie theater imply a complicity with the global economic system of competition and exploitation? Is enjoying a movie about teenagers fighting to the death similarly unethical as Capitol members taking pleasure in following this kind of violence for entertainment? Taking a more cynical stance, some commenters also suggested that since Lionsgate was already part of the capitalist machinery, it seemed fitting (or perhaps simply honest) that the production company would be so blunt about the fact that they were first and foremost thinking about profit: "Is it totally ironic?" Ashley Leckwold writes. "Oh hell yes. We've pretty much bought into the Capitol in this process."[63]

Author Suzanne Collins herself explicitly agreed with the assessment of the campaign as self-reflexive satire when she actually voiced her own opinion in 2013, perhaps motivated by the controversy around the marketing campaign:

> It's appropriately disturbing and thought-provoking how the campaign promotes "Catching Fire" while simultaneously promoting the Capitol's punitive forms of entertainment. The stunning image of Katniss in her wedding dress that we use to sell tickets is just the kind of thing the Capitol would use to rev up its audience for the Quarter Quell. That dualistic approach is very much in keeping with the books.[64]

Of course, Collins' description of the *Hunger Games* campaign as "thought-provoking and disturbing" means to measure the campaign's success against its potential to make viewers uncomfortable enough to distance themselves from the consumer practices associated with the Capitol. And at least to some extent, the campaign did seem to inspire reactions of alienation among its recipients. On *Jezebel*, one fan admits: "I feel kind of weird reading the Hunger Games tumblr/magazine. It makes me feel like a Capital [*sic*] Dweller ... and that creeps me out." In a different comment under the same article, another reader suggests that the disturbing, unsettling effect of *Capitol Couture* is due to its striking similarity with the imagery of real-life mainstream fashion magazines: "I see ridiculous, out-of-touch shit like that in Vogue all the time."[65] This fan draws attention to the fact that the *Capitol Couture* Tumblr, which extended the illusion of the fictional Capitol's wealth into the fans' own lived experience, presented an unsettlingly familiar discourse of glamor and fashion. The similarity between the aesthetic practices of *Capitol Couture* and real-life fashion magazines allowed consumers to draw parallels to the more problematic aspects of the fashion world, such as the frequent use

of colonialist, sexist imagery in fashion design, or the exploitative practice of low-cost production in developing countries common in the fashion
industry.

In this regard, *Capitol Couture* is both similar to and different from
another movie marketing campaign that forced consumers to reflect on
their own position regarding the ethical dilemma raised by the text. Not
as far-reaching in scope as Lionsgate's *Hunger Games* campaign, but still
very noticeable were the billboards advertising for Neill Blomkamp's
post-apocalyptic science-fiction film *District 9* (2009), which warned
drivers on U.S. highways not to pick up non-human hitchhikers: "Pick-
ing up non-humans is forbidden. $10,000 fine. Report it here 1-866-666-
6001."[66]

These posters did not simply draw attention to the product they were
advertising. In fact, although the billboards included a URL leading to a
website with information about the film, the ads were presumably still con-
fusing to those who had not already heard about the film. Positioned in
the public space, the posters created the illusion that passersby were in fact
part of the fictional universe. They made drivers think about their behavior
toward hitchhikers, their definition of what counts as human, as well as the
question whether they would ever prioritize their personal moral compass
over the law. The billboards' strategy of forcing the spectator to consider
their own stance toward these issues certainly seemed appropriate, considering that they were marketing a movie with not-so-subtle references to the
South-African apartheid system.

While the *District 9* posters were designed to inspire ethical rumi-
nations even in those not already familiar with the movie, however, the
Capitol Couture billboards presumably appeared to the uninitiated as just
another fashion ad. Furthermore, there was another, potentially more critical, difference between the campaigns: whereas the *District 9* billboards
only advertised for the actual movie, *Capitol Couture,* with its mix of fiction, journalism and product placement, was meant to market far more
than that.

Hypocrisy

This aspect in particular was what a second group of fans considered
the main issue with the *Capitol Couture* campaign. These fans did to some
extent acknowledge or even appreciate the self-reflexive potential of the
Capitol Couture website. However, they argued that the interpretation of
the *Hunger Games* marketing as a clever piece of satire was significantly
complicated by Lionsgate's tie-in partnerships. On Tor.com, one commenter explains:

It's one thing to have the designs and the marketing as part of the viral campaign to promote the movie—that's extending the satire and commentary of the story. But to actually produce the line for sale? That's *becoming* The Capitol, not mocking it or warning against it.[67]

These fans pointed out that Collins' *Hunger Games* novels and the movies critique precisely the unequal distribution of wealth that allows a minority of the population to afford the kind of luxury items promoted by Lionsgate's marketing campaign. Consequently, the tie-in products undermined the core of what these fans perceived to be the essential message of the fictional text. "I feel bad for Suzanne Collins," one reader of *The Mary Sue* remarks, "because she wrote something amazing and the studio is turning into the exact thing she spoke against in the books."[68]

Beyond their general displeasure with what they saw as Lionsgate's blatant encouragement of consumerism, fans also criticized more specific aspects of the tie-ins. Some were unhappy that the *Hunger Games* campaign was such an obvious example of gendered marketing in its clichéd association of female audiences with fashion, make-up, and chocolate. This seemed especially troubling because the *Hunger Games'* female protagonist is popular among girls and women precisely because she rebuffs traditional gender roles and does not show any interest in make-up and fashion. As one fan states: "Well it would help if they weren't trying to sell make-up using a character whose in-story 'beautifying' was clearly a negative experience for her and is specifically to make her more appealing to the masses who hold her life in their hands."[69]

This is significant in comparison to the strategy used by the toy company Hasbro, which in 2013 took the immense success of *The Hunger Games* (and Disney's 2012 movie *Brave*) as inspiration to release Nerf Rebelle, their first ever toy weapon line for girls.[70] The Nerf Rebelle toys, which included compound and crossbows as well as various Nerf guns in a pink and purple flowery design, did face criticism for being so obviously gendered. Still, unlike Lionsgate, Hasbro at least seemed to acknowledge that for many young girls, the appeal of texts like *The Hunger Games* and *Brave* was the non-traditional representation of femininity that was not merely defined by heteronormative romance.

Other *Hunger Games* fans primarily criticized that the tie-in products were high-end luxury goods and appeared to address an audience with the financial means to spend $200 on a box of chocolates. Not only, they complained, did the marketing campaign encourage fans' identification with the upper classes in the storyworld, it also excluded low-income or even middle-class fans from its target audience. "[T]hese are technically young adult books and most teens don't have $900 disposable income to blow on a dress,"[71] one fan commented on *The Mary Sue*, and on the *Hunger Games* fansite *Victor's Village*, one of the contributors stated in an article about Summerville's upcoming *Hunger Games* clothing line: "The clothes will probably be beautiful. We may even want to buy some but ... again, we can't. Both because we're poor and because it just *feels wrong*."[72]

A number of social justice grassroots organizations reacted to Lionsgate's campaign with attempts to steer the audience's attention away from the consumerism-focused marketing and back to what they saw as the resistant potential of the novels. The SPARK Action Squad (SAS), a group of young U.S. and UK feminist activists, targeted CoverGirl's make-up line *Capitol Beauty* with their satirical Tumblr blog *Capitol Cuties*. In a mockery of CoverGirl's *Capitol Beauty* ads featuring models in fantastical over-the-top hairdos and make-up, *Capitol Cuties* presents photos of girls in grotesque make-up, accompanied by satirical texts that expose the problematic implications of a celebration of mass consumerism in the face of a society ruled by exploitation and violence. "Your suffering is not a problem to solve, but an inspiration for the look of the day!" the profile page announces, and one of the contributors quips sarcastically:

> I am so over the protests from all of the poor districts. You are all ruining the games for everyone else and it is embarrassing. Some of us actually *enjoy* the fantastic games our wonderful Capitol provide us every year. It's free, fun, and fabulous. Stop acting like peasants. Taking the fun out of the games for everyone else. I was going to talk about how much fun I am having with the Covergirl Capitol Collection, but I am not feeling as festive at this current time. I heard there was a really big riot breakout in District 11? Well anyways, thank you Covergirl, for reminding us the real purpose of the Games, makeup. Panem today. Panem tomorrow. Panem forever.[73]

Equally sarcastic, albeit less explicit in its social criticism was the response of the website for the *Hunger Games* parody *The Hunger but Mainly Death Games*,[74] which offered their own take on China Glaze's nail polish line. Their line-up included colors like "Definitely-Not-Poison Teal" (with the description: "Wow, a gift from a rival tribute's sponsor! Well, whatever it is, it's definitely not poison, that's for sure. So go ahead and eat it!") and "President Snow Red" ("Inspired by the blood of your execution if you ever make fun of President Snow for wearing nail polish").[75]

The non-profit fan organization Harry Potter Alliance very explicitly set out to "hack" Lionsgate's campaign by drawing attention toward issues such as poverty and income inequality. In an opinion piece in the *LA Times*, Harry Potter Alliance co-founder Andrew Slack wrote:

> We can't produce our own multimillion-dollar marketing campaign, but we can hack Lionsgate's. Wherever the studio and its promotional partners post an advertisement for the movie, you'll see our members posting pictures of

themselves doing the three-finger salute—the Districts' symbol for solidarity in the face of the Capitol. Instead of letting the studio's campaign silence or distort the film's message, activists will draw attention to the reality of economic inequality in America and to organizations that are working to end it.[76]

In an awareness-raising fan video with the title "The Hunger Games are Real,"[77] the Harry Potter Alliance criticized Lionsgate's spotlight on luxury and excess in their marketing campaign, as well as the media's focus on the love triangle between Katniss, Peta (Josh Hutcherson) and Gale (Liam Hemsworth) in their coverage of the *Hunger Games* movies. The video message suggested that popular media distracted viewers from the main message of the texts, and tried to counteract this trajectory by drawing spectators' attention to the social issues of poverty and inequality. In addition to the video and the accompanying social media campaign "Odds in Our Favor," the Harry Potter Alliance also directly encouraged *Hunger Games* fans to move their protests to the streets by supporting workers in the service industry during their protests for minimum wages in 2014. Once again, social media like Twitter and Facebook were used to document the protests and spread the images across the Internet.

Bread and Circuses

Unlike these fans and organizations, who felt the need to "rescue" the fictional text from its appropriation by the marketing machinery, a considerable number of voices did not perceive the Lionsgate campaign to be at odds with the stance of the text and therefore did not feel as conflicted or jaded about it. Fans in this group were most likely to get into arguments with representatives of the second group in online discussions about the marketing campaign, and the two groups clashed rather forcefully several times. For some representatives of this last group, the issue of accepting the marketing campaign was merely a question of the separation between fiction and reality. They categorized the marketing campaign and the tie-in products as "fiction" or "art," and argued that there was a difference between enjoying things for entertainment and approving of them in real life. "You may fully understand what the Capitol represented and still love ridiculous, ostentatious garb,"[78] one fan argued on *Jezebel*. On Tor.com, a commenter similarly stated: "[F]ashion is supposed to be FUN! Don't take it so seriously. How do you read so far into fantastical, whimsical costumes?"[79]

Another subsection of fans, however, did not only dismiss the real-life impact of advertising, but in fact explicitly embraced the identificatory potential of the transmedia campaign. These fans were outspoken about their conscious identification with the members of the Capitol. Granted, the fans in this group were not the only ones to think of themselves as

"Capitol citizens," but for representatives of the "Irony" and "Hypocrisy" fractions, this reluctant identification was usually a shameful, guilty experience: "Not to take this too seriously," one commenter on *The Mary Sue* wrote,

> but we actually do live in the real Hunger Games. Most of us (who have computer, internet, etc.) actually live in the Capitol. There really are children out there dying from starvation in much of the world. And children are forced to kill other children, they are called child soldiers. And the gap between rich and poor gets bigger everyday.[80]

Those who embraced the campaign's offer of identification, however, rejected the suggestion that this role should come with automatic social responsibility, and vehemently disagreed with fans who criticized the marketing campaign for being too focused on consumerism. "What exactly are you implying?," one commenter on Tor.com asked. "That wealth and luxury are inherently bad things, and never, ever should they be in any way glorified? I strongly disagree [...] and frankly, I have always been strongly against the notion that the so called excesses of the might and wealthy are somehow evil or decadent."[81] On Tumblr, a fan remarked with reference to the *Hunger Games* make-up line:

> So I'm gonna extend kudos to the thinking kid who buys that nail polish. Heck yeah. Because it's okay to have shallow desires. It's okay to like a little bit of glittering pretty, and to want something tangible in your hand that associates with a story you love. And with my eyes open, I know that no one's gonna suffer for the purchase of that polish. No kid's gonna get killed. No oppressive government is going to prosper. 'Cause who gets the money ultimately? Merchants. Producers. Investors. People who worked or risked to make the story real. It's a paradox designed to make us THINK, but we don't have to wallow in guilt or decry the people who seem to play along a little more than others. We just have to remember that we're all human in the end.[82]

These fans defended their position with references to the fictional text just as the critics of the marketing campaign, and took care to justify their perspective by providing textual evidence for their argument. The commenter cited above for example identified with Octavia, a woman from the Capitol, and provided a detailed character analysis to explain her actions:

> Octavia is part of the Capitol. Octavia exaggerates, fangirls, goes out and buys the Hunger Games nail-polish, writes smutty fanfic about the starcrossed lovers of District 12 (Don't look at me like that, you know she did.), and carries on about her favorite celebrities having FEELS about them, all while obliviously not comprehending their real problems, and generally being blind to a lot of the things that are so wrong with the world she's in. But Octavia is no heartless bitch. Octavia's eyes can be opened once everything is made personal. When it is her victor, her FRIEND, who's [sic] life is going back under the chopping block,

she cries. And maybe hates the Capitol (herself) too. And Gale treating her like she isn't human is WRONG.

This emphatic identification with representatives of the Capitol may come as a surprise: after all, the novels appear to spell out very explicitly the relationship between the luxurious lifestyle in the Capitol and an economic system of exploitation, and not very subtly establish parallels to our contemporary globalized economy. Rather than following the typical pattern of popular Western epic narratives, however, Collins avoids putting the blame for social inequality on specific individuals and falling back onto simplistic oppositions of good vs. evil. Instead, the author depicts a political system of structural inequality that cannot be significantly improved without fundamental changes to its economic structure. As Tompkins explains, "the final film suggests that the back-and-forth melodramatic cycle of class war will continue so long as the tyrannical conditions of class domination remain."[83]

However, Brianna Burke argues that Collins' exposure of systemic inequality, as opposed to a focus on individual blame, is precisely what may open the novels up for alternative interpretations.

> Collins shows throughout the novel that the feeling of privilege and entitlement—to foodstuffs as well as to material wealth—is inculcated into the population in order to reinforce and maintain the created system. Because of this, one could easily argue that Collins excuses the ignorance of the citizens of the Capitol, in turn simultaneously alleviating readers' complicity in global hunger.[84]

The reaction of the last group of fans toward the novels, the film adaptations, and the marketing campaign seems to support Burke's argument with regard to the reception of Collins' work. Because the novels represent inequality as systemic rather than personal, some fans felt absolved from responsibility for the existence of injustice in the world. A similar interpretation of the *Hunger Games'* message was reflected in the Instagram posts of a J. Crew executive who had celebrated with colleagues after spending the day laying off 175 coworkers in the summer of 2015. He tagged the pictures of their drunken celebrations with hashtags referencing *The Hunger Games*, indicating that he, too, did not feel individual guilt over his role in the system that caused his coworkers to lose their jobs.[85]

John Fiske has discussed at length the polysemic nature of popular texts, which makes them open to alternative interpretations. Popular texts, he argues, aim to reach not a small and exclusive but rather an audience as broad as possible. Therefore, they need to provide access for identification by different groups of recipients.[86] This is certainly true for contemporary entertainment franchises such as the *Hunger Games*. Further, these franchises are made up of an archive of constantly evolving texts with collective authorship. Neither one single author nor one narrative element can claim authority over the interpretation of the story, which firmly positions these popular franchises outside the discourse of originality and authorship that has influenced the production and reception of Western "high culture" since the 18th century. In the case of *The Hunger Games*, the text was opened up to alternative readings precisely by the author's attempt at a more complex and less clear-cut representation of political structures. It is noteworthy, however, that the heated controversy about alternative readings of the texts seemed to emerge only in response to Lionsgate's marketing campaign—both because it directly addressed fans as citizens of Panem and thus extended the *Hunger Games*' diegetic storyworld beyond the purely fictional realm of fantasy, and because fans were put in the position to determine whether the content of the campaign should be treated as a canonical element of the "text."

Conclusion

The different reactions toward *Capitol Couture* and its tie-in merchandise not only divided the *Hunger Games* fanbase in their reception of the marketing campaign, but also revealed alternative readings of the fictional text and different opinions regarding the relationship between fiction, marketing, and politics.

Both the "Irony" and the "Hypocrisy" fractions among the fans ultimately distanced themselves from the marketing campaign's offer for identification, even though the consequences they drew from their interpretation of the campaign differed. Both groups seemed to agree that the "text itself" (which primarily meant the novels and to a lesser degree the film adaptations) conveyed an important message about the contemporary global political economy. For the "Irony" fraction, the marketing for the movie adaptations simply proved the point they felt the novels were trying to make, namely that it is practically impossible to not become complicit in the global system of exploitation, willingly or not. For the "Hypocrisy" fraction, on the other hand, the novels were not only taking stock of the current situation but rather represented a call for action; the marketing campaign for the films was an example of corporate appropriation that only made the need to act seem more urgent. The two groups had in common that they distinguished between text and marketing, that is, they considered *Capitol Couture* to be a paratext that did not considerably influence their initial interpretation of the text. Yet, their reception of said paratext led them to different conclusions: for one group, the marketing provided an intelligent commentary on the issues raised by the text; for the other, it was a crude distortion of the message the text was trying to convey.

Capitol Couture also called to a third group of fans who approached the campaign from an alternative reading of the text. For these fans, Lionsgate's marketing campaign served as reaffirmation for an already existing alternative interpretation of the novels—one that allowed them to embrace their position as members of the wealthy class and absolved them from social responsibility. For these fans, the transmedia storytelling elements of *Capitol Couture* became part of the diegetic universe, that is, *Capitol Couture* was seen not so much as a paratext but rather as part of the text itself, because it fit into their general understanding of the diegetic universe.

The example of Lionsgate's marketing campaign demonstrates how corporate transmedia storytelling significantly complicates the relationship between text and paratext: a piece of storytelling might be considered a paratext by some but read as part of the actual text by others. This decision is not necessarily determined, but is certainly influenced by a recipient's previous reading of the text. Depending on whether a specific transmedia element complies with their previous understanding of the text, they will be more likely to accept additional elements of storytelling as canonical, or reject them as merely paratextual. Gray proposes that paratexts influence the reception of texts in crucial ways: "they create texts, they manage them, they fill them with many of the meanings we associate with them."[87] In the case of the *Hunger Games* marketing campaign, however, it was the textual archive that influenced the reception of the paratext, and the question of whether a piece of storytelling is considered a paratext at all.

Fans' reactions to the *Hunger Games* marketing campaign also seriously complicate common assumptions about dominant and alternative readings. In his seminal 1980 essay "Encoding/Decoding," Stuart Hall develops a theory of textual reception based on the linguistic model of decoding messages.[88] Depending on social context and the position of the reader/spectator, Hall suggests, one and the same message will be decoded (read) in rather different ways. Hall offers three different main categories of decoding, the "dominant/hegemonic position" (reading the text the way it was intended), the "negotiated position" (reading the text in some ways the way it was intended, but not in others), and the "oppositional position" (reading the text against the grain). Presumably because Hall developed his theory based on the example of public television news programming, he suggested that the dominant reading would be aligned with hegemonic politics, while the oppositional position represents an attitude of political resistance.

But *The Hunger Games* and the alternative readings it has brought forth undermine this automatic association of dominant readings with hegemonic politics. On the one hand, the dominant reading of the textual archive, which by now has developed into an enormous multimedia franchise, happens to align itself with resistant politics to the point where the text became a political reference for different activist groups all over the globe, from anti-racism activists in the U.S. to anti-government protesters in Thailand. On the other hand, fans' responses to the marketing campaign for the film adaptations revealed an alternative reading of the text that reflects hegemonic politics, showing that alternative readings are certainly not automatically politically resistant. Thus, this example can serve as a reminder that alternative, non-dominant readings are not always transgressive or subversive, but might in fact align themselves with hegemonic positions, even as they resist the dominant reading of the fictional text. The debate about the *Hunger Games* marketing also offers another example of the tensions between fans for whom popular consumption and fan activity are embedded into broader political conflicts, and those who reject the notion that textual consumption and fannish identity come with social responsibility.

The different reactions to Lionsgate's marketing also raise another question. Critics of the campaign were certainly justified in criticizing *Capitol Couture* for its explicit encouragement of excessive consumerism, and its promotion of luxury goods. However, this critique assumes, at least implicitly, that there could have been a different kind of marketing strategy that would have not only better represented the political philosophy of the novels, but also better served the interests of those affected by inequality. The frequent references to *The Hunger Games* by political activists seem to imply that a campaign focusing on issues of social injustice might have been able to draw increased attention to those issues among audiences of the *Hunger Games* films. However, even if the marketing strategy had chosen to focus on different content, this would not have changed the fact that it was ultimately promoting a multi-million-dollar franchise, and inevitably would have meant for the franchise to capitalize on what appears—at least on paper—as an appeal for revolutionary change.

The State of Fandom

An Outlook

At this point in time, the United States of Fandom, the Nation of Geekdom that Gernsbackian science-fiction fans already dreamed of in the 1920s and that John Scalzi outlined in 2012 in his vision of Comic-Con, is still very much a utopian fantasy.

Between the fans spraying revolutionary graffiti and the fans buying *Hunger Games*–inspired nail polish, the disagreement about Lionsgate's marketing accompanying the *Hunger Games* movie releases shows very clearly that there is no universally shared common ground even among the fans of a franchise that at first glance seems to promote a relatively unambiguous political message. The heated debate about the *Hunger Games* marketing campaign as well as the other fannish controversies discussed in this book support the argument that the history of self-organized fandom is not a linear chronological development from a centrist-conservative organization to a progressive-inclusive "safe space." It would be misleading to suggest that the political consciousness of fans has steadily increased over time, or that fandom has continuously moved toward a more tolerant and inclusive communicative culture. Rather, the history of fannish controversies appears as a dialectic narrative of perpetually returning conflicts playing out in somewhat different ways over and over again. Since the beginnings of self-organized fandom in the early 20th century, these conflicts have revolved more or less around the same dichotomies that continue to divide fan communities to this day: the cohesion of the community vs. the ideal of tolerance, the concept of a hierarchically structured constituency vs. the sprawling network of an alternative public, and the emphasis on aesthetic value and entertainment vs. an engagement with social and political concerns. Many of these controversies played out in particular along the line of demarcation between fans for whom popular consumption and fannish activity are embedded into broader social and political contexts, and those who reject the notion that textual consumption and fannish identity come with social responsibility. The conflicts around the nominations and elections for the World Science Fiction Society's Hugo Awards between 2014 and 2019 revolved at their core around the question what role politics should play in fandom, and what the notion of a "politicized fandom" means in the first place. But in many ways, the polarized discussions about the purpose of the Hugo Awards and the role of the World Science Fiction Society mirrored the arguments that were brought forth during the First Exclusion in 1939 and the Great Breen Boondoggle of 1964, and once again during the RaceFail '09 debates and the disagreements over the *Hunger Games* marketing campaign.

Still, the dynamics between different fannish fractions as well as the nature of fans' relationship with both the entertainment industry and political movements have also significantly changed over time. The fannish landscape in 2020 is not the same as it was in the 1930s, the 1960s, or even the first years of the 21st century. The network of transformative fandom has gained, over the past 10 to 15 years, in public recognition as well as in self-confidence to a degree that for the first time in fandom history, transformative fans are starting to appear as equal to, and in some ways even more influential than the affirmational fans of literary science fiction and fantasy. Yet this development has not caused the different groups within fandom to grow closer together over time. Rather, over the past two decades the divide between politically progressive and politically conservative fractions of fandom has in fact deepened once more, and the feuds that are carried out between different camps in the fannish sphere are more directly and openly connected to national and global political developments than perhaps ever before in fandom history.

What all this means for the future development of fandom is difficult to say, especially since the past 15 years have made it clear that the influence of real-life political changes on fandom discourses cannot be underestimated, and thus the future of fandom may very well be dependent on the future of global politics. It has certainly become obvious at this point that the optimistic predictions about youth-centric activism and fan-based citizenship that fan studies scholars made just mere years ago in publications with hopeful titles such as *By Any Media Necessary: The New Youth Activism*[1] (2016) or *Politics for the Love of Fandom: Fan-Based Citizenship in a Digital World*[2] (2019) have not fully come to pass. In fact, rather than becoming the safe haven that John Scalzi envisioned for his Nation of Geekdom in his 2012 essay,[3] some corners of geekdom actually appear to bear increasingly high risks for members of vulnerable or underrepresented groups. The fannish conflicts of the 21st century, from RaceFail '09 to Puppygate, show that the very same communal, technological, and industrial structures that equipped transformative fans with the sense of ownership and agency they needed to engage with sociopolitical issues as actors in the public sphere also made it possible for politically conservative fans to foreground and disseminate their agenda, and in fact prepared the ground for the infiltration of fan spaces by white supremacists and men's rights activist groups. The consequences of this development are not limited to uncomfortable arguments on social media, but in fact affect the lives of those targeted in very real ways: death and rape threats, doxing, and swatting have become widespread strategies of attack. Swatting in particular, the practice of placing a fake 911 call with the intention of having a SWAT team deployed to an opponent's house, has become far too common in the gaming community and can have fatal consequences, as in the 2018 case of a man in Ohio who was shot to death by law enforcement because his address had been named in a swatting prank that was the result of a dispute between *Call of Duty* players.[4]

On the flipside, many fans continue to use their networking and media literacy skills as a way to channel their concern with sociopolitical issues into action. The format of the fanworks auction[5] for example, which seemed to have mostly disappeared with fandom's migration from the journal-based platforms of LiveJournal et al. to newer platforms such as Tumblr or Discord, has made a comeback on Tumblr. The most prominent among the recent wave of Tumblr-based fan auctions is "Fandom Trumps Hate,"[6] which was started in November 2016 in direct response to the presidential election, as a way for fans to raise money for a number of causes affected by the legislative and executive measures of the Trump administration.

K-Pop fans emerged as one unlikely group of actors who purposefully inserted themselves into the fraught political climate of 2020, when racial tensions in the USA and several other countries coincided not only with fears about the Covid pandemic but also with natural disasters brought forth by global warming. During the protests against police violence in the spring and summer of 2020, sparked by the death of George Floyd and other victims of law enforcement, the Dallas Police Department promoted their app iWatch Dallas on Twitter and explicitly encouraged citizens to report protesters engaged in "illegal activity." In a somewhat unexpected twist of events, K-Pop fans responded by rallying online and flooding the app with K-Pop fancams[7] as a way to derail the original purpose of the app. Within two hours of fans bombarding the DPD with videos of Korean pop stars, the app was down due to "technical difficulties." The fans also made sure to diminish the app's effectiveness beyond the duration of their spontaneous action by reviewing it negatively online: "The app did eventually go back online, though it presently has a one-star rating in Apple's App Store, which makes it far less likely to be featured or to appear in a search."[8]

Shortly after, K-Pop fans also joined forces with users of the video-sharing platform TikTok to undermine President Trump's rally in Tulsa on June 20 by making a concerted effort to register for the rally with no intention to actually appear in person. When only about 6,000 out of 19,000 seats in the event space filled during the actual event, TikTokers and K-Pop fans claimed to be responsible at least partly for the seeming failure of the event.[9]

What makes these actions fascinating is not necessarily their long-lasting or far-reaching impact, which is certainly difficult to assess, but the things they tell us about fans' self-awareness as public actors at the end of the second decade of the 21st century. For one thing, K-Pop fans' actions stand out for their reliance on a combination of (a) pre-existing fannish networks, (b) organizing strategies resembling those used by contemporary political activists in political protests, and (c) their use of trolling as a practice meant to undermine earnest discourse. Unlike the malicious trolling of alt-right-adjacent fans in conflicts such as Gamergate and Puppygate,[10] however, their version of trolling was a more cheerfully chaotic kind, meant to disrupt but not to harm.

Equally significantly, their efforts to undermine the presidential rally were an explicit effort to insert themselves into party politics. This is not the first time fans (in their role *as fans*) explicitly side with or against a political party: as we have seen in Chapter 1, one of the first major conflicts that divided literary science-fiction fandom in the 1930s revolved around a group of actively and openly socialist fans. Yet it bears remembering that the Great Exclusion of 1939 happened right as the world was on the brink of what was to become World War II, and it may not be a coincidence that fans found it necessary to take an explicit stance in favor of or against politicians and parties at a moment in time when so much appeared to be at stake.

In this politically charged context, Matt Hills' suggestion that fan studies as a discipline should attempt a measured analysis of both sides and not resort to a "moral demand for the-taking-of-sides"[11] in its study of fannish controversies necessarily has to fall flat. Those who have actively tried to take a politically "neutral" approach to the interrogation of recent fannish conflicts inevitably end up excusing at least implicitly the racist, homophobic, and misogynist rhetoric that is rampant in the parts of fandom that have been overtaken by alt-right actors and sympathizers. In their attempt to rehabilitate the arguments of the Sad Puppy movement,[12] Stevens/van der Merwe for example perpetuate the myth of "Actually it's about ethics in gaming journalism"[13] when they suggest that the Sad Puppies' hateful rhetoric is only superficial bluster that obscures legitimate concerns about the future of genre publishing. Similarly, William Proctor dismisses accusations of racism in *Star Wars* fandom by arguing that those opposed to the casting of Black actor John Boyega as stormtrooper Finn in the *Star Wars* sequels were primarily concerned with "canonical fidelity,"[14] but overlooks the fact that the argument of canonical authenticity has been used frequently and repeatedly as a way to derail and dismiss efforts to talk about systemic racism in popular culture and fandom alike, as Albert Fu has laid out in his analysis of online discussions about a Black Spider-Man.[15] This is not meant to suggest that the conservative movements in fandom and their motivations and practices should not be treated to a careful cultural analysis, nor that fan studies should make a U-turn from uncritical praise of fandom's progressive potential to an equally uncritical condemnation of fandom's regressive tendencies. It does mean, however, that fan studies—like any discipline with a claim to societal relevance—needs to remain conscious of the fact that academic scholarship is embedded in the same political power structures that fandom is situated in, and that taking an observer position outside of politics is simply not possible. Suzanne Scott explains this succinctly when she agrees with Matt Hills that fan studies "need more nuanced models of cultural power, but what is somewhat obscured in Hills's call is how fans' lived experience of these power dynamics, as well as their tendencies towards 'resistant' behavior, is shaped by their real-world identities."[16] As Mel Stanfill phrases it, "Fandom Is Political (and Politics Are Fannish),"[17] and this means that fan studies is by necessity political itself. Stuart Hall, figurehead of the Birmingham School of Cultural Studies and forefather of fan studies, laid much of the groundwork for understanding the political implications of popular culture, and it's up to contemporary fan studies scholars not to forget his insights, which are still highly relevant to this day.

Whether fandom will be able, in the long run, to retain at least some of the resistant-subversive potential that fascinated and attracted fan studies scholars in the first place, or whether the creative forces of fan communities will eventually be entirely absorbed by the interests of corporations or political organizations remains to be seen. Either way, the fact that the States of Fandom are currently a highly visible, *public* battlefield whose players are coveted by various corporations and political movements can only mean that the political and cultural relevance of the field of fan studies is higher than ever before.

Chapter Notes

Introduction

1. John Scalzi, "Who Gets to Be a Geek? Anyone Who Wants to Be," *Whatever.Scalzi*, July 26, 2012.

2. Derek Johnson, "Fan-tagonism: Factions, Institutions, and Constitutive Hegemonies of Fandom," in *Fandom: Identities and Communities in a Mediated World*, ed. Jonathan Gray and others (New York: New York University Press, 2007), 285.

3. Scalzi, "Who Gets to Be a Geek?"

4. Joe Peacock, "Booth Babes Need Not Apply," *Geek Out! CNN Blogs*, July 24, 2012.

5. For early seminal texts on fan culture, see for example: Camille Bacon-Smith, *Enterprising Women: Television Fandom and the Creation of Popular Myth* (Philadelphia: University of Pennsylvania Press, 1992); Miriam Hansen, *Babel and Babylon: Spectatorship in American Silent Film* (Cambridge: Harvard University Press, 1991); Henry Jenkins, *Textual Poachers: Television Fans & Participatory Culture* (New York: Routledge, 1992); Lisa A. Lewis, ed., *The Adoring Audience: Fan Culture and Popular Media* (London: Routledge, 1992); Constance Penley, *Nasa/Trek: Popular Science and Sex in America* (London: Verso, 1997); Jackie Stacey, *Star Gazing: Hollywood Cinema and Female Spectatorship* (London: Routledge, 1994).

6. See for example: Henry Jenkins and Sangita Shresthova, eds., "Special Issue: Transformative Works and Fan Activism," *Transformative Works and Cultures*, no. 10 (2012); Henry Jenkins et al., eds., *By Any Media Necessary* (New York: New York University Press, 2016); Ashley Hinck, *Politics for the Love of Fandom: Fan-Based*

Citizenship in a Digital World (Baton Rouge: Louisiana State University, 2019).

7. Alyssa Rosenberg, "How 'Harry Potter' Fans Won a Four-Year Fight Against Child Slavery," *The Washington Post*, January 13, 2015.

8. Henry Jenkins, "Youth Voice, Media, and Political Engagement: Introducing the Core Concepts," in *By Any Media Necessary*, ed. Henry Jenkins et al. (New York: New York University Press, 2016), 1.

9. Hinck, *Politics for the Love of Fandom*, 7.

10. Neta Kligler-Vilenchik, "'Decreasing World Suck': Harnessing Popular Culture for Fan Activism," in *By Any Media Necessary*, ed. Henry Jenkins et al. (New York: New York University Press, 2016), 116.

11. Jenkins, "Youth Voice," 9.

12. People for Bernie, "Casey Knows a Political Revolution When She Sees One. She Voted Early in Wisconsin! #FeelTheBern," *Twitter*, April 3, 2016.

13. Jenkins, "Youth Voice," 9.

14. See Chapter 3.

15. Jake Swearingen, "Steve Bannon Saw the 'Monster Power' of Angry Gamers While Farming Gold in *World of Warcraft*," *NY Magazine*, July 18, 2017.

16. Sean Cashbaugh, "A Paradoxical, Discrepant, and Mutant Marxism: Imagining a Radical Science Fiction in the American Popular Front," *Journal for the Study of Radicalism*, no. 10.1 (2016): 69.

17. Johnson, "Fan-tagonism," 286.

18. See for example: Melissa Click, ed., *Anti-Fandom: Dislike and Hate in the Digital Age* (New York: New York University Press, 2019); Jonathan Gray, "Antifandom and the Moral Text," *American Behavioral Scientist*, no. 48.7 (2005): 840–58; Sarah

Harman and Bethan Jones, "Fifty Shades of Ghey: Snark Fandom and the Figure of the Anti-Fan," *Sexualities*, no. 16.8 (2013): 951–68.

19. Matt Hills, "An Extended Foreword: From Fan Doxa to Toxic Fan Practices," *Participations*, no. 15.1 (2018): 105.

20. CarrieLynn Reinhard, *Fractured Fandoms: Contentious Communication in Fan Communities* (Lanham: Lexington Books, 2018), 3.

21. E.E. Buckels, P.D. Trapnell, and D.L. Paulhus, "Trolls Just Want to Have Fun," *Personality and Individual Differences*, no. 67 (2014): 101.

22. Reinhard, *Fractured Fandoms*, 15.

23. J. Richard Stevens and Rachel Lara van der Merwe, "The Imagined Communities of Toxic Puppies: Considering Fan Community Discourse in the 2015 Hugo Awards 'Puppygate' Controversy," *Participations* 15.1 (2018): 208.

24. Hills, "An Extended Foreword," 116.

25. Mel Stanfill, "Introduction: The Reactionary in the Fan and the Fan in the Reactionary," *Television & New Media*, no. 21.2 (2020): 126.

26. Lisa Nakamura, "Race In/For Cyberspace: Identity Tourism and Racial Passing on the Internet," in *Reading Digital Culture*, ed. David Trend (Malden: Blackwell, 2001), 226–35.

27. Rukmini Pande, *Squee from the Margins: Fandom and Race* (Iowa City: University of Iowa Press, 2018); Benjamin Woo, "The Invisible Bag of Holding: Whiteness and Media Fandom," in *The Routledge Companion to Media Fandom*, ed. Melissa Click and Suzanne Scott (New York: Routledge, 2018), 245–252.

28. Sarah Banet-Weiser, *Empowered: Popular Feminism and Popular Misogyny* (Durham and London: Duke University Press, 2018); Megan Condis, *Gaming Masculinity: Trolls, Fake Geeks, and the Gendered Battle for Online Culture* (Iowa City: University of Iowa Press, 2018); Anastasia Salter and Bridget Blodgett, *Toxic Geek Masculinity in Media: Sexism, Trolling, and Identity Politics* (London: Palgrave McMillan, 2017).

29. Henry Jenkins, *Convergence Culture* (New York: New York University Press, 2006), 23.

30. Kristina Busse, "Geek Hierarchies, Boundary Policing, and the Gendering of the Good Fan," *Participations* 10.1 (2013): 77.

31. Donatella della Porta and Alice Mattoni, "Cultures of Participation in Social Movements," in *The Participatory Cultures Handbook*, ed. Aaron Delwiche and Jennifer Henderson (New York: Routledge, 2013), 176.

32. Matt Hills, "Torchwood's Trans-Transmedia: Media Tie-Ins and Brand 'Fanagement,'" *Participations*, no. 9.2 (2012): 409–28; Suzanne Scott, "Authorized Resistance: Is Fan Production Frakked?," in *Cylons in America: Critical Studies in Battlestar Galactica*, ed. Tiffany Potter and C.W. Marshall (New York: Continuum, 2008), 210–23.

Chapter 1

1. Gregg Calkins, "Untitled," *The Rambling Fap*, no. 36 (February 1965).

2. Pacificon is the name that was given to World Science Fiction Conventions (Worldcons) held in California (that is, on the Pacific Coast). Pacificon I was held in Los Angeles in 1946, Pacificon II took place in Oakland in 1964.

3. Calkins, "Untitled."

4. Ferdinand Tönnies, *Community and Society*, transl. by Charles P. Loomis (New York: Dover, 2011), 53; Ferdinand Tönnies, *Gemeinschaft und Gesellschaft: Abhandlung des Communismus und des Socialismus als empirischer Culturformen* (Leipzig: Fues, 1887).

5. Robert Booth Fowler, *The Dance with Community: The Contemporary Debate in American Political Thought* (Lawrence: University Press of Kansas, 1991), 4.

6. Georges van den Abbeele, "Introduction," in *Community at Loose Ends*, ed. Miami Theory Collective (Minneapolis: University of Minnesota Press, 1991), ix.

7. Robert D. Putnam, *Bowling Alone: The Collapse and Revival of American Community* (New York: Simon & Schuster, 2000), 22.

8. Miranda Joseph, *Against the Romance of Community* (Minneapolis: University of Minnesota Press, 2002), xvii.

9. Iris Marion Young, "The Ideal of Community and the Politics of Difference," *Social Theory and Practice*, no. 12.1 (1986): 2.

10. Jean-Luc Nancy, *The Inoperative*

Community, transl. by Peter Connor et al. (Minneapolis: University of Minnesota Press, 1991), 1; Jean-Luc Nancy, "La Communauté désœuvrée," *Aléa*, no. 4 (1983): 11.

11. Fredric Jameson, "Reification and Utopia in Mass Culture," *Social Text*, no. 1 (1979): 134.

12. Fowler, *The Dance with Community*, 161.

13. *Ibid.*, 15.

14. Joseph, *Against the Romance*, vii.

15. Nancy, *The Inoperative Community*, 10.

16. Tönnies, *Community and Society*, 43. The translation referenced here uses the phrase "invisible scene or meeting," but the original "unsichtbare Ortschaft" more literally translates into "invisible township/village": "So empfinden sich, gleich Kunst- und Standesgenossen, einander kennenden, auch die in Wahrheit Glaubensgenossen sind, überall als durch ein geistiges Band verbunden, und an einem gemeinsamen Werk arbeitend. [...] so bildet hingegen die geistige Freundschaft eine Art von unsichtbarer Ortschaft, eine mystische Stadt und Versammlung, welche nur durch so etwas als eine künstlerische Intuition, durch einen schöpferischen Willen lebendig ist." Tönnies, *Gemeinschaft und Gesellschaft*, 18.

17. For a discussion of the nation state as "imagined community," see Benedict R. Anderson, *Imagined Communities: Reflections on the Origin and Spread of Nationalism* (London: Verso, 1991).

18. Joseph, *Against the Romance*, xxvi.

19. Jürgen Habermas, *The Structural Transformation of the Public Sphere: An Inquiry Into a Category of Bourgeois Society*, transl. by Thomas Burger (Cambridge: MIT Press, 1989); Jürgen Habermas, *Strukturwandel der Öffentlichkeit: Untersuchungen zu einer Kategorie der bürgerlichen Gesellschaft* (Frankfurt: Suhrkamp, 1990).

20. Putnam, *Bowling Alone*, 149.

21. Anderson, *Imagined Communities*, 35.

22. Max Horkheimer and Theodor W. Adorno, *Dialectic of Enlightenment*, transl. by John Cumming (New York: Herder and Herder, 1972); Max Horkheimer and Theodor W. Adorno, *Dialektik der Aufklärung: philosophische Fragmente* (Frankfurt am Main: Suhrkamp, 1981). Further, see Janice Radway, *Reading the Romance: Women, Patriarchy and Popular Literature* (Chapel

Hill: University of North Carolina Press, 1984) for a discussion of romance novel readers' reputation; Joli Jensen, "Fandom as Pathology: The Consequences of Characterization," in *The Adoring Audience: Fan Culture and Popular Media*, ed. Lisa A. Lewis (London: Routledge, 1992), 301–14, for the negative stereotyping of fans; Richard Shusterman, "Popular Art and Education," in *The New Scholarship on Dewey*, ed. James W. Garrison (Dordrecht: Kluwer, 1995), 35–44, for the academic bias toward popular art; Ken Gelder, *Popular Fiction: The Logics and Practices of a Literary Field* (London: Routledge, 2004), for the academic and public distinction between high literature and popular fiction; Melissa Click, "Understanding Twilight Fangirls and the Gendered Politics of Fandom," *Flow*, no. 11.4 (2009), for the media's problematic portrayal of *Twilight* readers. For the debate about popular consumption, see also Chapters 2 and 3.

23. Cashbaugh, "A Paradoxical," 65.

24. Liesbet van Zoonen, *Entertaining the Citizen: When Politics and Popular Culture Converge* (Lanham: Rowman & Littlefield, 2005), 53.

25. Neta Kligler-Vilenchik, "'Decreasing World Suck,'" 107.

26. Johnson, "Fan-tagonism," 285–86.

27. Cashbaugh's account paints a similar picture of the beginnings of science-fiction fandom: "Gernsbackian utopianism provided the raw material for the formation of a community that responded to the contingencies of the 1930s, providing a means of collective empowerment and possibilities of professional mobility." (Cashbaugh, "A Paradoxical," 69–70.)

28. Camille Bacon-Smith, *Science Fiction Culture* (Philadelphia: University of Pennsylvania Press, 2000), 12–13.

29. *Ibid.*, 14.

30. *Ibid.*, 34.

31. Sam Moskowitz, *The Immortal Storm: A History of Science Fiction Fandom* (Atlanta: Atlanta Science Fiction Organization Press, 1954); Damon Knight, *The Futurians* (New York: John Day, 1977); Lester Del Rey, *The World of Science Fiction, 1926–1976: The History of a Subculture* (New York: Garland Pub, 1980).

32. Donald Franson, *Some Historical Facts About Science Fiction Fandom* (N3F Fandbook Publication, 1962).

33. Bacon-Smith, *Science Fiction Culture*, 12.

34. Fans corresponded with each other within and beyond national borders from early on. The changing location of the World Science Fiction Convention throughout the early decades reveals the development of networks between different local/regional/national groups. The Worldcon was held not only all over the USA, but also abroad: In 1948 and 1973, the Worldcon took place in Toronto, Canada; in 1957 and 1965, it came to London, and in 1979 to Brighton, UK; the 1970 Worldcon took place in Heidelberg, Germany. In 1975 and 1985, the event moved to Melbourne, Australia. Since the 1980s, the convention has been held in Canada, the UK, and Australia, as well as Japan, the Netherlands, and Finland.

35. Edward E. Smith, "What Does This Convention Mean?" (Worldcon, Chicago, Ill., 1940).

36. Cashbaugh, "A Paradoxical," 68f.

37. Bill Bridget, AJ Bridget, and Julie Wilhoit, "Unanniversary Slumber Party," *News from F*****-up Fandom*, June 1979.

38. Leslie Crouch, "The Good Old Days," *Ad Astra*, no. 1.3 (September 1939).

39. "Trufen," for "true fans," was a fannish slang term that referred to the "most Serious Fans": fans in the traditional literary community used it to set themselves apart from those fans with an interest in science-fiction television and cinema.

40. Paul Abelkis, "SOTF," *Sound-Off*, no. 1 (March 2, 1979).

41. Johnson, "Fan-tagonism," 285–86.

42. *Ibid.*, 286.

43. MOO is short for "MUD (multi-user dungeon), object-oriented" and refers to a text-based multi-player virtual world.

44. Julian Dibbell, "A Rape in Cyberspace; Or: How an Evil Clown, a Haitian Trickster Spirit, Two Wizards, and a Cast of Dozens Turned a Database Into a Society," *The Village Voice*, December 23, 1993: 200.

45. Del Rey, *The World*, 146.

46. Robert Lowndes, "The Futurians and New Fandom," *Futurian Society of New York*, October 1939.

47. Compared to contemporary mass conventions like San Diego Comic-Con, these early conventions were attended by a mere handful of people. Precise numbers for the "Third Eastern" are difficult to

find, but based on the list of names given by Moskowitz, *Immortal Storm*, 116ff., the gathering appears to have attracted about 30 people, perhaps more. The following year, this number had grown to 125 (see Moskowitz, *Immortal Storm*, 151), indicating the rapid growth of science-fiction fandom during those early years.

48. John B. Michel, "Mutation or Death" (Third Eastern Science Fiction Convention, Philadelphia, October 1937).

49. Hugo Gernsback, the "father of science fiction," started publishing *Amazing Stories,* the first English-language science-fiction magazine, in 1926. This magazine also provided the starting point for organized science-fiction fandom when fans began to get in touch with each other via the letter column in *Amazing Stories*: "Since the addresses were usually printed together with the names of the writers, other fans were encouraged to write to the man who had his letter published. In some areas, such as the larger cities, the addresses made it possible for fans to find friends with similar interests. This was the original nucleus of organized fandom" (Del Rey, *The World*, 71–72).

50. Cashbaugh, "A Paradoxical," 64.

51. *Ibid.*, 68.

52. *Ibid.*, 67.

53. Del Rey, *The World*, 142.

54. Bacon-Smith, *Science Fiction Culture*, 13.

55. Donald Wollheim and John B. Michel, "Futurian House," *Science Fiction Progress*, no. 2 (September 1939).

56. John B. Michel, *The Foundation of the CPASF* (New York: CPASF, 1939).

57. Sam Moskowitz, "There Are Two Sides," *Science Fiction Collector*, no. 5.2 (August 1939).

58. Also known as the First National Science Fiction Convention.

59. Lowndes, "The Futurians" (emphasis in original).

60. The title of the original pamphlet is mentioned in: Donald Wollheim and John B. Michel, "Convention Booklets," *Science Fiction Progress*, no. 2 (September 1939), but I have not seen an actual copy of the pamphlet. However, the text was reprinted in the fanzine *Alchemist* the following year, see: Robert Lowndes, "Dead End," *Alchemist*, no. 1.4 (December 1940): 5–13.

61. Robert Lowndes, *An Amazing Story*

(New York: CPASF, 1939); Douglas W.F. Meyer, *The Purpose of Science Fiction: Speech Held at the Second Convention of the Science Fiction Association in London, UK, on April 10, 1938* (New York: CPASF, 1939); Michel, *The Foundation*; Upton Sinclair, *Science-fiction Turns to Life* (New York: Michel-Wollheim Publications, 1939).

62. Dave Kyle, "A Warning," July 2, 1939.

63. Dave Kyle, "The Great Exclusion Act of 1939," *Mimosa*, no. 6 (1989).

64. Moskowitz, "Two Sides" (emphasis in original).

65. Knight, *The Futurians*, 40.

66. Moskowitz, *Immortal Storm*, 214.

67. Robert Lowndes, "Sykora Starts Riot: QSFL Meeting Ends in Brawl," *Le Vombiteur*, no. 3.11 (January 6, 1941): 1.

68. A regional convention in Philadelphia, hosted by the Philadelphia Science Fiction Society. The vote on the location for the 1940 Worldcon was held at Philcon 1939.

69. Donald Wollheim and John B. Michel, "The Philadelphia Convention," *Science Fiction Progress*, no. 4 (November 1, 1939).

70. Damon Knight, "Unite or Fie!," *Fanfare*, no. 1.4 (October 1940).

71. Smith, "What Does."

72. Knight, *The Futurians*, 41.

73. John Boston, "Untitled," *Tightbeam*, no. 27 (September 1964).

74. Deirdre Saoirse Moen, "Marion Zimmer Bradley: It's Worse Than I Knew," *Sounds Like Weird*, June 10, 2014.

75. See Katessa S. Harkey, "In the Midst of Avalon: Casualties of the Sexual Revolution," in *Pagan Consent Culture*, ed. Christine Hoff Kraemer and Yvonne Arburrow (Hubbardston, MA: Asphodel Press, 2016), 194–213; Charles Morgan and Hubert Walker, "Confronting Breen," *CoinWeek*, November 3, 2015.

76. Fanac is a fannish slang term from the era of traditional science-fiction fandom, referring to work done by fans that serves the fan community, including the publication of fanzines or the organization of fan conventions.

77. They separated in 1979 and were divorced in 1990.

78. During his time at Columbia Medical School, where Breen attended pre-med classes in the early/mid 1950s, he interviewed juveniles identifying as homosexual and/or transgender about their childhood sexual behaviors and collected data on their genitals, for what was presented as research on "gifted children"; various poems, plays, and literary texts produced in the 1950s/1960s explicitly reference sex with children (for both, see Walter Breen, *Walter H. Breen Papers*, 1950–ca. 1992. Coll. 7755. Division of Rare and Manuscript Collections, Carl A. Kroch Library, Cornell University). In 1964, he published *Greek Love*, a defense of man/boy love, under the pseudonym J.Z. Eglinton (New York: Oliver Layton Press, 1964).

79. It should be stated at this point that there is, from a current perspective, no doubt that Breen had a long history of child molestation, spanning several decades and including dozens of victims. In 1954, he was arrested for child molestation in Atlantic City and received a probationary sentence. He was arrested again in 1990 after being reported by his daughter Moira and other victims. The following trial ended in another probationary sentence; a year later he was rearrested for another transgression and sentenced to 13 years in prison, where he died of cancer the following year.

80. Bill Donaho, "The Great Breen Boondoggle or All Berkeley Is Plunged Into War," 1964.

81. Bill Donaho et al., "Untitled," *RPM*, no. 8 (August 1964).

82. George Scithers, "Pacificon II Report," 1964 (emphasis in original).

83. Bruce Pelz, "Untitled," *Ankus*, no. 11 (May 1964).

84. Prentiss Choate, "The Great Breen-donaho Boon," *Postmortem*, May 1964.

85. Richard Brown and Dave Van Arnam, "Untitled," *Poor Richard's Almanach*, no. 17 (April 1964).

86. Knight, *The Futurians*, 225.

87. Richard Bergeron, "Untitled," *Warhoon*, no. 20 (1964).

88. Pelz, "Untitled."

89. Brown/Van Arnam, "Untitled."

90. Choate, "The Great."

91. Rusty Hevelin, "The Despicable Donhao Doggery," *Phineas Pinkham Pallograph*, August 1964.

92. Robert Coulson and Juanita Coulson, "Untitled," *Yandro*, no. XII.5 (May 1964).

93. Chuck Hansen, "Untitled," *Damballa*, no. 2.3 (May 1965).

94. Bill Donaho, "Apologia," August 22, 1964.

95. Sam Moskowitz, "What to Do About Undesirables," *Noreascon III Program Book*, 1989.

96. Rebecca Lesses, "Untitled," *It Can't Happen Here*, no. 32 (October 1974).

97. Gene Roddenberry, *Star Trek* (NBC, 3 seasons, 1966–1969).

98. George Lucas, *Star Wars IV: A New Hope* (Lucasfilm/20th Century–Fox, 1977).

99. Harlan Ellison (born 1934) was (and is), like many members of the science-fiction community, both an active fan and an acclaimed professional writer of novels and short stories.

100. Matt Hickmann, "Untitled," *Tightbeam*, no. 3 (1978).

101. See Bacon-Smith, *Enterprising Women*; Francesca Coppa, "A Brief History of Media Fandom," in *Fan Fiction and Fan Communities in the Age of the Internet*, ed. Kristina Busse and Karen Hellekson (Jefferson, NC: McFarland, 2006), 41–59; Joan Marie Verba, *Boldly Writing: A Trekker Fan and Zine History 1967–1987* (Minnetonka, MN: FTL Publications, 1996). See also Chapter 2.

102. Bev Lorenstein and Judith Gran, "Welcome," *Organia*, no. 1 (July 1982).

Chapter 2

1. Short for "Science Fiction and Fantasy."

2. N.K. Jemisin, "Why I Think RaceFail Was the Bestest Thing Evar for SFF," *NKJemisin*, January 18, 2010.

3. tablesaw, "O HAI RACEFAILZ: Notes On Reading An Internet Conflict," *LiveJournal*, March 9, 2009.

4. Pande, *Squee from the Margins*, 33.

5. Bacon-Smith, *Enterprising Women*; Coppa, "A Brief History"; Verba, *Boldly Writing*.

6. Pande, *Squee from the Margins*, 8.

7. Habermas, *Structural Transformation*.

8. This was partly due also to the rather belated translation of Habermas' influential work from 1962 into English in 1989, as well as a revised edition of the German text that appeared in 1990 with a new introduction that directly engaged with the criticism directed at the original text: Habermas, *Strukturwandel*.

9. Warwick Mules, "Media Publics and the Transnational Public Sphere," *Critical Arts: A South-North Journal of Cultural & Media Studies*, no. 12.1/2 (1998): 24.

10. Others have summarized the different criticisms comprehensively and in detail, see: Craig J. Calhoun, ed., *Habermas and the Public Sphere* (Cambridge: MIT Press, 1992); Peter Uwe Hohendahl and Marc Silberman, "Critical Theory, Public Sphere and Culture. Jürgen Habermas and His Critics," *New German Critique*, no. 16 (1979): 89–118; Robert C. Holub, *Jürgen Habermas: Critic in the Public Sphere* (London: Routledge, 1991).

11. "Der Status eines Privatmannes kombiniert die Rolle des Warenbesitzers mit der des Familienvaters, die des Eigentümers mit der des 'Menschen' schlechthin" (Habermas, *Strukturwandel*, 88). In translation: "The status of private man combined the role of owner of commodities with that of head of the family, that of property owner with that of 'human being' per se" (Habermas, *Structural Transformation*, 29).

12. It does need to be said that Habermas himself not only acknowledged, but at least partly agreed with some of those criticisms in the introduction to the new edition, although he wasn't interested in fundamentally reassessing his theory (Habermas, *Strukturwandel*, 11–50).

13. See Nancy Fraser, "Rethinking the Public Sphere: A Contribution to the Critique of Actually Existing Democracy," *Social Text*, no. 25/26 (1990): 56–80; Joan B. Landes, "Women and the Public Sphere," *Social Analysis Gender and Social Life*, no. 15 (1984): 20–31.

14. Alexander Kluge and Oskar Negt, *Öffentlichkeit und Erfahrung: Zur Organisationsanalyse von bürgerlicher und proletarischer Öffentlichkeit* (Frankfurt: Suhrkamp, 1972).

15. Kluge/Negt, *Öffentlichkeit*.

16. Landes, "Women."

17. L.F. Selzer, "Angela Nissel from Blog to Books: Authorship and the Digital Public Sphere," *Auto/Biography Studies*, no. 27.1 (2012): 127–52.

18. Michael Warner, *Publics and Counterpublics* (New York: Zone Books, 2002).

19. *Ibid.*, 51.

20. Of course, the implicit barriers of internet access and basic literacy need to be kept in mind—even the (relatively) low

access barriers to online communication advantage those with access to primary and secondary education and public internet access. Today, more than 40% of the entire world population have access to the internet, in 1999 it was only 5% ("Internet Users," *Internet Live Stats*). This means that more than half of the world's population is still excluded from online communication.

21. Henry Jenkins and David Thorburn, "Introduction: The Digital Revolution, the Informed Citizen, and the Culture of Democracy," in *Democracy and New Media*, ed. Henry Jenkins, David Thorburn, and Brad Seawell (Cambridge: MIT Press, 2003), 1–13; Marita Sturken and Lisa Cartwright, *Practices of Looking: An Introduction to Visual Culture* (Oxford: Oxford University Press, 2001), 333–42.

22. Jodi Dean, "Why the Net Is Not a Public Sphere," *Constellations*, no. 10.1 (2003): 95–112.

23. James Brook and Iain Boal, *Resisting the Virtual Life: The Culture and Politics of Information* (San Francisco: City Lights, 1995).

24. Mark Poster, "Cyberdemocracy: The Internet and the Public Sphere," in *Reading Digital Culture*, ed. David Trend (Malden, MA: Blackwell Publishers Ltd, 2001), 259–71.

25. Nancy Fraser, *Scales of Justice: Reimagining Political Space in a Globalizing World* (New York: Columbia University Press, 2009), 76.

26. *Ibid.*, 93.

27. *Ibid.*, 91.

28. Thomas Olesen, "Transnational Publics: New Spaces of Social Movement Activism and the Problem of Global Long-Sightedness," *Current Sociology*, no. 53.3 (2005): 420.

29. Della Porta/Mattoni, "Cultures of Participation," 172.

30. Theodor W. Adorno, "Culture Industry Reconsidered," transl. by Anson G. Rabinbach, *New German Critique*, no. 6 (1975): 12–19; Theodor W. Adorno, "Resümee über die Kulturindustrie," in *Gesammelte Schriften Band 10.1: Kulturkritik Und Gesellschaft I: Prismen. Ohne Leitbild* (Frankfurt: Suhrkamp, 1977), 337–45; Adorno/Horkheimer, *Dialectic of Enlightenment*.

31. "Damit entstand eine neue Kategorie von Einfluß, nämlich eine Medienmacht, die, manipulativ eingesetzt, dem Prinzip der Publizität seine Unschuld raubte" (Habermas, *Strukturwandel*, 28; transl. by author).

32. "Kurzum, meine Diagnose einer geradlinigen Entwicklung vom politisch aktiven zum privatistischen, 'vom kulturrässonierenden zum kulturkonsumierenden' Publikum greift zu kurz. Die Resistenzfähigkeit und vor allem das kritische Potential eines in seinen kulturellen Gewohnheiten aus Klassenschranken hervortretenden, pluralistischen, nach innen weit differenzierten Massenpublikum habe ich seinerzeit zu pessimistisch beurteilt" (Habermas, *Strukturwandel*, 30; transl. by author).

33. Radway, *Reading the Romance*.

34. John Fiske, *Understanding Popular Culture* (Boston: Unwin Hyman, 1989); Stuart Hall, "Encoding/Decoding," in *Culture, Media, Language: Working Papers in Cultural Studies, 1972–79*, ed. The Centre for Contemporary Cultural Studies, University of Birmingham (London: Hutchinson, 1980), 128–38.

35. Matt Hills, *Fan Cultures* (London: Routledge, 2002); Alan McKee, "The Fans of Cultural Theory," in *Fandom: Identities and Communities in a Mediated World*, ed. Jonathan Gray et al. (New York: New York University Press, 2007), 88–97; Roberta Pearson, "Bachies, Bardies, Trekkies, and Sherlockians," in *Fandom: Identities and Communities in a Mediated World*, ed. Jonathan Gray et al. (New York: New York University Press, 2007), 98–109.

36. obsession_inc, "Affirmational Fandom Vs. Transformational Fandom," *Dreamwidth*, June 1, 2009.

37. Fannish slang for: costume play; fans dressing up as fictional characters and performing as these characters in public spaces (such as conventions).

38. Fannish slang; borrows from the term "folk music" and is used to describe music/songs about fictional texts or characters.

39. Abigail Derecho, "Archontic Literature: A Definition, a History, and Several Theories of Fanfiction," in *Fan Fiction and Fan Communities in the Age of the Internet*, ed. Kristina Busse and Karen Hellekson (Jefferson, NC: McFarland, 2006), 61–78.

40. Michel de Certeau, *The Practice of Everyday Life*, transl. by Steven Rendall (Berkeley: University of California Press,

1984); Michel de Certeau, *L'invention du quotidien 1: Arts de faire* (Paris: Gallimard, 1990).

41. Henry Jenkins, "Star Trek Rerun, Reread, Rewritten: Fan Writing as Textual Poaching," in *Close Encounters: Film, Feminism, and Science Fiction*, ed. Constance Penley et al. (Minneapolis: University of Minnesota Press, 1991), 171–204.

42. centrumlumina, "AO3 Census: Masterpost," *Tumblr*, October 5, 2013.

43. melannen, "Science, Y'all," *Dreamwidth*, January 16, 2010.

44. Bacon-Smith, *Enterprising Women*; Coppa, "A Brief History"; Verba, *Boldly Writing*.

45. Rukmini Pande and Samira Nadkarni, "From a Land Where 'Other' People Live: Perspectives from an Indian Fannish Experience," in *Fic: Why Fanfiction Is Taking Over the World*, ed. Anne Jamison (Dallas: BenBella Books, 2013), 350.

46. Karen Hellekson, "A Fannish Field of Value: Online Fan Gift Culture," *Cinema Journal*, no. 48.8 (2009): 113–18.

47. Exceptions are occasionally made for the sake of charity auctions, in which the money raised with commissioned fanworks is donated to a specific cause (see also Chapter 4).

48. See Jenkins, *Convergence Culture*, 177; Henry Jenkins, "Transforming Fan Culture Into User-Generated Content: The Case of FanLib," *Confessions of an Aca-Fan*, May 22, 2007.

49. geekturnedvamp, "Untitled Comment," *LiveJournal*, May 18, 2007.

50. Abigail De Kosnik, "Should Fan Fiction Be Free?," *Cinema Journal*, no. 48.4 (2009): 118–24; Tiziana Terranova, "Free Labor: Producing Culture for the Digital Economy," *Social Text*, no. 18.2 (2000): 33–58.

51. Bacon-Smith, *Enterprising Women*; Verba, *Boldly Writing*.

52. Francesca Coppa, "An Editing Room of One's Own: Vidding as Women's Work," *Camera Obscura*, no. 26.77 (2011): 123–30.

53. Many terms now widely associated with social networking sites, like the verbs "to friend" or "to friends-lock," likely originated on LJ.

54. This doesn't mean that all transformative fans used these platforms to interact: The community around Wizard Rock,

for example, a filk music genre in *Harry Potter* fandom, was primarily connected via *MySpace*.

55. Rebecca Lucy Busker, "On Symposia: LiveJournal and the Shape of Fannish Discourse," *Transformative Works and Cultures*, no. 1 (2008): 1.5.

56. *Ibid.*, 1.3.

57. *Ibid.*, 2.4.

58. Polyfannish: Fannish slang that describes the simultaneous interest in and engagement with different textual sources.

59. musesfool, "Nothing New Under the Sun," *Frail and Bedazzled. LiveJournal*, September 9, 2003.

60. Busker, "On Symposia," 2.2.

61. Alice Marwick, "LiveJournal Users: Passionate, Prolific and Private" (LiveJournal Inc., 2008): 1.

62. Rhiannon Bury et al., "'From Usenet to Tumblr: The Changing Role of Social Media,'" *Participations: Journal of Audience and Reception Studies*, no. 10.1 (March 2013): 301–02.

63. van Zoonen, *Entertaining the Citizen*.

64. Hansen, *Babel and Babylon*, 260.

65. Catherine Coker, "The Angry!Textual!Poacher! Is Angry! Fan Works as Political Statements," in *Fan Culture: Theory/Practice*, ed. Katherine Larsen and Lynn Zubernis (Newcastle upon Tyne: Cambridge Scholars Publishing, 2012), 83.

66. Verba, *Boldly Writing*.

67. Jonathan Gray et al., "Introduction: Why Study Fans?," in *Fandom: Identities and Communities in a Mediated World* (New York: New York University Press, 2007), 2.

68. Jenkins, *Convergence Culture*, 140.

69. *Ibid.*, 194.

70. kate-nepveu, "Diana Gabaldon & Fanfic Followup," *Incidents and Accidents, Hints and Allegations. LiveJournal*, May 10, 2010.

71. Gray et al., "Introduction," 4.

72. Della Porta/Mattoni, "Cultures of Participation," 176.

73. astolat, "An Archive of One's Own," *LiveJournal*, May 17, 2007.

74. Francesca Coppa, "An Archive of Our Own: Fanfiction Writers Unite!," in *Fic: Why Fanfiction Is Taking Over the World*, ed. Anne Jamison (Dallas: BenBella Books, 2013), 302–08.

75. Data retrieved on August 30, 2021.

76. Henry Jenkins, Anne Kustritz, and

Derek Johnson, "Gender and Fan Culture (Round Thirteen, Part One): Anne Kustritz and Derek Johnson," *Confessions of an Aca-Fan*, August 30, 2007.

77. Selzer, "Angela Nissel"; Elke Siegel, "Remains of the Day: Rainald Goetz's Internet Diary Abfall Für Alle," *The Germanic Review*, no. 81.3 (2006): 235–54.

78. Warner, *Publics*.

79. Busker, "On Symposia," 3.4.

80. *Ibid.*

81. British term for: masturbation.

82. Anne Jamison, *Fic: Why Fanfiction Is Taking Over the World* (Dallas: BenBella Books, 2013), 233.

83. See Chapter 1.

84. See for example Bacon-Smith, *Enterprising Women*; Justine Larbalestier, *The Battle of the Sexes in Science Fiction* (Middletown: Wesleyan University Press, 2002); Helen Merrick, "The Readers Feminism Doesn't See: Feminist Fans, Critics and Science Fiction," in *Trash Aesthetics: Popular Culture and Its Audience*, ed. Deborah Cartmell et al. (London: Pluto Press, 1997), 48–65.

85. Consuela Francis and Alison Piepmeier, "My Hair Stood on End!: Talking with Joanna Russ About Slash, Community, and Female Sexuality," *Journal of Popular Romance Studies*, no. 1.2 (2011): n.p. See also Verba, *Boldly Writing*; Bacon-Smith, *Enterprising Women*.

86. André M. Carrington, *Speculative Blackness: The Future of Race in Science Fiction* (Minneapolis: University of Minnesota Press, 2016), 30.

87. *Ibid.*, 48.

88. Fraser, "Rethinking," 64.

89. Amitai Etzioni, "Are Virtual and Democratic Communities Feasible?," in *Democracy and New Media*, ed. Henry Jenkins and David Thorburn (Cambridge: MIT Press, 2003), 85–100.

90. Banet-Weiser, *Empowered*, 32.

91. Rebecca MacKinnon and Hae-in Lim, "Google Plus Finally Gives Up on Its Ineffective, Dangerous Real-Name Policy," *Slate*, July 17, 2014.

92. Ellen Moll, "What's in a Nym? Gender, Race, Pseudonymity, and the Imagining of the Online Persona," *M/C Journal*, no. 17.3 (2014).

93. ithiliana, "A Minor Issue, Perhaps...," *The Heart of the Maze. LiveJournal*, March 7, 2009.

94. Jamison, *Fic*, 112.

95. Woo, "The Invisible Bag of Holding," 248.

96. Nakamura, "Race In/For Cyberspace," 226.

97. *Ibid.*, 230.

98. *Ibid.*, 227.

99. Mimi Nguyen, "Tales of an Asiatic Geek Girl: Slant from Paper to Pixels," in *Technicolor: Race, Technology and Everyday Life*, ed. Alondra Nelson and Thuy Linh N Tu (New York: New York University Press, 2001), 186.

100. Woo, "The Invisible Bag of Holding," 247.

101. Elizabeth Bear, "Whatever You're Doing, You're Probably Wrong," *Throw Another Bear in the Canoe. LiveJournal*, January 12, 2009.

102. *Ibid.*

103. Deepa D., "I Didn't Dream of Dragons," *Dreamwidth*, January 13, 2009.

104. In screen media, "whitewashing" refers to the practice of casting characters of color with white actors and/or completely erasing their racial origins. The TV adaptation of Ursula Le Guin's *Earthsea* novels is a notorious example of whitewashing in speculative fiction; see Ursula K. Le Guin, "A Whitewashed Earthsea," *Slate*, December 16, 2004; for more examples of whitewashing, see Amanda Scherker, "Whitewashing Was One of Hollywood's Worst Habits: So Why Is It Still Happening?," *Huffington Post*, July 10, 2014.

105. Elizabeth Bear, *Blood and Iron* (New York: ROC, 2006).

106. seeking-avalon, "Open Letter: To Elizabeth Bear," *Seeking Avalon*, January 13, 2009.

107. obsession_inc, "Affirmational Fandom."

108. Lois McMaster Bujold, "Untitled Comment," *LiveJournal*, May 9, 2009.

109. delux_vivens, "Wild Unicorn Herd Check In," *LiveJournal*, May 11, 2009. Unicorn: Slang term to describe a person whose character traits are rare and elusive (and thus perceived/depicted as the exception to the norm).

110. Robin Anne Reid, "'The Wild Unicorn Herd Check-In': The Politics of Race in Science Fiction Fandom," in *Black and Brown Planets: The Politics of Race in Science Fiction*, ed. Isaiah Lavender (Jackson: University Press of Mississippi, 2014), 230.

111. Sarah Monette, "Untitled Comment," *LiveJournal*, January 15, 2009.

112. bossymarmalade, "Untitled," *Dreamwidth*, January 18, 2009.

113. Alexis Lothian et al., "Pattern Recognition: A Dialogue on Racism in Fan Communities," *Transformative Works and Cultures*, no. 3 (2009): 5.2.

114. veejane, "Untitled," *LiveJournal*, March 2, 2009.

115. Elizabeth Bear, "Cease Fire," *Throw Another Bear in the Canoe*. *LiveJournal*, March 5, 2009.

116. bossymarmalade, "Sees Fire," *I Don't Like Angry Future Romulans*. *LiveJournal*, March 4, 2009.

117. seeking-avalon, "Open Letter."

118. Black speculative fiction author Nalo Hopkinson has talked openly about how a teaching position at UC Riverside helped her leave behind a life of poverty as an independent writer. Nalo Hopkinson, John Joseph Adams, and David Barr Kirtley, "Interview: Nalo Hopkinson," *Lightspeed Magazine*, June 18, 2013.

119. Danga was the name of Fitzpatrick's company that developed the LJ code. The other mentioned platforms are DW (Dreamwidth), IJ (Insanejournal), and JF (Journalfen), all LJ "spin-offs" based on the open-source LJ code.

120. Jemisin, "Why I Think."

121. Pande/Nadkarni, "From a Land," 347–48.

122. Fabio Fernandes and Djibril Al-Ajad, eds., *We See a Different Frontier: A Postcolonial Speculative Fiction Anthology* (Futurefire, 2013); Rose Fox and Daniel José Older, eds., *Long Hidden: Speculative Fiction from the Margins of History* (Framingham: CrossedGenres, 2014).

123. Albert Fu, "Fear of a Black Spider-Man: Racebending and the Colour-Line in Superhero (Re)Casting," *Journal of Graphic Novels and Comics*, no. 6.3 (2015): 276.

124. Dan Harmon, *Community* (NBC/Yahoo!, 6 seasons, 2009–2015).

125. Bob Persichetti et al., *Spider-Man: Into the Spider-Verse* (Columbia Pictures/SONY, 2018).

126. Lori Morimoto and Louisa Ellen Stein, "Tumblr and Fandom," *Transformative Works and Cultures*, Special issue: Tumblr and Fandom, ed. Lori Morimoto and Louisa Ellen Stein, no. 27 (2018): 2.1.

127. Elli E. Bourlai, "'Comments in Tags, Please!' Tagging Practices on Tumblr," *Discourse, Context & Media*, no. 22 (2018): 47.

128. Ibid., 46–56.

129. Morimoto/Stein, "Tumblr and Fandom," 2.5.

130. For more on Tumblr fandom, see also, for example: Lori Morimoto, "Roundtable: Tumblr and Fandom," *Transformative Works and Cultures*, Special issue: Tumblr and Fandom, ed. Lori Morimoto and Louisa Ellen Stein, no. 27 (2018); Line Nybro Petersen, "*Sherlock* Fans Talk: Mediatized Talk on Tumblr," *Northern Lights*, no. 12 (2014): 87–104; Lily Winterwood, "Discourse Is the New Wank: A Reflection on Linguistic Change in Fandom," *Transformative Works and Cultures*, Special issue: Tumblr and Fandom, ed. Lori Morimoto and Louisa Ellen Stein, no. 27 (2018).

Chapter 3

1. nenya_kanadka, "Untitled Comment," *AO3*, September 19, 2019.

2. See Chapter 1.

3. Bernadette Lynn Bosfey and Arthur D. Hlauaty, "Fandom," in *Women in Sciencefiction and Fantasy*, ed. Robin Ann Reid (Westport: Greenwood Press, 2009), 286.

4. See Chapter 2.

5. Cashbaugh, "Paradoxical," 68.

6. Stevens/van der Merwe, "The Imagined Communities," 221.

7. Hinck, *Politics*, 10.

8. Chris Weitz, *The Twilight Saga: New Moon* (Temple Hill Entertainment/Summit Entertainment, 2009).

9. Suzanne Scott, *Revenge of the Fanboy: Convergence Culture and the Politics of Incorporation* (University of Southern California, 2011), 125.

10. See Chapter 2.

11. Alexander Abad-Santos, "How the Nerds Lost Comic-Con," *The Atlantic*, July 13, 2013.

12. Paul Abbott, *Shameless* (Showtime, 2011–2021).

13. Lori Weisberg, "Comic-Con Is Staying in San Diego—at Least Through 2024," *San Diego Union-Tribune*, July 5, 2019.

14. Stephenie Meyer, *Twilight*, 4 volumes (New York: Little, Brown and Company, 2005–2008).

15. For more on the figure of the

anti-fan, see for example: Click (ed.), *Anti-Fandom*.

16. Jacqueline Pinkowitz, "'The Rabid Fans That Take [Twilight] Much Too Seriously': The Construction and Rejection of Excess in Twilight Antifandom," *Transformative Works and Cultures*, no. 7 (2011).

17. Elizabeth Spires, "'Enthusiasm,' by Polly Shulman and 'Twilight,' by Stephenie Meyer," *New York Times*, February 12, 2006.

18. David Cox, "Twilight: The Franchise That Ate Feminism," *The Guardian*, July 12, 2010.

19. Ashley Renfro, "Time to Set Bella Down: A Feminist Critique of Twilight," *Medium*, February 15, 2017.

20. Pierre Bourdieu, *Distinction: A Social Critique of the Judgement of Taste*, transl. by Richard Nice (Cambridge: Harvard University Press, 1984); Pierre Bourdieu, *La Distinction: Critique Sociale Du Jugement* (Paris: Éditions de Minuit, 1979).

21. Robert W. Jones, *Gender and the Formation of Taste in Eighteenth-Century Britain* (Cambridge: Cambridge University Press, 1998), 5.

22. Siegfried Kracauer, "Little Shopgirls Go to the Movies," in *The Mass Ornament*, transl. by Thomas Levin (Cambridge: Harvard University Press, 1995), 300; Siegfried Kracauer, "Die kleinen Ladenmädchen gehen ins Kino," in *Das Ornament der Masse* (Frankfurt am Main: Suhrkamp, 1977), 279–94.

23. Andrea Braithwaite, "It's About Ethics in Games Journalism? Gamergaters and Geek Masculinity," in *Gender, Race, and Class in Media*, ed. Gail Dines et al. (Thousand Oaks: Sage Publications, 2018), 537–38.

24. Banet-Weiser, *Empowered*, 131.

25. Hansen, *Babel and Babylon*, 254.

26. Gene Kelly and Stanley Donen, *Singin' in the Rain* (MGM/Loew's, 1952).

27. Barbara Ehrenreich, Elizabeth Hess, and Gloria Jacobs, "Beatlemania: Girls Just Want to Have Fun," in *The Adoring Audience: Fan Culture and Popular Media*, ed. Lisa Lewis (London: Routledge, 1992), 87.

28. Melissa Click, "'Rabid,' 'Obsessed,' and 'Frenzied': Understanding Twilight Fangirls and the Gendered Politics of Fandom," *Flow*, no. 11.4 (December 2009).

29. Screen Junkies, "Honest Trailers—Twilight," *YouTube*, March 22, 2012.

30. Suzanne Collins, *The Hunger Games* (New York: Scholastic Press, 2008); Gary Ross, *The Hunger Games* (Color Force/Lions Gate Films, 2012); for a more detailed discussion of *The Hunger Games*, see also Chapter 5.

31. Salter/Blodgett, *Toxic Geek Masculinity*, 148.

32. Lauren Faust, *My Little Pony: Friendship Is Magic* (Discovery Family, 2010–2019).

33. A neologism created from a combination of the words "Bros" and "Ponies"; for more about the history of the Bronies, see also Patrick Edwards et al., *Meet the Bronies: The Psychology of the Adult My Little Pony Fandom* (Jefferson: McFarland, 2019).

34. Salter/Blodgett, *Toxic Geek Masculinity*, 148.

35. *Ibid.*

36. Busse, "Geek Hierarchies," 73.

37. Peacock, "Booth Babes' Need Not Apply."

38. Jenkins, "Star Trek Rerun."

39. Scott, *Revenge of the Fanboy*, 81.

40. *Ibid.*

41. Condis, *Gaming Masculinity*, 63.

42. Xillionous, "Idiot Nerd Girl," *Know Your Meme*, June 9, 2010.

43. Hugh Jackman is not a superhero called "X-man"; he is the actor playing the character Wolverine, who is a member of the *X-men*, a group of mutant heroes in a transmedia franchise owned by Marvel Entertainment.

44. Scott, *Fake Geek Girls*, 98–99.

45. Scalzi, "Who Gets to Be a Geek?"

46. Salter/Blodgett, *Toxic Geek Masculinity*, 132.

47. *Ibid.*, 152.

48. Scalzi, "Who Gets to Be a Geek?"

49. Rebecca Lucy Busker, "Fandom and Male Privilege: Seven Years Later," *Transformative Works and Cultures*, Special Issue: Appropriating, Interpreting, and Transforming Comic Books, ed. Matthew J. Costello, no. 13 (2013): 1.9.

50. Scott, *Revenge of The Fanboy*, 87.

51. Roddenberry, *Star Trek*.

52. See also Chapters 1 and 2.

53. Robert Runte, ed. *The NCF Guide to Canadian Science Fiction and Fandom* (Edmonton: New Canadian Fandom, 1988).

54. Bacon-Smith, *Science Fiction Culture*, 12–13.

55. Suzanne Scott, "Fangirls in Refrigerators: The Politics of (In)visibility in Comic Book Culture," *Transformative Works and Cultures*, Special issue: Appropriating, Interpreting, and Transforming Comic Books, ed. Matthew J. Costello, no. 13 (2013): 2.3.

56. Jennifer S. Light, "When Computers Were Women," *Technology and Culture*, no. 40.3 (1999): 483.

57. *Ibid.*, 455.

58. Michael Salter, "From Geek Masculinity to Gamergate: The Technological Rationality of Online Abuse," *Crime Media Culture*, no. 14.2 (2018): 249.

59. Light, "When Computers," 482.

60. Scott, *Revenge of the Fanboy*, 124.

61. Busse, "Geek Hierarchies," 77.

62. See Chapter 2.

63. Scott, "Fangirls in Refrigerators," 1.3.

64. comicbookGRRRL, "Women in Comics: The New 52 and the Batgirl of San Diego," *comicbookGRRRL*, July 24, 2011.

65. *The Hawkeye Initiative*, Tumblr, 2014.

66. For additional context, see Braithwaite, "It's About Ethics."

67. Paul Feig, *Ghostbusters: Answer the Call* (Columbia Pictures/Sony Pictures, 2016).

68. The anti–*Ghostbusters* protests were an organized campaign against Paul Feig's 2016 *Ghostbusters* reboot with an all-female main cast. Male fans on YouTube and Reddit voiced their resentment about what they saw as a cult object and sacred childhood memory being ruined by efforts to make the reboot of the original 1984 *Ghostbusters* more "politically correct." One of the prominent voices in the discussion was conservative vlogger James Rolfe who stated outright that he was going to boycott the film (James Rolfe, "Ghostbusters 2016. No Review. I Refuse," *Cinemassacre*, May 17, 2016). For more information, see Peter C. Bryan and Brittany R. Clark, "#NotMyGhostbusters: Adaptation, Response, and Fan Entitlement in 2016's Ghostbusters," *Journal of American Culture* no. 42.2 (2019): 147–58.

69. The Fappening refers to an incident in 2014, during which nude pictures of female celebrities (most famously Jennifer Lawrence, the main actress in the *Hunger Games* franchise) were obtained by hacking Apple's iCloud and then distributed via the social media platforms 4chan and Reddit.

For additional context, see for example Adrienne Massanari, "#Gamergate and the Fappening: How Reddit's Algorithm, Governance, and Culture Support Toxic Technocultures," *New Media & Society*, no. 19.3 (2017): 329–46.

70. Alongside the Nebula Awards, which have been awarded by the Science Fiction and Fantasy Writers of America since 1966.

71. G.R.R. Martin, "Puppygate," *Not a Blog*. LiveJournal, April 8, 2015.

72. Jo Walton, *An Informal History of the Hugos: A Personal Look Back at the Hugo Awards, 1953–2000* (New York: Tor Books 2018), 397.

73. Noreascon was the name given to the Worldcons held in Boston, Massachusetts. The name is derived from the geographical identifier "Northeast."

74. Noreascon Organizing Committee, "Hugo Statement," *recs.arts.sf-lovers*, June 16, 1989.

75. See also: Mike Glyer, "Source Materials About the 1989 Hugo Controversy," *File 770*, September 25, 2017.

76. Larry Correia, "Sad Puppies 2: The Illustrated Edition," *Monster Hunter Nation*, January 14, 2014.

77. Larry Correia, "How to Get Correia Nominated for a Hugo Part 2: A Very Special Message," *Monster Hunter Nation*, January 16, 2013.

78. *Ibid.*

79. Correia, "Sad Puppies 2."

80. Brad Torgersen, "Announcing SAD PUPPIES 3!" *Brad R. Torgersen: Blue Collar Speculative Fiction*, January 7, 2015.

81. Jim Hines, "Puppies in Their Own Words," *Jim C. Hines*, June 7, 2015.

82. Martin, "Puppygate."

83. Total membership numbers were 6,060 in 2013, 10,718 and 10,350 in 2014 and 2015 respectively, and 7,338 in 2016.

84. Tasha Robinson, "How the Sad Puppies Won—By Losing," *NPR*, August 26, 2015.

85. *Ibid.*

86. Vann Newkirk II, "N.K. Jemisin and the Politics of Prose," *The Atlantic*, September 2, 2016.

87. Robinson, "How the Sad Puppies Won."

88. Buckels et al., "Trolls Just Want to Have Fun," 97.

89. Worldcon '75 Organizing Com-

mittee, "The Hugo Awards—What's New in 2017," *Worldcon 75*, not dated.

90. Condis, *Gaming Masculinity*, 15.

91. Ibid., 1.

92. Stevens/van der Merwe, "The Imagined Communities," 209.

93. Suzanne Scott, *Fake Geek Girls: Fandom, Gender, and the Convergence Culture Industry* (New York: New York University Press, 2019), 4.

94. Banet-Weiser, *Empowered*, 126.

95. See Chapter 1.

96. Banet-Weiser, *Empowered*, 118.

97. Abby Ohlheiser, "Just How Offensive Did Milo Yiannopoulos Have to Be to Get Banned from Twitter?" *Washington Post*, July 21, 2016.

98. Jeff Kaplan et al., *World of Warcraft* (Blizzard Entertainment, 2004).

99. Swearingen, "Steve Bannon."

100. Salter, "From Geek Masculinity," 255–56.

101. Rebecca Alter, "The Largest My Little Pony Fan Site Bans Your Horse-Crap Racist Fan Art," *Vulture*, June 23, 2020; Kaitlyn Tiffany, "My Little Pony Fans Are Ready to Admit They Have a Nazi Problem," *The Atlantic*, June 23, 2020.

102. Krystman, "Actually It's About Ethics," *Know Your Meme*, October 24, 2014.

103. Banet-Weiser, *Empowered*, 145.

104. See Chapter 2.

105. Isaac Walwyn, "The Hoffman Electronic Ads 1962," *Sevagram*, July 28, 2013.

106. Jo Walton, *An Informal History*, 78–79.

107. Ibid., 316.

108. Ibid., 402.

109. obsession-inc, "Affirmational Fandom."

110. synecdochic, "Untitled Comment," *AO3*, September 17, 2019.

111. obsession-inc, "Affirmational Fandom."

112. Naomi Novik, *Acceptance Speech at the Hugo Award Ceremony*, August 18, 2019, at the Worldcon in Dublin, Ireland.

113. Ruth EJ Booth, "Untitled," *Twitter*, August 18, 2019.

114. Nagaina, "Untitled Comment," *AO3*, September 16, 2019.

115. Standback, "Untitled Comment," *File 770*, July 28, 2019.

116. Kendall, "Untitled Comment," *File 770*, July 29, 2019.

117. JJ, "Untitled Comment," *File 770*, July 27, 2019.

118. Kaila Hale-Stern, "Everyone Who Contributed to Fanfiction Site 'Archive of Our Own' Is Now a Hugo Award Winner," *The Mary Sue*, August 19, 2019.

119. Source remains unnamed to protect the creator.

120. Source remains unnamed to protect the creator.

121. AO3 Team, "Hugo Award—What It Means," *AO3*, September 13, 2019.

122. JJ, "Untitled Comment," *File 770*, September 16, 2019.

123. Olav Rokne, "Untitled Comment," *File 770*, September 14, 2019.

124. 20Books to 50K is a business plan initiative for independent self-published authors who aim to make a living from their writing by publishing 20 books that bring in at least $7.50/day. See Michael Anderle, *20Booksto50K. Facebook*, February 7, 2016.

125. JJ, "Untitled Comment," *File 770*, July 28, 2019.

126. Steve Davidson, "Untitled Comment," *File 770*, July 28, 2019.

127. Anonymous, "Untitled Comment," *Failfandomanon. Dreamwidth*, September 19, 2019.

128. DragonessEclectic, "Untitled Comment," *AO3*, September 19, 2019.

129. Teaberryblue, "Untitled Comment," *AO3*, September 20, 2019.

130. peoriapeoria, "Untitled Comment," *AO3*, September 20, 2019.

131. LadyGoat, "Untitled Comment," *AO3*, September 17, 2019.

132. Anonymous, "Untitled Comment," *AO3*, September 17, 2019.

133. Muccamukk, "Untitled Comment," *File 770*, September 16, 2019.

134. Anonymous, "Untitled Comment," *AO3*, September 18, 2019.

135. Muccamukk, "Untitled Comment," *File 770*, September 16, 2019.

136. Meredith, "Untitled Comment," *File 770*, September 15, 2019.

137. Nagaina, "Untitled Comment," *AO3*, September 16, 2019.

138. Fairestcat, "One More Hugos Thing." *Just Off the Key of Reason. Dreamwidth*, September 17, 2019.

139. Anonymous, "Untitled Comment," *Failfandomanon. Dreamwidth*, September 18, 2019.

Chapter 4

1. Ryan Murphy, "Extraordinary Merry Christmas," *Glee* (FOX, December 13, 2011).

2. Tamila Gresham et al., *Box Scene Project*; now *Represent*.

3. See Joss Whedon, *Serenity* (Universal Pictures, 2005); Joss Whedon, *Firefly* (FOX, 1 season, 2002/2003); Sheilah O'Connor and Stephanie Leasure, *Can't Stop the Serenity: The Global Sci-Fi Charity Event*, 2006; Yasmeen Hassan et al., *Equality Now*, 1992.

4. "Sweet Charity" (2006, down since 2011); "Help Haiti: A Fandom Auction to Help Haiti Recover," *LiveJournal*, 2010; "Help for Japan: March 2011 Relief Charity Auction," *Dreamwidth*, 2011.

5. Melissa Anelli et al., *The Harry Potter Alliance*, 2005.

6. See Ashley Hinck, "Theorizing a Public Engagement Keystone: Seeing Fandom's Integral Connection to Civic Engagement Through the Case of the Harry Potter Alliance," *Transformative Works and Cultures*, Special issue: Transformative Works and Fan Activism, ed. Henry Jenkins and Sangita Shresthova, no. 10 (2012); Neta Kligler-Vilenchik et al., "Experiencing Fan Activism: Understanding the Power of Fan Activist Organizations Through Members' Narratives," *Transformative Works and Cultures*, Special issue: Transformative Works and Fan Activism, ed. Henry Jenkins and Sangita Shresthova, no. 10 (2012).

7. Ian Brownwell, Harry Potter Alliance, and Walmart Watch, *Harry Potter and the Dark Lord Waldemart* (2006).

8. A fan convention organized by the *Harry Potter* fansite *The Leaky Cauldron*.

9. Andrew Slack et al., "Can Fandom Change the World?" Panel at LeakyCon 2013, Portland, 2013.

10. For example Kligler-Vilenchik et al., "Experiencing Fan Activism"; Hinck, "Theorizing"; Tanya R. Cochran, "'Past the Brink of Tacit Support': Fan Activism and the Whedonverses," *Transformative Works and Cultures*, Special issue: Transformative Works and Fan Activism, ed. Henry Jenkins and Sangita Shresthova, no. 10 (2012). For an overview of the early scholarship on fan activism, see also Lucy Bennett, "Fan Activism for Social Mobilization: A Critical Review of the Literature," *Transformative Works and Cultures*, Special issue:

Transformative Works and Fan Activism, ed. Henry Jenkins and Sangita Shresthova, no. 10 (2012).

11. Cochran, "Past the Brink," 1.4.

12. Kligler-Vilenchik et al., "Experiencing Fan Activism," 5.2.

13. Karen Ann Yost, "It Is Better to Give…: A Look at Fandoms and Their Relationships with Charities," *Strange New Worlds*, March 1994.

14. A media fandom convention focusing on the television show *Starsky & Hutch* (and later also other buddy shows), which was held from 1979 to 2007 in Chicago and Kalamazoo.

15. Bennett, "Fan Activism."

16. Jared Padalecki, "What Does the Fandom Mean to Me?", in *Family Don't End with Blood*, ed. Lynn Zubernis (Dallas: Ben-Bella Books, 2017), 217–48.

17. Kligler-Vilenchik et al., "Experiencing Fan Activism," 5.2.

18. See Hellekson, "A Fannish Field."

19. See Chapter 2.

20. Cochran, "Past the Brink," 4.4.

21. Rhonda Wilcox, "Whedon, Browncoats, and the Big Damn Narrative: The Unified Meta-Myth of Firefly and Serenity," in *Science Fiction Double Feature: The Science Fiction Film as Cult Text*, ed. J.P. Telotte and Gerald Duchovnay (Liverpool: Liverpool University Press, 2015), 99.

22. *Ibid.*, 100.

23. Joss Whedon, "Safe," *Firefly* (FOX, November 8, 2002).

24. Wilcox, "Whedon, Browncoats," 110.

25. Joss Whedon, *Buffy the Vampire Slayer* (The WB/UPN, 7 seasons, 1997–2003).

26. Wilcox, "Whedon, Browncoats," 105.

27. Kai Cole, "Joss Whedon Is a 'Hypocrite Preaching Feminist Ideals,' Ex-Wife Kai Cole Says (Guest Blog)," *The Wrap*, August 20, 2017.

28. Years before the scandal about the revelations of Whedon's ex-wife, Natasha Simons was one of the voices explaining rather pointedly why Whedon's "street cred" as feminist should be reevaluated: Natasha Simons, "Reconsidering the Feminism of Joss Whedon," *The Mary Sue*, April 7, 2011.

29. Laura Browning, "Joss Whedon Was Never a Feminist," *AV Club*, August 21, 2017.

30. Anelli et al., *Harry Potter Alliance*.

31. Hinck, "Theorizing," 7.3.

32. van Zoonen, *Entertaining the Citizen*, 53.

33. J.K. Rowling, "J.K. Rowling Writes About Her Reasons for Speaking Out on Sex and Gender Issues," *JKRowling.com*, June 10, 2020.

34. Julia Jacobs, "Harry Potter Fans Imagine a World Without J.K. Rowling After Transphobia Row," *Independent*, June 13, 2020.

35. Hannah Yasharoff, "How Trans Harry Potter Fans Are Grappling with J.K. Rowling's Legacy After Her Transphobic Comments," *USA Today*, July 31, 2020.

36. Melissa Anelli, "Addressing J.K. Rowling's Recent Statements," *The Leaky Cauldron*, July 1, 2020.

37. A. Marwick, M.L. Gray, and M. Ananny, "'Dolphins Are Just Gay Sharks': Glee and the Queer Case of Transmedia as Text and Object," *Television & New Media*, no. XX(X) (February 26, 2013): 16.

38. Ryan Murphy and John Scott, "Acafellas," *Glee* (FOX, September 16, 2009).

39. Ryan Murphy and Elodie Keene, "Mash-Up," *Glee* (FOX, October 21, 2009).

40. Electricpurplearmor, "In Defense of Gleeks, Part Two: But, Why Glee?" *A Sense of Humor Is Needed Armor*, April 4, 2012.

41. Kevin Tancharoen, *Glee: The 3D Concert Movie* (Ryan Murphy Productions/20th Century–Fox, 2011).

42. "I Heart Glee" (Sky 1, March 10, 2013).

43. Dan Savage, *It Gets Better Project: Give Hope to LGBT Youth*, 2010.

44. Lee Hirsch, *Bully* (The Bully Project/Where We Live Films, 2011); *The BULLY Project*, 2011.

45. U.S. Department of Health & Human Services, *StopBullying.gov*, 2012.

46. Meghan Barr, "4 Bullied Teen Deaths at Ohio School," *Huffington Post*, December 8, 2010.

47. Roger C. Aden, *Popular Stories and Promised Lands: Fan Cultures and Symbolic Pilgrimages* (Tuscaloosa: University of Alabama Press, 1999); Nick Couldry, "On the Set of the Sopranos: 'Inside' a Fan's Construction of Nearness," in *Fandom: Identities and Communities in a Mediated World*, ed. Jonathan Gray and et al. (New York: New York University Press, 2007), 139–48; Hills, *Fan Cultures*.

48. Ryan Murphy and Brad Falchuk, "Preggers," *Glee* (FOX, September 23, 2009).

49. Ryan Murphy, "Theatricality," *Glee* (FOX, May 25, 2010).

50. Larry Teng, "Hana I Wa 'Ia," *Hawaii Five-0* (CBS, January 21, 2013).

51. Ryan Murphy and Brad Falchuk, "The New Rachel," *Glee* (FOX, September 13, 2012).

52. Ryan Murphy and Brad Falchuk, "New York," *Glee* (FOX, May 24, 2011).

53. Tim Stack, "'Glee': The Show Heard Round the World," *Entertainment Weekly*, May 28, 2010.

54. "Glee: Keep on Believin'," *Biography* (BIO Channel (now fyi), April 10, 2012).

55. Chris Colfer et al., *Panel at New Yorker Festival 2011* (New York, 2011).

56. Chris Colfer, "Q&A with Chris Colfer," *Chris-Colfer.com*, not dated. CEHS = Clovis East High School.

57. Murphy/Falchuk, "New York."

58. Murphy/Falchuk, "Preggers."

59. Chelsea Handler, "Guest: Chris Colfer," *Chelsea Lately* (E!, December 3, 2009).

60. Dianna Agron, "Chris Colfer: Song-and-Dance Man," *TIME*, May 2, 2011.

61. Frederik Dhaenens, "Teenage Queerness: Negotiating Heteronormativity in the Representation of Gay Teenagers in 'Glee,'" *Journal of Youth Studies*, no. 16.3 (2013): 304–17; Lynne Joyrich, "Queer Television Studies: Currents, Flows, and (Main)streams," *Cinema Journal*, no. 53.2 (2014): 133–39.

62. Versusthefans, "The Trouble with 'Glee,'" *Versus the Fans*, September 30, 2013.

63. Fannish term for the romantic relationship between two fictional characters that fans are particularly invested in. This can be both a relationship actually depicted in the text, or one that fans would like to see or create fanworks about.

64. lulzychan, "How Klaine Changed the World" (*YouTube* 2012).

65. troutymouth, "What Glee Means to Me," *Trouty Mouth*, August 2, 2012.

66. Gleek is a mash-up of the words Glee and geek.

67. In his study on *X-files* fans, Will Brooker describes rituals of fan viewing as a form of symbolic pilgrimage, as a "rite de passage" that marks the fans' transition to a place of belonging. Watching

Glee, and being a *Glee* fan, generated a similar sense of belonging. Will Brooker, "A Sort of Homecoming: Fan Viewing and Symbolic Pilgrimage," in *Fandom: Identities and Communities in a Mediated World*, ed. Jonathan Gray and et al. (New York: New York University Press, 2007), 149–64.

68. Tancharoen, *3D Concert Movie*.

69. Hills, *Fan Cultures*, 146.

70. "The Glee Project Casting Promo" (Oxygen, August 2011).

71. Matthias Stork, "The Cultural Economics of Performance Space: Negotiating Fan, Labor, and Marketing Practice in Glee's Transmedia Geography," *Transformative Works and Cultures*, Special issue: Fandom and/as Labor, ed. Mel Stanfill and Megan Condis, no. 15 (2014).

72. See Cathy Applefeld Olson, "Can 'Glee' Make a Splash in Music Class?," *Teaching Music*, no. 19.1 (2011): 32–34, 36; Jaime J. Weinman, "A Song in Their Hearts," *Maclean's*, November 22, 2010.

73. Christopher Loudon, "The Glee Effect," *JazzTimes*, September 16, 2010.

74. Stork, "The Cultural Economics."

75. Adam Anders et al., "Loser Like Me" (Columbia, 2011).

76. Naomi Lesley, "Character Education and the Performance of Citizenship in Glee," *Children's Literature*, no. 41 (2013): 12.

77. *Ibid.*, 15–16; 21.

78. See also Chapter 2.

79. Ryan Murphy and Eric Stoltz, "Opening Night," *Glee* (FOX, April 22, 2014).

80. troutymouth, "What Glee."

81. versusthefans, "The Trouble."

82. Ryan Murphy and Alfonso Gomez-Rejon, "Born This Way," *Glee* (FOX, April 26, 2011).

83. Lady Gaga, "Born This Way" (Streamline/Kon Live/Interscope, 2011). Lady Gaga explicitly dedicated her hit to the members of different underrepresented groups facing discrimination. Part of the sales of her "Born This Way—The Country Road Version" remix went to the Gay, Lesbian and Straight Education Network, and in 2011, the artist and her mother founded the Born This Way Foundation, dedicated to the promotion of tolerance and the fight against bullying: Lady Gaga and Cynthia Germanotta, *Born This Way Foundation*, 2012.

84. Showrunner Ryan Murphy endeared himself to his fans when he released the deleted scene via YouTube/Twitter half a year later, in the summer of 2012 (Ryan Murphy, "Untitled," *Twitter*, August 1, 2012).

85. Ryan Murphy and Bradley Buecker, "The First Time," *Glee* (FOX, November 8, 2011).

86. Tamila Gresham et al., *Represent*, 2011.

87. Which in turn angered fans also because the episode showed Rachel demanding an unrealistic amount of Christmas presents from her boyfriend, despite her being Jewish, something that fans perceived as an ethno-religious whitewashing of her character. For a discussion of whiteness and Jewishness on *Glee*, see also Rachel E. Dubrofsky, "Jewishness, Whiteness, and Blackness on Glee: Singing to the Tune of Postracism," *Communication, Culture & Critique*, no. 6.1 (March 2013): 82–102.

88. John Tulloch and Henry Jenkins, *Science Fiction Audiences: Watching Doctor Who and Star Trek* (London: Routledge, 1995), 111.

89. Gene Roddenberry, *Star Trek—The Next Generation* (CBS, 7 seasons, 1987–1994).

90. In fact, it was not until the theatrical release of the feature film *Star Trek Beyond* (Justin Lin, Skydance Media/Paramount Pictures 2016) that the first openly queer character was introduced into the *Star Trek* universe in a very minor, blink-and-you'll-miss-it subplot.

91. See Chapter 2.

92. "Mary Sue" is a fannish term referring to an original character in fanfiction who is very obviously a stand-in of the writer's own personality. The name of the blog is therefore an explicit reference to the fan practices of female fans in transformative fandom, thus establishing a link between fan practices and professional journalism.

93. Fannish term for the action of expressing delight over an element of popular culture that meets the fan's emotional or intellectual needs or desires.

94. Tamila Gresham et al., *Fandom for Equality*, 2013.

95. "GleeEqualityProject," *Tumblr*, 2012.

Chapter 5

1. Daniel Bates, "Ferguson Protesters Scrawl Hunger Games Slogan on Landmark as Tense Town Waits for Grand Jury Decision on Indicting Officer Darren Wilson Over Killing of Michael Brown," *Daily Mail Online*, November 24, 2014.

2. Suzanne Collins, *The Hunger Games: Mockingjay* (London: Scholastic, 2010), 100.

3. Don Latham and Jonathan Hollister, "The Games People Play: Information and Media Literacies in the Hunger Games Trilogy," *Children's Literature in Education*, no. 45 (2014): 33.

4. Laurie Skrivan, "Vandal Damages Statue Near Shaw Neighborhood of St. Louis: News," *St Louis Post Dispatch*, November 24, 2014.

5. Suzanne Goldenberg, "'Terror Charges Faced by Oklahoma Fossil Fuel Protesters 'Outrageous,'" *The Guardian*, January 10, 2014.

6. Index, middle, and ring finger held up together.

7. Reeves Wiedeman, "#Activism," *The New Yorker*, December 22, 2014; Ashoka, "Protesters Fighting for Higher Wages," *Forbes*, December 5, 2014.

8. Francis Lawrence, *The Hunger Games: Mockingjay Part I* (Lions Gate Films, 2014).

9. Seth Mydans, "Thai Protesters Are Detained After Using 'Hunger Games' Salute," *New York Times*, November 20, 2014.

10. Latham/Hollister, "Games People Play."

11. Brianna Burke, "'Reaping' Environmental Justice Through Compassion in the Hunger Games," *Interdisciplinary Studies in Literature and Environment*, no. 22.3 (2015): 1–24.

12. *Ibid.*, 8.

13. Amber M. Simmons, "Class on Fire: Using the Hunger Games Trilogy to Encourage Social Action," *Journal of Adolescent & Adult Literacy*, no. 56.1 (2012): 23.

14. Jon Stewart, *The Daily Show* (Comedy Central, April 27, 2015).

15. People for Bernie, "Casey Knows."

16. Jonathan Hardy, "Mapping Commercial Intertextuality: HBO's True Blood," *Convergence: The International Journal of Research Into New Media Technologies*, no. 17.1 (2011): 7–17.

17. Leigh Edwards, "Transmedia Storytelling, Corporate Synergy, and Audience Expression—ProQuest," *Global Media Journal*, no. 12.20 (2012): 1–12; Hardy, "Mapping Commercial"; Hills, "Torchwood's Trans-Transmedia"; Henry Jenkins, *Convergence*; Henry Jenkins, "Transmedia Storytelling 101," *Confessions of an Aca-Fan*, March 22, 2007; Henry Jenkins, "Transmedia 202: Further Reflections," *Confessions of an Aca-Fan*, August 1, 2011; Andrea Phillips, "Transmedia Storytelling, Fan Culture and the Future of Marketing," *Knowledge@Wharton UPenn*, July 3, 2012.

18. Lana and Lilly Wachowski, *The Matrix; The Matrix Reloaded; the Matrix Revolutions* (Warner Bros./Village Roadshow Pictures, 1999–2003).

19. Jenkins, Convergence, 96.

20. Hills, "Torchwood's Trans-Transmedia."

21. Ianto Jones dies in the last episode of Season 3. Russell T. Davies, "Day Five," *Torchwood: Children of the Earth* (BBC, July 10, 2009).

22. Hills, "Torchwood's Trans-Transmedia," 416.

23. James Goss, "The House of the Dead," *The Lost Files* (BBC/AudioGo, 2011).

24. A fix-it is a piece of fanfiction (or art, or video) which reworks parts of a narrative that left fans particularly dissatisfied, like the death of a beloved character or the break-up of a couple fans were deeply invested in.

25. J.K. Rowling, *Pottermore*, 2012.

26. Cassie Brummitt, "Pottermore: Transmedia Storytelling and Authorship in Harry Potter," *The Midwest Quarterly*, no. 58.1 (2016): 116.

27. Bethan Jones, "Pottermore: Encouraging or Regulating Participatory Culture?" *Magic Is Might 2012: Proceedings of the International Conference*, eds. L. Ciolfi and G. O'Brien (Limerick/Sheffield: University of Limerick/Sheffield Hallam University, 2013), 170.

28. Jason Thibeault, "Is Transmedia Storytelling the New Digital Marketing?," *Jason Thibeault*, October 17, 2013.

29. Dustin Lance Black, *El SMS* (Coca Cola, 2015).

30. Hardy, "Mapping Commercial."

31. Jonathan Gray, *Show Sold Separately: Promos, Spoilers, and Other Media Paratexts*

(New York: New York University Press, 2010), 3.

32. Rowling, *Pottermore*. In the case of *Harry Potter*, most fans might agree that the "text" includes, at the very least, seven novels (1997–2007) and eight movie adaptations (2001–2011); for some, it might also include the prequel/spin-off *Fantastic Beasts and Where to Find Them* (2001) and the films loosely based on that book, as well as the sequel stage play *Harry Potter and the Cursed Child*, written by J.K. Rowling, Jack Thorne and John Tiffany (2016); while others might reject or ignore these later additions to the universe. See J.K. Rowling, *Harry Potter Hardcover Boxed Set*, 7 volumes (New York: Arthur A. Levine Books, 2007); Chris Columbus et al., *Harry Potter 1–8* (Warner Bros., 2001–2011); J.K Rowling, *Fantastic Beasts and Where to Find Them* (London: Bloomsbury, 2001); David Yates, *Fantastic Beasts and Where to Find Them* and *Fantastic Beasts: The Crimes of Grindelwald* (both Warner Bros., 2016 and 2018); Jack Thorne, *Harry Potter and the Cursed Child* (New York: Arthur A. Levine Books, 2017; Stage Premiere July 30, 2016 at the Palace Theatre, London).

33. Gray, *Show Sold Separately*, 46.

34. This distinction between "text" and "paratext" to some extent overlaps with but also diverges from the distinction between "canon" and "fanon" that is used in fan communities to determine the significance or value of narrative elements. The canon comprises the entirety of facts and information that most fans agree on as being "officially" part of the fictional storyworld; whereas fanon encompasses assumptions about characters or events that a majority of the fan community believes to be true, even though the text has never explicitly stated it. This does not mean that the opinion on what is part of canon is always univocal. In the case of the *Star Trek* franchise, most viewers will agree that information conveyed by the television show and the tie-in feature films are canon, whereas opinions might differ in regard to the tie-in novels.

35. Ignition Creative, *Capitol Couture*, 2012; Ignition Creative, *The Capitol*, 2012.

36. Ross, *The Hunger Games*; Francis Lawrence, *The Hunger Games: Catching Fire* (Lions Gate Films, 2013); Lawrence, *The Hunger Games: Mockingjay Part I*; Francis Lawrence, *The Hunger Games: Mockingjay Part II* (Lions Gate Films, 2015).

37. Ignition Creative, *Capitol Couture*.

38. "User-generated content" is a term generally used to describe the corporate strategy of appropriating free labor employed by consumers in order to generate profit—fan videos, for example, have served as an unofficial, non-commercial kind of advertising for decades, but more recently companies have begun to incorporate these works into their own marketing efforts: for companies, this has the advantage of both being provided with free content and giving fans the impression that their voices and creative output are valued (see Jenkins, "Transforming").

39. Joe Tompkins, "The Makings of a Contradictory Franchise: Revolutionary Melodrama and Cynicism in the Hunger Games," *JCMS: Journal of Cinema and Media Studies* no. 58.1 (2018): 84.

40. "Shop Capitol Couture at NET-A-PORTER," *Net-a-Porter*, 2013.

41. Lauren Smith, "The Hunger Games Capitol Couture Collection," *Glamour*, November 18, 2013.

42. See also Richard Berrigan, "The Case of the Missing Action Figure: Gender in Marketing," *Moviepilot*, May 3, 2015.

43. Suzanne Scott, "#Wheresrey? Toys, Spoilers, and the Gender Politics of Franchise Paratexts," *Critical Studies in Media Communication*, no. 34.2 (2017): 138–47.

44. Sarah Luoma, "How the Hunger Games Franchise Wins Fans with Content Marketing," *Strategist Magazine*, February 24, 2015.

45. Seth Soulstein, Interview about the Odds in Our Favor campaign, May 7, 2015.

46. Steven Spielberg, *A.I.—Artificial Intelligence* (Amblin Entertainment/Warner Bros., 2001).

47. Jay Bushman, "Cloudmaker Days: A Memoir of the A.I. Game," in *Well Played 2.0: Video Games, Value and Meaning*, ed. Drew Davidson and et al. (ETC Press, 2010); Charles Herold, "Game Theory: Tracking an Elusive Film Game Online," *New York Times*, May 3, 2001; CarrieLynn Reinhard, "Gameplay Marketing Strategies as Audience Co-optation: The Story of the Dark Knight, the Cloverfield Monster, and Their Brethren," *International Journal of Communication*, no. 5 (2011): 56.

48. Phillips, "Transmedia Storytelling."

49. Reinhard, "Gameplay Marketing Strategies."

50. Christopher Nolan, *The Dark Knight* (Warner Bros., 2008).

51. Reinhard, "Gameplay Marketing Strategies," 68.

52. Dodai Stewart, "Volunteering for the Hunger Games? Don't Forget the CoverGirl Lipgloss," *Jezebel*, May 17, 2013.

53. Tumblr, an image-friendly micro-blogging platform with a predominantly young membership. For more about Tumblr, see Chapter 2.

54. *The Mary Sue*, a well-known online media journal that focuses on the intersection of geek culture and feminism. *The Mary Sue* attracts by definition a fannish audience that seems predominantly, but not exclusively, female, and is age-wise more diverse than the fannish participants on Tumblr. For more about the blog, see Chapter 4.

55. *Jezebel*, a feminist media blog with a focus on popular culture and celebrities. Because of their shared interests in women/feminism and popular culture, there is presumably some overlap in audiences between *Jezebel* and *The Mary Sue* (and I found occasional references to *Jezebel* in comments on *The Mary Sue*).

56. Tor.com, a science-fiction and fantasy online journal. Tor.com differs from the above-mentioned sites in that it publishes original fiction and is geared toward those with a professional interest in literary science fiction (authors, editors, publishers).

57. *Victor's Village*, a Wordpress-based fan-run fansite for *The Hunger Games*. In contrast to the transformative fans on Tumblr, *Victor's Village* appears to represent a more affirmative brand of fandom.

58. Blog of the SPARK Action Squad (SAS), an organization of young feminist activists.

59. *The Diary of a Dimension Hopper*, Leckwold's blog. Leckwold identifies as "'media enthusiast' (or 'fangirl,' if you prefer)," and is on the staff for *Nerdophiles*, a Nerd Culture online magazine.

60. *The Lone Wolf*, Riordan's blog. He identifies as "22 year old writer from Ireland, Gay, Irish/ Thai, Hufflepuff Pride!"

61. *In medias unrest*, O'Flynn's blog. She introduces herself: "I teach. I write. I track emerging trends, innovations & disruptions in digital culture. I advise on interactive storytelling and experience design."

62. Stewart, "Volunteering."

63. Ashley Leckwold, "Hunger Games Month: The Brilliant Irony of Lionsgate's Marketing," *The Diary of a Dimension Hopper*, March 17, 2012.

64. Mark Graser, "Suzanne Collins Breaks Silence to Support 'The Hunger Games: Catching Fire,'" *Variety*, October 29, 2013.

65. Dodai Stewart, "There Are McQueen Shoes on the Hunger Games Fashion Tumblr!," *Jezebel*, January 24, 2012.

66. Katie Riley, *Viral Marketing Campaign: District 9*, not dated.

67. Emily Asher-Perrin, "Is the Capitol Couture Clothing Line Sending the Wrong Message to Hunger Games Fans?," *Tor.com*, September 18, 2013.

68. Victoria McNally, "Update: Lionsgate Still Trying to Make the Hunger Games Theme Park Happen," *The Mary Sue*, August 20, 2014.

69. Jill Pantozzi, "District Fashions Are on Display in the Latest Hunger Games Couture Offerings," *The Mary Sue*, June 19, 2014.

70. Hillary Busis, "Hasbro Launches 'Rebelle' Nerf Line for Girls," *Entertainment Weekly's EW.com*, February 8, 2013.

71. Rebecca Pahle, "Hunger Games Clothing Line Is Available for Purchase Despite a Serious Lack of Butterfly Dresses," *The Mary Sue*, December 31, 2013.

72. The Girl with the Pearl, "Crossing the (Fashion) Line," *Victor's Village*, September 5, 2013.

73. SPARK Action Squad, *Capitol Cuties*, not dated.

74. "The Hunger but Mainly Death Games Nail Polish," *The Hunger but Mainly Death Games*, December 2011.

75. Michelle Mismas, "China Glaze Capitol Colours—Hunger Games Collection Update," *All Lacquered Up*, December 13, 2011.

76. Andrew Slack, "Ad Campaign (Lip) Glosses Over 'Hunger Games' Message," *Los Angeles Times*, November 25, 2013.

77. The Harry Potter Alliance, "The Hunger Games Are Real" (*YouTube* 2013).

78. Laura Beck, "Want to Dress Like You Live in Panem? Capitol Couture Is Here!," *Jezebel*, September 19, 2013.

79. Asher-Perrin, "Is the Capitol Couture."

80. Susana Polo, "The Internet Has Done It: We've Found the Dumbest Hunger Games Tie In," *The Mary Sue*, November 8, 2013.

81. Asher-Perrin, "Is the Capitol Couture."

82. Allinablur, "You Know What's Ironic About the Hunger Games?" *Tumblr*, January 11, 2012.

83. Tompkins, "Contradictory Franchise," 79.

84. Burke, "Reaping Environmental Justice," 13.

85. Jana Kasperkevic, "J Crew Executive Posts Hunger Games Jokes Online After Hundreds of Layoffs," *The Guardian*, June 18, 2015.

86. Fiske, *Understanding*, 392–94.

87. Gray, "Show Sold Separately," 6.

88. Hall, "Encoding/Decoding."

The State of Fandom

1. Jenkins et al., *By Any Media*.

2. Hinck, *Politics*.

3. Scalzi, "Who Gets to Be a Geek?"

4. Brendan Koerner, "It Started as an Online Gaming Prank: Then It Turned Deadly," *Wired*, October 23, 2018.

5. See Chapter 4.

6. Bamfinacuddlyjumper et al., "Fandom Trumps Hate," *Tumblr*, 2017.

7. Short videos of K-Pop stars performing on stage.

8. Amanda Petrusich, "K-Pop Fans Diffuse Racist Hashtags," *The New Yorker*, June 5, 2020.

9. Taylor Lorenz, Kellen Browning and Sheera Frenkel, "TikTok Teens and K-Pop Stans Say They Sank Trump Rally," *New York Times*, June 21, 2020.

10. See Chapter 3.

11. Hills, "An Extended Foreword," 123.

12. Stevens/van der Merwe, "The Imagined Community"

13. Krystman, "Actually It's About Ethics"; Braithwaite, "It's About Ethics in Games Journalism?"

14. William Proctor, "'I've seen a lot of talk about the #blackstormtrooper outrage, but not a single example of anyone complaining': *The Force Awakens*, Canonical Fidelity And Non-toxic Fan Practices," *Participations*, 15.1 (2018): 160–79.

15. Fu, "Fear of a Black Spider-Man"

16. Scott, "Fake Geek Girls," 35.

17. Stanfill, "The Reactionary in the Fan," 126.

Bibliography

Print and Online Sources

Abad-Santos, Alexander. "How the Nerds Lost Comic-Con." *The Atlantic*, July 13, 2013. https://www.theatlantic.com/entertainment/archive/2013/07/how-nerds-lost-comic-con/313106/

Abelkis, Paul. "SOTF." *Sound-Off*, no. 1 (March 2, 1979).

Aden, Roger C. *Popular Stories and Promised Lands: Fan Cultures and Symbolic Pilgrimages.* Tuscaloosa: University of Alabama Press, 1999.

Adorno, Theodor W. "Culture Industry Reconsidered." Translated by Anson G. Rabinbach. *New German Critique*, no. 6 (1975): 12–19.

_____. "Resümee über die Kulturindustrie." In *Gesammelte Schriften Band 10.1: Kulturkritik Und Gesellschaft I: Prismen. Ohne Leitbild*, 337–45. Frankfurt: Suhrkamp, 1977.

Adorno, Theodor W., and Max Horkheimer. *Dialectic of Enlightenment.* Translated by John Cumming. New York: Herder and Herder, 1972.

_____. *Dialektik der Aufklärung: philosophische Fragmente.* Frankfurt am Main: Suhrkamp, 1981.

Agron, Dianna. "Chris Colfer: Song-and-Dance Man." *TIME*, May 2, 2011.

allinablur (now shiningsobrightly). "You Know What's Ironic About the Hunger Games?" *Tumblr*, January 11, 2012.

Alter, Rebecca. "The Largest My Little Pony Fan Site Bans Your Horse-Crap Racist Fan Art." *Vulture*, June 23, 2020. https://www.vulture.com/2020/06/the-largest-my-little-pony-fan-site-bans-racist-fan-art.html

Anderle, Michael. *20Booksto50K. facebook*, February 7, 2016. https://www.facebook.com/groups/20Booksto50k/

Anderson, Benedict R. *Imagined Communities: Reflections on the Origin and Spread of Nationalism.* London/New York: Verso, 1991.

Anelli, Melissa. "Addressing J.K. Rowling's Recent Statements." *The Leaky Cauldron*, July 1, 2020. http://www.the-leaky-cauldron.org/2020/07/01/addressing-j-k-rowlings-recent-statements/

Anelli, Melissa, et al. *The Harry Potter Alliance*, 2005. http://www.thehpalliance.org/ (redirects to https://fandomforward.org/ since June 2021).

Anonymous. "Untitled Comment." *AO3*, September 17, 2019.

_____. "Untitled Comment." *AO3*, September 18, 2019.

_____. "Untitled Comment." *Failfandomanon. Dreamwidth*, September 18, 2019.

_____. "Untitled Comment." *Failfandomanon. Dreamwidth*, September 19, 2019.

AO3 Team. "Hugo Award—What It Means." *AO3*, September 13, 2019. https://archiveofourown.org/admin_posts/13766

Applefeld Olson, Cathy. "Can 'Glee' Make a Splash in Music Class?" *Teaching Music*, no. 19.1 (2011): 32–34, 36.

Asher-Perrin, Emily. "Is the Capitol Couture Clothing Line Sending the Wrong Message to Hunger Games Fans?" *Tor.com*, September 18, 2013. http://www.tor.com/blogs/2013/09/is-the-capitol-couture-clothing-line-sending-the-wrong-message-to-hunger-games-fans

Ashoka (Contributor). "Hunger Games Salute Used by Black Friday Protesters Fighting for Higher Wages." *Forbes*, December 5, 2014. http://www.forbes.com/sites/ashoka/2014/12/05/hunger-games-salute-used-by-black-friday-protesters-fighting-for-higher-wages/

astolat. "An Archive of One's Own." *LiveJournal*, May 17, 2007.

Bacon-Smith, Camille. *Enterprising Women: Television Fandom and the Creation of Popular Myth*. Philadelphia: University of Pennsylvania Press, 1992.

_____. *Science Fiction Culture*. Philadelphia: University of Pennsylvania Press, 2000.

bamfinacuddlyjumper et al. "Fandom Trumps Hate." *Tumblr*, 2017.

Banet-Weiser, Sarah. *Empowered. Popular Feminism and Popular Misogyny*. Durham and London: Duke University Press, 2018.

Barr, Meghan. "4 Bullied Teen Deaths at Ohio School." *Huffington Post*, December 8, 2010. http://www.huffingtonpost.com/2010/10/08/4-bullied-teen-deaths-at-_n_755461.html

Bates, Daniel. "Ferguson Protesters Scrawl Hunger Games Slogan on Landmark as Tense Town Waits for Grand Jury Decision on Indicting Officer Darren Wilson Over Killing of Michael Brown." *Daily Mail Online*, November 24, 2014. http://www.dailymail.co.uk/news/article-2847503/Ferguson-protesters-scrawl-Hunger-Games-slogan-landmark-tense-town-waits-grand-jury-decision-indicting-Darren-Willson-killing-Michael-Brown.html

Bear, Elizabeth. *Blood and Iron*. New York: ROC, 2006.

_____. "Cease Fire." *Throw Another Bear in the Canoe. LiveJournal*, March 5, 2009.

_____. "Whatever You're Doing, You're Probably Wrong." *Throw Another Bear in the Canoe. LiveJournal*, January 12, 2009.

Beck, Laura. "Want to Dress Like You Live in Panem? Capitol Couture Is Here!" *Jezebel*, September 19, 2013. http://jezebel.com/this-i-wouldnt-wanna-live-in-say-victorian-england-1350326568

Bennett, Lucy. "Fan Activism for Social Mobilization: A Critical Review of the Literature." *Transformative Works and Cultures*, Special issue: Transformative Works and Fan Activism, edited by Henry Jenkins and Sangita Shresthova, no. 10 (2012). http://journal.transformativeworks.org/index.php/twc/article/view/346

Bergeron, Richard. "Untitled." *Warhoon*, no. 20 (1964).

Berrigan, Richard. "The Case of the Missing Action Figure: Gender in Marketing." *Moviepilot*, May 3, 2015. http://moviepilot.com/posts/2905218

Booth, Ruth EJ. "Untitled." *Twitter*, August 18, 2019. https://twitter.com/RuthEJBooth/status/1163195012504576001

Bosfey, Bernadette Lynn, and Arthur D. Hlauaty. "Fandom." In *Women in Science-Fiction and Fantasy*, edited by Robin Ann Reid, 278–89. Westport: Greenwood Press, 2009.

bossymarmalade. "Sees Fire." *I Don't Like Angry Future Romulans. LiveJournal*, March 4, 2009.

_____. "Untitled." *Dreamwidth*, January 18, 2009.

Boston, John. "Untitled." *Tightbeam*, no. 27 (September 1964): 9–10.

Bourdieu, Pierre. *Distinction: A Social Critique of the Judgement of Taste*, translated by Richard Nice. Cambridge: Harvard University Press, 1984.

_____. *La Distinction: Critique Sociale du Jugement*. Paris: Éditions de Minuit, 1979.

Bourlai, Elli E. "'Comments in Tags, Please!' Tagging Practices on Tumblr." *Discourse, Context & Media*, no. 22 (2018): 46–56.

Bowles, Nellie, and Michael Keller. "Video Games and Online Chats Are 'Hunting Grounds' for Sexual Predators." *New York Times*, December 7, 2019. https://www.nytimes.com/interactive/2019/12/07/us/video-games-child-sex-abuse.html

Braithwaite, Andrea. "It's About Ethics in Games Journalism? Gamergaters and Geek Masculinity." In *Gender, Race, and Class in Media*, edited by Gail Dines et al., 536–47. Thousand Oaks: Sage Publications, 2018.

Breen, Walter (under pseudonym J.Z. Eglinton). *Greek Love*. New York: Oliver Layton Press, 1964.

_____. *Walter H. Breen Papers*, 1950–ca. 1992. Coll. 7755. Division of Rare and Manuscript Collections, Carl A. Kroch Library. Cornell University.

Bridget, Bill, AJ Bridget, and Julie Wilhoit. "Unanniversary Slumber Party." *News from F*****-up Fandom* (June 1979).

Brook, James, and Iain Boal. *Resisting the Virtual Life: The Culture and Politics of Information.* San Francisco: City Lights, 1995.

Brooker, Will. "A Sort of Homecoming: Fan Viewing and Symbolic Pilgrimage." In *Fandom. Identities and Communities in a Mediated World,* edited by Jonathan Gray and et al., 149–64. New York/London: New York University Press, 2007.

Brown, Richard, and Dave Van Arnam. "Untitled." *Poor Richard's Almanach,* no. 17 (April 1964).

Browning, Laura. "Joss Whedon Was Never a Feminist." *AV Club,* August 21, 2017. https://aux.avclub.com/joss-whedon-was-never-a-feminist-1798346253

Brummitt, Cassie. "Pottermore: Transmedia Storytelling and Authorship in Harry Potter," *The Midwest Quarterly,* no. 58.1 (2016): 112–32.

Bryan, Peter C., and Brittany R. Clark. "#NotMyGhostbusters: Adaptation, Response, and Fan Entitlement in 2016's Ghostbusters." *Journal of American Culture* 42.2 (2019): 147–58.

Buckels, E.E., P.D. Trapnell, and D.L. Paulhus. "Trolls Just Want to Have Fun." *Personality and Individual Differences,* no. 67 (2014): 97–102.

The BULLY Project, 2011. http://www.thebullyproject.com/

Burke, Brianna. "'Reaping' Environmental Justice Through Compassion in the Hunger Games." *Interdisciplinary Studies in Literature and Environment,* no. 22.3 (2015): 1–24.

Bury, Rhiannon, Ruth Deller, Adam Greenwood, and Bethan Jones. "'From Usenet to Tumblr: The Changing Role of Social Media.'" *Participations. Journal of Audience and Reception Studies,* no. 10.1 (March 2013). http://www.participations.org/Volume%2010/Issue%201/contents.htm

Bushman, Jay. "'Cloudmaker Days: A Memoir of the A.I. Game.'" In *Well Played 2.0: Video Games, Value and Meaning,* edited by Drew Davidson and et al. ETC Press, 2010. http://press.etc.cmu.edu/content/i-game-jay-bushman

Busis, Hillary. "Hasbro Launches 'Rebelle' Nerf Line for Girls." *Entertainment Weekly's EW.com,* February 8, 2013. http://www.ew.com/article/2013/02/08/hasbro-introduces-nerf-rebelle-line-for-girls-starting-with-the-heartbreaker-bow-exclusive

Busker, Rebecca Lucy. "Fandom and Male Privilege: Seven Years Later." *Transformative Works and Cultures,* Special Issue: Appropriating, Interpreting, and Transforming Comic Books, edited by Matthew J. Costello, no. 13 (2013). https://journal.transformativeworks.org/index.php/twc/article/view/473/353

———. "On Symposia: LiveJournal and the Shape of Fannish Discourse." *Transformative Works and Cultures,* no. 1 (2008). http://journal.transformativeworks.org/index.php/twc/article/view/49/23

Busse, Kristina. "Geek Hierarchies, Boundary Policing, and the Gendering of the Good Fan." *Participations,* no. 10.1 (2013): 73–91.

Calhoun, Craig J., ed. *Habermas and the Public Sphere.* Cambridge: MIT Press, 1992.

Calkins, Gregg. "Untitled." *The Rambling Fap,* no. 36 (February 1965).

Carrington, André M. *Speculative Blackness: The Future of Race in Science Fiction.* Minneapolis: University of Minnesota Press, 2016.

Cashbaugh, Sean. "A Paradoxical, Discrepant, and Mutant Marxism: Imagining a Radical Science Fiction in the American Popular Front." *Journal for the Study of Radicalism,* no. 10.1 (2016): 63–106.

centrumlumina. "AO3 Census: Masterpost." *Tumblr,* October 5, 2013.

Choate, Prentiss. "The Great Breendonaho Boon." *Postmortem* (May 1964).

Click, Melissa, ed. *Anti-Fandom. Dislike and Hate in the Digital Age.* New York University Press, 2019.

———. "'Rabid,' 'Obsessed,' and 'Frenzied': Understanding Twilight Fangirls and the Gendered Politics of Fandom." *Flow,* no. 11.4 (2009). http://www.flowjournal.org/2009/12/rabid-obsessed-and-frenzied-understanding-twilight-fangirls-and-the-gendered-politics-of-fandom-melissa-click-university-of-missouri/

Cochran, Tanya R. "'Past the Brink of Tacit Support': Fan Activism and the Whedonverses." *Transformative Works and Cultures,* Special issue: Transformative Works and Fan Activism, edited by Henry Jenkins and Sangita Shresthova, no. 10 (2012). http://journal.transformativeworks.org/index.php/twc/article/view/331

Coker, Catherine. "The Angry! Textual! Poacher! Is Angry! Fan Works as Political Statements." In *Fan Culture: Theory/Practice,* edited by Katherine Larsen and Lynn Zubernis, 81–96. Newcastle upon Tyne: Cambridge Scholars Publishing, 2012.

Cole, Kai. "Joss Whedon Is a 'Hypocrite Preaching Feminist Ideals,' Ex-Wife Kai Cole Says (Guest Blog)." *The Wrap,* August 20, 2017. https://www.thewrap.com/joss-whedon-feminist-hypocrite-infidelity-affairs-ex-wife-kai-cole-says/amp/

Colfer, Chris. "Q&A with Chris Colfer." *Chris-Colfer.com,* not dated. http://chris-colfer.com/qa_chris (website down, accessible via Wayback Machine).

Colfer, Chris, et al. *Panel at New Yorker Festival 2011.* New York, 2011.

Collins, Suzanne. *The Hunger Games.* New York: Scholastic Press, 2008.

_____. *The Hunger Games: Catching Fire.* London: Scholastic Press, 2009.

_____. *The Hunger Games: Mockingjay.* London: Scholastic, 2010.

comicbookGRRRL. "Women in Comics: The New 52 and the Batgirl of San Diego." *comicbookGRRRL,* July 24, 2011. http://www.comicbookgrrrl.com/2011/07/24/women-in-comics-the-new-52-and-the-batgirl-of-san-diego/

Condis, Megan. *Gaming Masculinity: Trolls, Fake Geeks, and the Gendered Battle for Online Culture.* Iowa City: University of Iowa Press, 2018.

Coppa, Francesca. "An Archive of Our Own. Fanfiction Writers Unite!" In *Fic. Why Fanfiction Is Taking Over the World,* edited by Anne Jamison, 302–08. Dallas: BenBella Books, 2013.

_____. "A Brief History of Media Fandom." In *Fan Fiction and Fan Communities in the Age of the Internet,* edited by Kristina Busse and Karen Hellekson, 41–59. Jefferson, NC: McFarland, 2006.

_____. "An Editing Room of One's Own: Vidding as Women's Work." *Camera Obscura,* No. 16.77 (2011): 123–30.

Correia, Larry. "How to Get Correia Nominated for a Hugo Part 2: A Very Special Message." *Monster Hunter Nation,* January 16, 2013. http://monsterhunternation.com/2013/01/16/how-to-get-correia-nominated-for-a-hugo-part-2-a-very-special-message/

_____. "Sad Puppies 2: The Illustrated Edition." *Monster Hunter Nation,* January 14, 2014. http://monsterhunternation.com/2014/01/14/sad-puppies-2-the-illustrated-edition/

Couldry, Nick. "On the Set of the Sopranos: 'Inside' a Fan's Construction of Nearness." In *Fandom. Identities and Communities in a Mediated World,* edited by Jonathan Gray and et al., 139–48. London/New York: New York University Press, 2007.

Coulson, Robert, and Juanita Coulson. "Untitled." *Yandro,* no. XII.5 (May 1964).

Cox, David. "Twilight: The Franchise That Ate Feminism." *The Guardian,* July 12, 2010. https://www.theguardian.com/film/filmblog/2010/jul/12/twilight-eclipse-feminism

Crouch, Leslie. "The Good Old Days." *Ad Astra,* no. 1.3 (September 1939).

Davidson, Steve. "Untitled Comment." *File 770,* July 28, 2019.

Dean, Jodi. "Why the Net Is Not a Public Sphere." *Constellations,* no. 10.1 (2003): 95–112.

De Certeau, Michel. *The Practice of Everyday Life.* Translated by Steven Rendall. Berkeley: University of California Press, 1984.

_____. *L'Invention du Quotidien 1: Arts de Faire.* Paris: Gallimard, 1990.

Deepa D. "I Didn't Dream of Dragons." *Dreamwidth,* January 13, 2009.

De Kosnik, Abigail. "Should Fan Fiction Be Free?" *Cinema Journal,* no. 48.4 (2009): 118–24.

Del Rey, Lester. *The World of Science Fiction, 1926–1976: The History of a Subculture.* New York: Garland Pub, 1980.

della Porta, Donatella, and Alice Mattoni. "Cultures of Participation in Social Movements." In *The Participatory Cultures Handbook,* edited by Aaron Delwiche and Jennifer Henderson, 171–81. New York: Routledge, 2013.

delux_vivens. "Wild Unicorn Herd Check In." *LiveJournal,* May 11, 2009.

Derecho, Abigail. "Archontic Literature: A Definition, a History, and Several Theories of Fanfiction." In *Fan Fiction and Fan Communities in the Age of the Internet,* edited by Kristina Busse and Karen Hellekson, 61–78. Jefferson, NC: McFarland, 2006.

Dhaenens, Frederik. "Teenage Queerness: Negotiating Heteronormativity in the Representation of Gay Teenagers in 'Glee.'" *Journal of Youth Studies,* no. 16.3 (2013): 304–17.

Dibbell, Julian. "A Rape in Cyberspace; Or: How an Evil Clown, a Haitian Trickster Spirit, Two Wizards, and a Cast of Dozens Turned a Database Into a Society." *The Village Voice,* December 23, 1993.

Donaho, Bill. "Apologia" (August 22, 1964).
_____. "The Great Breen Boondoggle or All Berkeley Is Plunged Into War" (1964).
Donaho, Bill, Norm Metcalf, Alva Rogers, and Gordon Eklund. "Untitled." *RPM*, no. 8 (August 1964).
dragonessEclectic. "Untitled Comment." *AO3*, September 19, 2019.
Dubrofsky, Rachel E. "Jewishness, Whiteness, and Blackness on Glee : Singing to the Tune of Postracism." *Communication, Culture & Critique*, no. 6.1 (March 2013): 82–102.
Edwards, Leigh. "Transmedia Storytelling, Corporate Synergy, and Audience Expression." *Global Media Journal*, no. 12.20 (2012): 1–12.
Edwards, Patrick, et al. *Meet the Bronies: The Psychology of the Adult My Little Pony Fandom.* Jefferson, NC: McFarland, 2019.
Ehrenreich, Barbara, Elizabeth Hess, and Gloria Jacobs. "Beatlemania: Girls Just Want to Have Fun." In *The Adoring Audience: Fan Culture and Popular Media*, edited by Lisa Lewis, 84–106. London: Routledge, 1992.
electricpurplearmor. "In Defense of Gleeks, Part Two: But, Why Glee?" *A Sense of Humor Is Needed Armor*, April 4, 2012. http://electricpurplearmor.wordpress.com/2012/04/04/in-defense-of-gleeks-part-two-but-why-glee/
Etzioni, Amitai. "Are Virtual and Democratic Communities Feasible?" In *Democracy and New Media*, edited by Henry Jenkins and David Thorburn, 85–100. Cambridge: MIT Press, 2003.
Evans, Lilinaz, Georgia Luckhurst, and Melissa Campbell. "You'll Have to Kill a Child but at Least You'll Look Good Doing It." *SPARK Movement*, November 20, 2013. http://www.sparksummit.com/2013/11/20/youll-have-to-kill-a-child-but-at-least-youll-look-good-doing-it/
Fairestcat. "On Pearl-Clutching." *Just Off the Key of Reason. Dreamwidth*, September 17, 2019.
_____. "One More Hugos Thing." *Just Off the Key of Reason. Dreamwidth*, September 17, 2019.
Fernandes, Fabio, and Djibril Al-Ajad, eds. *We See a Different Frontier: A Postcolonial Speculative Fiction Anthology.* Futurefire, 2013.
Fiske, John. *Understanding Popular Culture.* Boston: Unwin Hyman, 1989.
Fowler, Robert Booth. *The Dance with Community: The Contemporary Debate in American Political Thought.* Lawrence: University Press of Kansas, 1991.
Fox, Rose, and Daniel José Older, eds. *Long Hidden: Speculative Fiction from the Margins of History.* Framingham: CrossedGenres, 2014.
Francis, Consuela, and Alison Piepmeier. "My Hair Stood on End!: Talking with Joanna Russ About Slash, Community, and Female Sexuality." *Journal of Popular Romance Studies*, no. 1.2 (2011): n.p. https://www.jprstudies.org/2011/03/interview-joanna-russ/
Franson, Donald. *Some Historical Facts About Science Fiction Fandom.* N3F Fandbook Publication, 1962.
Fraser, Nancy. "Rethinking the Public Sphere: A Contribution to the Critique of Actually Existing Democracy." *Social Text*, no. 25/26 (1990): 56–80.
_____. *Scales of Justice: Reimagining Political Space in a Globalizing World.* New York: Columbia University Press, 2009.
Fu, Albert. "Fear of a Black Spider-Man: Racebending and the Colour-Line in Superhero (Re) Casting." *Journal of Graphic Novels and Comics*, no. 6.3 (2015): 269–83.
geekturnedvamp. "Untitled Comment." *LiveJournal*, May 18, 2007.
Gelder, Ken. *Popular Fiction: The Logics and Practices of a Literary Field.* London: Routledge, 2004.
The Girl with the Pearl. "Crossing the (Fashion) Line." *Victor's Village*, September 5, 2013. http://victorsvillage.com/2013/09/05/crossing-the-fashion-line/ (website down, accessible via Wayback Machine).
"GleeEqualityProject." *Tumblr*, 2012. http://glee-equality-project.tumblr.com/?og=1
Glyer, Mike. "Baby Is 3, Jeffty Is 5, Now We Are Number 6, Who Is Number One?" *File 770*, July 27, 2019. http://file770.com/pixel-scroll-7-27-19-baby-is-3-jeffty-is-5-now-we-are-number-6-who-is-number-one/comment-page-1/#comments
_____. "Source Materials About the 1989 Hugo Controversy." *File 770*, September 25, 2017. http://file770.com/source-materials-about-the-1989-hugo-controversy/
_____. "The SJW Credential That Sleeps on You from Nowhere." *File 770*, September 19, 2019.

http://file770.com/pixel-scroll-9-19-19-the-sjw-credential-that-sleeps-on-you-from-nowhere/comment-page-1/#comments

_____. "We Are All in the Pixel, but Some of Us Are Looking at the Scroll." *File 770*, September 14, 2019. http://file770.com/pixel-scroll-9-14-19-we-are-all-in-the-pixel-but-some-of-us-are-looking-at-the-scrolls/comment-page-1/#comments

Goldenberg, Suzanne. "Terror Charges Faced by Oklahoma Fossil Fuel Protesters 'Outrageous.'" *The Guardian*, January 10, 2014. http://www.theguardian.com/environment/2014/jan/10/terror-charges-oklahoma-fossil-fuel-protest

Graser, Mark. "Suzanne Collins Breaks Silence to Support 'The Hunger Games: Catching Fire.'" *Variety*, October 29, 2013. http://variety.com/2013/film/news/suzanne-collins-breaks-silence-to-support-the-hunger-games-catching-fire-1200775202/

Gray, Jonathan. "Antifandom and the Moral Text." *American Behavioral Scientist*, no. 48.7 (2005): 840–58.

_____. *Show Sold Separately: Promos, Spoilers, and Other Media Paratexts*. New York: New York University Press, 2010.

Gray, Jonathan, et al., eds. *Fandom. Identities and Communities in a Mediated World*. London/New York: New York University Press, 2007.

_____. "Introduction: Why Study Fans?" In *Fandom. Identities and Communities in a Mediated World*, 1–16. London/New York: New York University Press, 2007.

Gresham, Tamila et al. *Box Scene Project*, 2011, http://www.theboxsceneproject.org/ (now *Represent*).

_____. *Fandom for Equality*, 2013. http://fandomforequality.tumblr.com/

_____. *Represent: Because Representation Matters*, 2011. http://www.werepresent.org/

Habermas, Jürgen. *The Structural Transformation of the Public Sphere: An Inquiry Into a Category of Bourgeois Society*. Translated by Thomas Burger. Cambridge: MIT Press, 1989.

_____. *Strukturwandel der Öffentlichkeit: Untersuchungen zu einer Kategorie der bürgerlichen Gesellschaft*. Frankfurt: Suhrkamp, 1990.

Hale-Stern, Kaila. "Everyone Who Contributed to Fanfiction Site 'Archive of Our Own' Is Now a Hugo Award Winner." *The Mary Sue*, August 19, 2019. https://www.themarysue.com/archive-of-our-own-hugo-award-winner/

Hall, Stuart. "Encoding/Decoding." In *Culture, Media, Language. Working Papers in Cultural Studies, 1972–79*, edited by The Centre for Contemporary Cultural Studies, University of Birmingham, 128–38. London et al.: Hutchinson, 1980.

Hansen, Chuck. "Untitled." *Damballa*, no. 2.3 (May 1965).

Hansen, Miriam. *Babel and Babylon: Spectatorship in American Silent Film*. Cambridge: Harvard University Press, 1991.

Hardy, Jonathan. "Mapping Commercial Intertextuality: HBO's True Blood." *Convergence: The International Journal of Research Into New Media Technologies*, no. 17.1 (2011): 7–17.

Harkey, Katessa S. "In the Midst of Avalon: Casualties of the Sexual Revolution." In *Pagan Consent Culture*, edited by Christine Hoff Kraemer and Yvonne Arburrow, 194–213. Hubbardston, MA: Asphodel Press, 2016.

Harman, Sarah, and Bethan Jones. "Fifty Shades of Ghey: Snark Fandom and the Figure of the Anti-Fan." *Sexualities*, no. 16.8 (2013): 951–68.

Hassan, Yasmeen, et al. *Equality Now*, 1992. http://www.equalitynow.org/

Havens, Timothy, et al. "Critical Media Industry Studies: A Research Approach." *Communication, Culture & Critique*, no. 2.2 (2009): 234–53.

The Hawkeye Initiative. Tumblr, 2014. https://thehawkeyeinitiative.tumblr.com/

Hellekson, Karen. "A Fannish Field of Value: Online Fan Gift Culture." *Cinema Journal*, no. 48.8 (2009): 113–18.

Hellekson, Karen, and Kristina Busse, eds. *Fan Fiction and Fan Communities in the Age of the Internet*. Jefferson, NC: McFarland, 2006.

"Help for Japan: March 2011 Relief Charity Auction." *Dreamwidth*, 2011.

"Help Haiti: A Fandom Auction to Help Haiti Recover." *LiveJournal*, 2010.

Herold, Charles. "'Game Theory: Tracking an Elusive Film Game Online.'" *New York Times*, May 3, 2001. http://www.nytimes.com/2001/05/03/technology/03GAME.html

Hevelin, Rusty. "The Despicable Donhao Doggery." *Phineas Pinkham Pallograph* (August 1964).

Hickmann, Matt. "Untitled." *Tightbeam*, no. 3 (1978): 29.

Hills, Matt. "An Extended Foreword: From Fan Doxa to Toxic Fan Practices." *Participations*, no. 15.1 (2018): 105–26.

_____. *Fan Cultures*. London/New York: Routledge, 2002.

_____. "Torchwood's Trans-Transmedia: Media Tie-Ins and Brand 'Fanagement.'" *Participations*, no. 9.2 (2012): 409–28.

Hinck, Ashley. *Politics for the Love of Fandom: Fan-based Citizenship in a Digital World*. Baton Rouge: Louisiana State University Press, 2019.

_____. "Theorizing a Public Engagement Keystone: Seeing Fandom's Integral Connection to Civic Engagement Through the Case of the Harry Potter Alliance." *Transformative Works and Cultures*, Special issue: Transformative Works and Fan Activism, edited by Henry Jenkins and Sangita Shresthova, no. 10 (2012). http://journal.transformativeworks.org/index.php/twc/article/view/311/

Hines, Jim. "Puppies in Their Own Words." *Jim C. Hines*, June 7, 2015. http://www.jimchines.com/2015/06/puppies-in-their-own-words/

Hohendahl, Peter Uwe, and Marc Silberman. "Critical Theory, Public Sphere and Culture. Jürgen Habermas and His Critics." *New German Critique*, no. 16 (1979): 89–118.

Holub, Robert C. *Jürgen Habermas: Critic in the Public Sphere*. London/New York: Routledge, 1991.

Hopkinson, Nalo, John Joseph Adams, and David Barr Kirtley. "Interview: Nalo Hopkinson." *Lightspeed Magazine*, June 18, 2013. http://www.lightspeedmagazine.com/nonfiction/interview-nalo-hopkinson/

"The Hunger but Mainly Death Games Nail Polish." *The Hunger but Mainly Death Games*, December 2011. http://hungergamesparody.com/new-parody-nail-polish-line/

Ignition Creative. *Capitol Couture*, 2012. http://capitolcouture.pn/ (website down, accessible via Wayback Machine).

_____. *The Capitol*, 2012. http://thecapitol.pn (website down, accessible via Wayback Machine).

"Internet Users." *Internet Live Stats*. http://www.internetlivestats.com/internet-users/

ithiliana. "A Minor Issue, Perhaps..." *The Heart of the Maze, LiveJournal*, March 7, 2009.

Jacobs, Julia. "Harry Potter Fans Imagine a World Without J.K. Rowling After Transphobia Row." *Independent*, June 13, 2020. https://www.independent.co.uk/arts-entertainment/music/news/jk-rowling-transphobia-twitter-harry-potter-fans-transgender-a9564431.html

Jameson, Fredric. "Reification and Utopia in Mass Culture." *Social Text*, no. 1 (1979): 130–48.

Jamison, Anne, ed. *Fic. Why Fanfiction Is Taking Over the World*. Dallas: BenBella Books, 2013.

Jemisin, N.K. "Why I Think RaceFail Was the Bestest Thing Evar for SFF." *NKJemisin*, January 18, 2010. http://nkjemisin.com/2010/01/why-i-think-racefail-was-the-bestest-thing-evar-for-sff/#sthash.bWAnVGMu.VRH6Lu7i.dpuf

Jenkins, Henry. *Convergence Culture. Where Old and New Media Collide*. New York: New York University Press, 2006.

_____. "'Out of the Closet and Into the Universe': Queers and Star Trek." *Science Fiction Audiences: Doctor Who, Star Trek, and Their Fans*, by John Tulloch and Henry Jenkins, 237–65. New York: Routledge, 1995.

_____. "Star Trek Rerun, Reread, Rewritten: Fan Writing as Textual Poaching." In *Close Encounters: Film, Feminism, and Science Fiction*, edited by Constance Penley and others, 171–204. Minneapolis: University of Minnesota Press, 1991.

_____. *Textual Poachers: Television Fans & Participatory Culture*. New York: Routledge, 1992.

_____. "Transforming Fan Culture Into User-Generated Content: The Case of FanLib." *Confessions of an Aca-Fan*, May 22, 2007. http://henryjenkins.org/2007/05/transforming_fan_culture_into.html

_____. "Transmedia 202: Further Reflections." *Confessions of an Aca-Fan*, August 1, 2011. http://henryjenkins.org/2011/08/defining_transmedia_further_re.html

_____. "Transmedia Storytelling 101." *Confessions of an Aca-Fan*, March 22, 2007. http://henryjenkins.org/2007/03/transmedia_storytelling_101.html

_____. "Youth Voice, Media, and Political Engagement: Introducing the Core Concepts." In *By Any Media Necessary,* edited by Henry Jenkins et al., 1–60. New York: New York University Press, 2016.

Jenkins, Henry, and David Thorburn. "Introduction: The Digital Revolution, the Informed Citizen, and the Culture of Democracy." In *Democracy and New Media,* edited by Henry Jenkins, David Thorburn, and Brad Seawell, 1–20. Cambridge: MIT Press, 2003.

Jenkins, Henry, Anne Kustritz, and Derek Johnson. "Gender and Fan Culture (Round Thirteen, Part One): Anne Kustritz and Derek Johnson." *Confessions of an Aca-Fan,* August 30, 2007. http://henryjenkins.org/2007/08/gender_and_fan_culture_round_t_2.html

Jenkins, Henry, et al., eds. *By Any Media Necessary. the New Youth Activism.* New York: New York University Press, 2016.

Jensen, Joli. "Fandom as Pathology: The Consequences of Characterization." In *The Adoring Audience: Fan Culture and Popular Media,* edited by Lisa A. Lewis, 301–14. London/New York: Routledge, 1992.

JJ. "Untitled Comment." *File 770,* July 27, 2019.

_____. "Untitled Comment." *File 770,* July 28, 2019.

_____. "Untitled Comment." *File 770,* September 16, 2019.

Johnson, Derek. "Fan-tagonism: Factions, Institutions, and Constitutive Hegemonies of Fandom." In *Fandom. Identities and Communities in a Mediated World,* edited by Jonathan Gray et al., 285–300. London/New York: New York University Press, 2007.

Jones, Bethan. "Pottermore: Encouraging or Regulating Participatory Culture?" *Magic Is Might 2012: Proceedings of the International Conference,* edited by L. Ciolfi and G. O'Brien, 159–71. Limerick/Sheffield: University of Limerick/Sheffield Hallam University, 2013.

Jones, Robert W. *Gender and the Formation of Taste in Eighteenth-Century Britain.* Cambridge: Cambridge University Press, 1998.

Joseph, Miranda. *Against the Romance of Community.* Minneapolis: University of Minnesota Press, 2002.

Kapur, Isabella. "CoverGirl Emphasizes Capitol Decadence for Their Hunger Games Makeup Line." *The Mary Sue,* August 16, 2013. http://www.themarysue.com/cover-girl-hunger-games/

Kasperkevic, Jana. "J Crew Executive Posts Hunger Games Jokes Online After Hundreds of Layoffs." *The Guardian,* June 18, 2015. http://www.theguardian.com/business/2015/jun/18/j-crew-executive-jokes-about-hunger-games-after-layoffs

kate-nepveu. "Diana Gabaldon & Fanfic Followup." *Incidents and Accidents, Hints and Allegations. LiveJournal,* May 10, 2010.

Kendall. "Untitled Comment." *File 770,* July 29, 2019.

Kligler-Vilenchik, Neta. "'Decreasing World Suck': Harnessi Popular Culture for Fan Activism." In *By Any Media Necessary,* edited by Henry Jenkins et al., 102–48. New York: New York University Press, 2016.

Kligler-Vilenchik, Neta, Joshua McVeigh-Schultz, Christine Weitbrecht, and Chris Tokuhama. "Experiencing Fan Activism: Understanding the Power of Fan Activist Organizations Through Members' Narratives." *Transformative Works and Cultures,* Special issue: Transformative Works and Fan Activism, edited by Henry Jenkins and Sangita Shresthova, no. 10 (2012). http://journal.transformativeworks.org/index.php/twc/article/view/322/273

Kluge, Alexander, and Oskar Negt. *Öffentlichkeit und Erfahrung: Zur Organisationsanalyse von bürgerlicher und proletarischer Öffentlichkeit.* Frankfurt: Suhrkamp, 1972.

Knight, Damon. *The Futurians.* New York: John Day, 1977.

_____. "Unite or Fie!" *Fanfare,* no. 1.4 (October 1940).

Koerner, Brendan. "It Started as an Online Gaming Prank. Then It Turned Deadly." *Wired,* October 23, 2018. https://www.wired.com/story/swatting-deadly-online-gaming-prank/

Kracauer, Siegfried. "Little Shopgirls Go to the Movies." In *The Mass Ornament,* translated by Thomas Levin, 291–306. Cambridge: Harvard University Press, 1995.

_____. "Die kleinen Ladenmädchen gehen ins Kino." In *Das Ornament der Masse,* 279–94. Frankfurt am Main: Suhrkamp, 1977.

Krystman. "Actually It's About Ethics." *Know Your Meme,* October 24, 2014. https://knowyourmeme.com/memes/actually-its-about-ethics

Kyle, Dave. "The Great Exclusion Act of 1939." *Mimosa,* no. 6 (1989). http://www.jophan.org/mimosa/m06/kyle.htm
_____. "A Warning." July 2, 1939.
Lady Gaga, and Cynthia Germanotta. *Born This Way Foundation,* 2012. https://bornthisway.foundation/
LadyGoat. "Untitled Comment." *AO3,* September 17, 2019.
Landes, Joan B. "Women and the Public Sphere." *Social Analysis Gender and Social Life,* no. 15 (1984): 20–31.
Larbalestier, Justine. *The Battle of the Sexes in Science Fiction.* Middletown: Wesleyan University Press, 2002.
Latham, Don, and Jonathan Hollister. "The Games People Play. Information and Media Literacies in the Hunger Games Trilogy." *Children's Literature in Education,* no. 45 (2014): 33–46.
Lavender, Isiah, ed. *Black and Brown Planets: The Politics of Race in Science Fiction.* Jackson: University Press of Mississippi, 2014.
Le Guin, Ursula K. "A Whitewashed Earthsea." *Slate,* December 16, 2004. http://www.slate.com/articles/arts/culturebox/2004/12/a_whitewashed_earthsea.html
Leckwold, Ashley. "Hunger Games Month: The Brilliant Irony of Lionsgate's Marketing." *The Diary of a Dimension Hopper,* March 17, 2012. https://lieselhindmann.wordpress.com/2012/03/17/hunger-games-month-the-brilliant-irony-of-lionsgates-marketing/
Lesley, Naomi. "Character Education and the Performance of Citizenship in Glee." *Children's Literature,* no. 41 (2013): 1–27.
Lesses, Rebecca. "Untitled." *It Can't Happen Here,* no. 32 (October 1974).
Lewis, Lisa A., ed. *The Adoring Audience: Fan Culture and Popular Media.* London/New York: Routledge, 1992.
Light, Jennifer S. "When Computers Were Women." *Technology and Culture,* no. 40.3 (1999): 455–83.
Lorenstein, Bev, and Judith Gran. "Welcome." *Organia,* no. 1 (July 1982).
Lorenz, Taylor, Kellen Browning, and Sheera Frenkel. "TikTok Teens and K-Pop Stans Say They Sank Trump Rally." *New York Times,* June 21, 2020. https://www.nytimes.com/2020/06/21/style/tiktok-trump-rally-tulsa.html
Lori Morimoto. "Roundtable: Tumblr and Fandom." *Transformative Works and Cultures.* Special issue: Tumblr and Fandom, edited by Lori Morimoto and Louisa Ellen Stein, no. 27 (2018).
Lothian, Alexis, et al. "Pattern Recognition: A Dialogue on Racism in Fan Communities." *Transformative Works and Cultures,* no. 3 (2009). http://journal.transformativeworks.org/index.php/twc/article/view/172
Loudon, Christopher. "The Glee Effect." *JazzTimes,* September 16, 2010. http://jazztimes.com/articles/26514-the-glee-effect
Lowndes, Robert. *An Amazing Story.* New York: CPASF, 1939.
_____. "Dead End." *Alchemist,* no. 1.4 (December 1940): 5–13.
_____. "The Futurians and New Fandom." Published by the Futurian Society of New York, October 1939.
_____. "Sykora Starts Riot. QSFL Meeting Ends in Brawl." *Le Vombiteur,* No. 3.11 (January 6, 1941): 1–2.
Luoma, Sarah. "How the Hunger Games Franchise Wins Fans with Content Marketing." *Strategist Magazine,* February 24, 2015. http://strategistmagazine.co/sarahluoma/hunger-games-mockingjay-1148
MacKinnon, Rebecca, and Hae-in Lim. "Google Plus Finally Gives Up on Its Ineffective, Dangerous Real-Name Policy." *Slate,* July 17, 2014. http://www.slate.com/blogs/future_tense/2014/07/17/google_plus_finally_ditches_its_ineffective_dangerous_real_name_policy.html
Martin, G.R.R. "Puppygate." *Not a Blog. LiveJournal,* April 8, 2015.
Marwick, A., M.L. Gray, and M. Ananny. "'Dolphins Are Just Gay Sharks': Glee and the Queer Case of Transmedia as Text and Object." *Television & New Media,* no. 15.7 (2014): 627–47.

Marwick, Alice. *LiveJournal Users: Passionate, Prolific and Private.* LiveJournal Inc., 2008.

Massanari, Adrienne. "#Gamergate and the Fappening: How Reddit's Algorithm, Governance, and Culture Support Toxic Technocultures." *New Media & Society,* no. 19.3 (2017): 329–46.

McKee, Alan. "The Fans of Cultural Theory." In *Fandom. Identities and Communities in a Mediated World,* edited by Jonathan Gray and et al., 88–97. New York/London: New York University Press, 2007.

McMaster Bujold, Lois. "Untitled Comment." *LiveJournal,* May 9, 2009.

McNally, Victoria. "Update: Lionsgate Still Trying to Make the Hunger Games Theme Park Happen." *The Mary Sue,* August 20, 2014. http://www.themarysue.com/hunger-games-still-theme-park-still-happening/#comment-1551596074

melannen. "Science, Y'all." *Dreamwidth,* January 16, 2010.

Meredith. "Untitled Comment." *File 770,* September 15, 2019.

Merrick, Helen. "The Readers Feminism Doesn't See: Feminist Fans, Critics and Science Fiction." In *Trash Aesthetics. Popular Culture and Its Audience,* edited by Deborah Cartmell et al., 48–65. London/Chicago: Pluto Press, 1997.

Meyer, Douglas W.F. *The Purpose of Science Fiction.* Speech presented at the Second Convention of the Science Fiction Association in London, UK, on April 10, 1938. New York: CPASF, 1939.

Meyer, Stephenie. *Twilight.* 4 volumes. New York: Little, Brown and Company, 2005–2008.

Miami Theory Collective, eds. *Community at Loose Ends.* Minneapolis: University of Minnesota Press, 1991.

Michel, John B. *The Foundation of the CPASF.* New York: CPASF, 1939.

———. "Mutation or Death." Speech presented at the Third Eastern Science Fiction Convention, Philadelphia, October 1937. http://www.fanac.org/fanzines/Sense_of_FAPA/Mutation_or_Death.html

Mismas, Michelle. "China Glaze Capitol Colours—Hunger Games Collection Update." *All Lacquered Up,* December 13, 2011. http://www.alllacqueredup.com/2011/12/china-glaze-colours-from-the-capital-hunger-games-collection-update.html

Moen, Deirdre Saoirse. "Marion Zimmer Bradley: It's Worse Than I Knew." *Sounds Like Weird* (June 10, 2014). https://deirdre.net/marion-zimmer-bradley-its-worse-than-i-knew/

Moll, Ellen. "What's in a Nym? Gender, Race, Pseudonymity, and the Imagining of the Online Persona." *M/C Journal* no. 17.3 (2014). http://journal.media-culture.org.au/index.php/mcjournal/article/view/816

Monette, Sarah. "Untitled Comment." *LiveJournal,* January 15, 2009.

Morgan, Charles, and Hubert Walker. "Confronting Breen." *CoinWeek,* November 3, 2015. http://www.coinweek.com/education/confronting-breen/

Morimoto, Lori, and Louisa Ellen Stein. "Tumblr and Fandom." *Transformative Works and Cultures,* Special issue: Tumblr and Fandom, edited by Lori Morimoto and Louisa Ellen Stein, no. 27 (2018). https://journal.transformativeworks.org/index.php/twc/article/view/1580/1826

Moskowitz, Sam. *The Immortal Storm: A History of Science Fiction Fandom.* Atlanta: Atlanta Science Fiction Organization Press, 1954.

———. "There Are Two Sides." *Science Fiction Collector,* no. 5.2 (August 1939): 4–18.

———. "What to Do About Undesirables." *Noreascon III Program Book,* 1989.

Muccamukk. "Untitled Comment." *File 770,* September 16, 2019.

———. "Untitled Comment." *File 770,* September 16, 2019.

Mules, Warwick. "Media Publics and the Transnational Public Sphere." *Critical Arts: A South-North Journal of Cultural & Media Studies,* no. 12.1/2 (1998): 24–44.

Murphy, Ryan. "Untitled." *Twitter,* August 1, 2012.

musesfool. "Nothing New Under the Sun." *Frail and Bedazzled. LiveJournal,* September 9, 2003.

Mydans, Seth. "Thai Protesters Are Detained After Using 'Hunger Games' Salute." *The New York Times,* November 20, 2014. http://www.nytimes.com/2014/11/21/world/asia/thailand-protesters-hunger-games-salute.html

Nagaina. "Untitled Comment." *AO3,* September 16, 2019.

———. "Untitled Comment." *AO3,* September 16, 2019.

Nakamura, Lisa. "Race In/For Cyberspace: Identity Tourism and Racial Passing on the Internet." In *Reading Digital Culture,* edited by David Trend, 226–35. Malden: Blackwell Publishers Ltd, 2001.

Nancy, Jean-Luc. *The Inoperative Community.* Translated by Peter Connor et al. Minneapolis: University of Minnesota Press, 1991.

———. "La Communauté désœuvrée." *Aléa,* no. 4 (1983): 11–49.

nenya_kanadka. "Untitled Comment." *AO3,* September 19, 2019.

Newkirk II, Vann. "N.K. Jemisin and the Politics of Prose." *The Atlantic,* September 2, 2016. https://www.theatlantic.com/entertainment/archive/2016/09/nk-jemisin-hugo-award-conversation/498497/

Nguyen, Mimi. "Tales of an Asiatic Geek Girl. Slant from Paper to Pixels." In *Technicolor. Race, Technology and Everyday Life,* edited by Alondra Nelson and Thuy Linh N Tu, 177–90. New York: New York University Press, 2001.

Noreascon Organzing Committee. "Hugo Statement." *recs.arts.sf-lovers,* June 16, 1989.

Novik, Naomi. "Acceptance Speech at the Hugo Award Ceremony." WorldCon in Dublin, Ireland, August 18, 2019.

obsession_inc. "Affirmational Fandom Vs. Transformational Fandom." *Dreamwidth,* June 1, 2009.

O'Connor, Sheilah, and Stephanie Leasure. *Can't Stop the Serenity. The Global Sci-Fi Charity Event,* 2006. http://www.cantstoptheserenity.com/

O'Flynn, Siobhan. "You Have to Love Lionsgate's Commitment to the Dark Side: Catching Fire's Misfired Marketing..." *In Medias Unrest,* August 30, 2013. http://siobhanoflynn.com/you-have-to-love-lionsgates-commitment-to-the-dark-side/

Ohlheiser, Abby. "Just How Offensive Did Milo Yiannopoulos Have to Be to Get Banned from Twitter?" *Washington Post,* July 21, 2016. https://www.washingtonpost.com/news/the-intersect/wp/2016/07/21/what-it-takes-to-get-banned-from-twitter/

Olesen, Thomas. "Transnational Publics: New Spaces of Social Movement Activism and the Problem of Global Long-Sightedness." *Current Sociology,* no. 53.3 (2005): 419–40.

Padalecki, Jared. "What Does the Fandom Mean to Me?" In *Family Don't End with Blood,* edited by Lynn Zubernis, 217–48. Dallas: BenBella Books, 2017.

Pahle, Rebecca. "Hunger Games Clothing Line Is Available for Purchase Despite a Serious Lack of Butterfly Dresses." *The Mary Sue,* December 31, 2013. http://www.themarysue.com/capitol-couture-clothing-line/#comment-1182604443

Pande, Rukmini. *Squee from the Margins. Fandom and Race.* Iowa City: University of Iowa Press, 2018.

Pande, Rukmini, and Samira Nadkarni. "From a Land Where 'Other' People Live. Perspectives from an Indian Fannish Experience." In *Fic. Why Fanfiction Is Taking Over the World,* edited by Anne Jamison, 344–52. Dallas: BenBella Books, 2013.

Pantozzi, Jill. "District Fashions Are on Display in the Latest Hunger Games Couture Offerings." *The Mary Sue,* June 19, 2014. http://www.themarysue.com/hunger-games-capitol-couture-disctrict-fashions/#comment-1445397934

Peacock, Joe. "Booth Babes Need Not Apply." *Geek Out! CNN Blogs,* July 24, 2012. http://geekout.blogs.cnn.com/2012/07/24/booth-babes-need-not-apply/

Pearson, Roberta. "Bachies, Bardies, Trekkies, and Sherlockians." In *Fandom. Identities and Communities in a Mediated World,* edited by Jonathan Gray, Cornel Sandvoss, and C. Lee Harrington, 98–109. New York/London: New York University Press, 2007.

Pelz, Bruce. "Untitled." *Ankus,* no. 11 (May 1964).

Penley, Constance. *Nasa/Trek. Popular Science and Sex in America.* London/New York: Verso, 1997.

People for Bernie. "Casey Knows a Political Revolution When She Sees One. She Voted Early in Wisconsin! #FeelTheBern." *Twitter,* April 3, 2016. https://twitter.com/People4Bernie/status/716731172223590401/photo/1

peoriapeoria. "Untitled Comment." *AO3,* September 20, 2019.

Petersen, Line Nybro. "Sherlock Fans Talk: Mediatized Talk on Tumblr." *Northern Lights,* no. 12 (2014): 87–104.

Petrusich, Amanda. "K-Pop Fans Diffuse Racist Hashtags." *The New Yorker,* June 5, 2020.

https://www.newyorker.com/culture/cultural-comment/k-pop-fans-defuse-racist-hashtags

Phillips, Andrea. "Transmedia Storytelling, Fan Culture and the Future of Marketing." *Knowledge@Wharton UPenn,* July 3, 2012. http://knowledge.wharton.upenn.edu/article/transmedia-storytelling-fan-culture-and-the-future-of-marketing/

Pinkowitz, Jacqueline. "'The Rabid Fans That Take [Twilight] Much Too Seriously': The Construction and Rejection of Excess in Twilight Antifandom." *Transformative Works and Cultures,* no. 7 (2011). https://journal.transformativeworks.org/index.php/twc/article/view/247/253

Polo, Susana. "The Internet Has Done It: We've Found the Dumbest Hunger Games Tie In." *The Mary Sue,* November 8, 2013. http://www.themarysue.com/hunger-games-subway/#comment-1114097179

Poster, Mark. "Cyberdemocracy: The Internet and the Public Sphere." In *Reading Digital Culture,* edited by David Trend, 259–71. Malden: Blackwell Publishers Ltd, 2001.

Proctor, William. "'I've Seen a Lot of Talk About the #blackstormtrooper Outrage, but Not a Single Example of Anyone Complaining': The Force Awakens, Canonical Fidelity and Non-toxic Fan Practices." *Participations,* 15.1 (2018): 160–79.

Putnam, Robert D. *Bowling Alone: The Collapse and Revival of American Community.* New York: Simon & Schuster, 2000.

Radway, Janice. *Reading the Romance: Women, Patriarchy and Popular Literature.* Chapel Hill: University of North Carolina Press, 1984.

Reid, Robin Anne. "'The Wild Unicorn Herd Check-In': The Politics of Race in Science Fiction Fandom." In *Black and Brown Planets: The Politics of Race in Science Fiction,* edited by Iasiah Lavender, 225–40. Jackson: University Press of Mississippi, 2014.

Reinhard, CarrieLynn. *Fractured Fandoms. Contentious Communication in Fan Communities.* Lanham: Lexington Books, 2018.

_____. "Gameplay Marketing Strategies as Audience Co-optation: The Story of *The Dark Knight,* the *Cloverfield* Monster, and Their Brethren." *International Journal of Communication,* no. 5 (2011): 51–77.

Renfro, Ashley. "Time to Set Bella Down: A Feminist Critique of Twilight." *Medium,* February 15, 2017. https://medium.com/@ashleyrenfro_31357/time-to-set-bella-down-a-feminist-critique-of-twilight-b695a728556e

Riley, Katie. *Viral Marketing Campaign: District 9,* not dated. http://district9campaign.weebly.com/

Riordan, Stephen. "Capitol Couture: Innovation or Complete Contradiction?" *The Lone Wolf,* September 23, 2013. https://lostteen07.wordpress.com/2013/09/23/capitol-couture-innovation-or-complete-contradiction/

Robinson, Tasha. "How the Sad Puppies Won—By Losing." *NPR,* August 26, 2015. https://www.npr.org/2015/08/26/434644645/how-the-sad-puppies-won-by-losing

Rokne, Olav. "Untitled Comment." *File 770,* September 14, 2019.

Rolfe, James. "Ghostbusters 2016. No Review. I Refuse." *Cinemassacre,* May 17, 2016. http://cinemassacre.com/2016/05/17/ghostbusters-2016-no-review-i-refuse/

Rosenberg, Alyssa. "How 'Harry Potter' Fans Won a Four-Year Fight Against Child Slavery." *The Washington Post,* January 13, 2015. http://www.washingtonpost.com/news/act-four/wp/2015/01/13/how-harry-potter-fans-won-a-four-year-fight-against-child-slavery/

Rowling, J.K. *Fantastic Beasts and Where to Find Them.* London: Bloomsbury, 2001.

_____. *Harry Potter Hardcover Boxed Set.* 7 volumes. New York: Arthur A. Levine Books, 2007.

_____. "J.K. Rowling Writes About Her Reasons for Speaking Out on Sex and Gender Issues." *JKRowling.com,* June 10, 2020. https://www.jkrowling.com/opinions/j-k-rowling-writes-about-her-reasons-for-speaking-out-on-sex-and-gender-issues/

_____. *Pottermore,* 2012. https://www.pottermore.com/

Runte, Robert, ed. *The NCF Guide to Canadian Science Fiction and Fandom.* Edmonton: New Canadian Fandom, 1988.

Salter, Anastasia, and Bridget Blodgett. *Toxic Geek Masculinity in Media. Sexism, Trolling, and Identity Politics.* London: Palgrave Macmillan, 2017.

Salter, Michael. "From Geek Masculinity to Gamergate: The Technological Rationality of Online Abuse." *Crime Media Culture*, no. 14.2 (2018): 247–64.

Savage, Dan. *It Gets Better Project. Give Hope to LGBT Youth*, 2010. http://www.itgetsbetter. org/

Scalzi, John. "Who Gets to Be a Geek? Anyone Who Wants to Be." *Whatever.Scalzi*, July 26, 2012. https://whatever.scalzi.com/2012/07/26/who-gets-to-be-a-geek-anyone-who-wants-to-be/

Scherker, Amanda. "Whitewashing Was One of Hollywood's Worst Habits. So Why Is It Still Happening?" *Huffington Post*, July 10, 2014. http://www.huffingtonpost.com/2014/07/10/hollywood-whitewashing_n_5515919.html

Scithers, George. "Pacificon II Report," 1964.

Scott, A.O. "The Death of Adulthood in American Culture." *The New York Times*, September 11, 2014. http://www.nytimes.com/2014/09/14/magazine/the-death-of-adulthood-in-american-culture.html

Scott, Suzanne. "Authorized Resistance: Is Fan Production Frakked?" In *Cylons in America. Critical Studies in Battlestar Galactica*, edited by Tiffany Potter and C.W. Marshall, 210–23. New York/London: Continuum, 2008.

_____. *Fake Geek Girls. Fandom, Gender, and the Convergence Culture Industry*. New York: New York University Press, 2019.

_____. "Fangirls in Refrigerators: The Politics of (In)visibility in Comic Book Culture." *Transformative Works and Cultures*, Special issue: Appropriating, Interpreting, and Transforming Comic Books, edited by Matthew J. Costello, no. 13 (2013). https://journal.transformativeworks.org/index.php/twc/article/view/460/384

_____. *Revenge of the Fanboy. Convergence Culture and the Politics of Incorporation*. Dissertation, University of Southern California, 2011.

_____. "#Wheresrey? Toys, Spoilers, and the Gender Politics of Franchise Paratexts." *Critical Studies in Media Communication*, no. 34.2 (2017): 138–47.

seeking-avalon. "Open Letter: To Elizabeth Bear." *Seeking Avalon*, January 13, 2009. http://seeking-avalon.blogspot.com/2009/01/open-letter-to-elizabeth-bear.html

Selzer, L.F. "Angela Nissel from Blog to Books: Authorship and the Digital Public Sphere." *Auto/Biography Studies*, no. 27.1 (2012): 127–52.

Sheffield, Jessica, and Elyse Merlo. "Biting Back: Twilight Anti-Fandom and the Rhetoric of Superiority." In *Bitten by Twilight. Youth Culture, Media, & the Vampire Franchise*, edited by Melissa Click, Jennifer Stevens Aubrey, and Elizabeth Behm-Morawitz, 207–22. New York et al.: Peter Lang, 2010.

"Shop Capitol Couture at NET-A-PORTER." *Net-a-Porter*, 2013. http://www.net-a-porter.com/Shop/Designers/Capitol_Couture_by_Trish_Summerville/All

Shusterman, Richard. "Popular Art and Education." In *The New Scholarship on Dewey*, edited by James W. Garrison, 35–44. Dordrecht/Boston: Kluwer, 1995.

Simmons, Amber M. "Class on Fire: Using the Hunger Games Trilogy to Encourage Social Action." *Journal of Adolescent & Adult Literacy*, no. 56.1 (2012): 22–34.

Simons, Natasha. "Reconsidering the Feminism of Joss Whedon." *The Mary Sue*, April 7, 2011. http://www.themarysue.com/reconsidering-the-feminism-of-joss-whedon/

Sinclair, Upton. *Science-Fiction Turns to Life*. New York: Michel-Wollheim Publications, 1939.

Skrivan, Laurie. "Vandal Damages Statue Near Shaw Neighborhood of St. Louis: News." *St Louis Post Dispatch*, November 24, 2014. http://www.stltoday.com/news/local/metro/vandal-damages-statue-near-shaw-neighborhood-of-st-louis/article_e3234aa0-fa6e-54f6-8e1b-4393a322186e.html

Slack, Andrew. "Ad Campaign (Lip) Glosses Over 'Hunger Games' Message." *Los Angeles Times*, November 25, 2013. http://www.latimes.com/opinion/op-ed/la-oe-1125-slack-hunger-games-covergirl-capitol-20131125-story.html

Slack, Andrew, et al. "Can Fandom Change the World?" *Panel at LeakyCon 2013*. Portland, 2013. https://www.youtube.com/watch?v=PVSn0Dgjy3M

Smith, Edward E. "What Does This Convention Mean?" Speech presented at the World Con, Chicago, 1940.

Smith, Lauren. "The Hunger Games Capitol Couture Collection." *Glamour*, November 18, 2013.

http://www.glamourmagazine.co.uk/fashion/shopping/2013/11/hunger-games-capitol-couture-by-trish-summerville-net-a-porter

Soulstein, Seth. Interview with Hannah Mueller about the Odds in Our Favor campaign, May 7, 2015.

SPARK Action Squad. *Capitol Cuties*, not dated. http://capitolcuties.tumblr.com/?og=1

Spires, Elizabeth. "'Enthusiasm,' by Polly Shulman and 'Twilight,' by Stephenie Meyer." *New York Times*, February 12, 2006. https://www.nytimes.com/2006/02/12/books/review/enthusiasm-by-polly-shulman-and-twilight-by-stephenie-meyer.html

Stacey, Jackie. *Star Gazing: Hollywood Cinema and Female Spectatorship*. London/New York: Routledge, 1994.

Stack, Tim. "'Glee': The Show Heard Round the World." *Entertainment Weekly's EW.com*, May 28, 2010. http://www.ew.com/ew/article/0,,20386845,00.html

Standback, "Untitled Comment," *File 770*, July 28, 2019.

Stanfill, Mel. "Introduction: The Reactionary in the Fan and the Fan in the Reactionary." *Television & New Media*, no. 21.2 (2020): 123–34.

Stevens, J. Richard, and Rachel Lara van der Merwe. "The Imagined Communities of Toxic Puppies: Considering Fan Community Discourse in the 2015 Hugo Awards 'Puppygate' Controversy." *Participations* 15.1 (2018): 207–30.

Stewart, Dodai. "There Are McQueen Shoes on the Hunger Games Fashion Tumblr!" *Jezebel*, January 24, 2012. http://jezebel.com/5878995/there-are-mcqueen-shoes-on-the-hunger-games-fashion-tumblr?comment=46332713

_____. "Volunteering for the Hunger Games? Don't Forget the CoverGirl Lipgloss." *Jezebel*, May 17, 2013. http://jezebel.com/volunteering-for-the-hunger-games-dont-forget-the-cove-508277061

Stork, Matthias. "The Cultural Economics of Performance Space: Negotiating Fan, Labor, and Marketing Practice in Glee's Transmedia Geography." *Transformative Works and Cultures*, Special issue: Fandom and/as Labor, edited by Mel Stanfill and Megan Condis, no. 15 (2014). http://journal.transformativeworks.org/index.php/twc/article/view/490/420

Sturken, Marita, and Lisa Cartwright. *Practices of Looking. an Introduction to Visual Culture*. Oxford: Oxford University Press, 2001.

sunnymodffa. "FFA DW Post #1164." *Failfandomanon. Dreamwidth*, September 17, 2019.

Swearingen, Jake. "Steve Bannon Saw the 'Monster Power' of Angry Gamers While Farming Gold in *World of Warcraft*." *NY Magazine*, July 18, 2017. http://nymag.com/intelligencer/2017/07/steve-bannon-world-of-warcraft-gold-farming.html

"Sweet Charity." http://www.sweet-charity.net/ (down since 2011).

synecdochic. "Untitled Comment." *AO3*, September 17, 2019.

tablesaw. "O HAI RACEFAILZ: Notes on Reading an Internet Conflict." *LiveJournal*, March 9, 2009.

Teaberryblue. "Untitled Comment." *AO3*, September 20, 2019.

Terranova, Tiziana. "Free Labor: Producing Culture for the Digital Economy." *Social Text*, no. 18.2 (2000): 33–58.

Thibeault, Jason. "Is Transmedia Storytelling the New Digital Marketing?" *Jason Thibeault*, October 17, 2013. http://jasonthibeault.com/2013/10/17/is-transmedia-storytelling-the-new-digital-marketing/

Thorne, Jack. *Harry Potter and the Cursed Child*. New York: Arthur A. Levine Books, 2017 (Stage Premiere July 30, 2016 at the Palace Theatre, London).

Tiffany, Kaitlyn. "*My Little Pony* Fans Are Ready to Admit They Have a Nazi Problem." *The Atlantic*, June 23, 2020. https://www.theatlantic.com/technology/archive/2020/06/my-little-pony-nazi-4chan-black-lives-matter/613348/

Tompkins, Joe. "The Makings of a Contradictory Franchise: Revolutionary Melodrama and Cynicism in the Hunger Games." JCMS: Journal of Cinema and Media Studies 58, no. 1 (2018): 70–90.

Tönnies, Ferdinand. *Community and Society*. Translated by Charles P. Loomis. New York: Dover, 2011.

_____. *Gemeinschaft und Gesellschaft: Abhandlung des Communismus und des Socialismus als empirischer Culturformen*. Leipzig: Fues, 1887.

Torgersen, Brad. "Announcing SAD PUPPIES 3!" *Brad R. Torgersen: Blue Collar Speculative Fiction,* January 7, 2015. https://bradrtorgersen.wordpress.com/2015/01/07/announcing-sad-puppies-3/

troutymouth. "What Glee Means to Me." *Trouty Mouth,* August 2, 2012. http://troutymouth.com/2012/08/what-glee-means-to-me.html (website down, accessible via Wayback Machine).

Tulloch, John, and Henry Jenkins. *Science Fiction Audiences. Watching Doctor Who and Star Trek.* London/New York: Routledge, 1995.

U.S. Department of Health & Human Services. *StopBullying.gov,* 2012. http://www.stopbullying.gov/

van den Abbeele, Georges. "Introduction." In *Community at Loose Ends,* edited by Miami Theory Collective, ix–xxvi. Minneapolis: University of Minnesota Press, 1991.

van Zoonen, Liesbet. *Entertaining the Citizen: When Politics and Popular Culture Converge.* Lanham: Rowman & Littlefield, 2005.

veejane. "Untitled." *LiveJournal,* March 2, 2009.

Verba, Joan Marie. *Boldly Writing: A Trekker Fan and Zine History 1967–1987.* Minnetonka: FTL Publications, 1996.

versusthefans. "The Trouble with 'Glee.'" *Versus the Fans,* September 30, 2013. http://versusthefans.com/2013/09/30/the-trouble-with-glee/

Walton, Jo. *An Informal History of the Hugos: A Personal Look Back at the Hugo Awards, 1953–2000.* New York: Tor Books 2018.

Walwyn, Isaac. "The Hoffman Electronic Ads 1962." *Sevagram,* July 28, 2013. http://www.icshi.net/sevagram/articles/hoffman.php

Warner, Michael. *Publics and Counterpublics.* New York: Zone Books, 2002.

Weinman, Jaime J. "A Song in Their Hearts." *Maclean's,* November 22, 2010.

Weisberg, Lori. "Comic-Con Is Staying in San Diego—at Least Through 2024." *San Diego Union-Tribune,* July 5, 2019. https://www.sandiegouniontribune.com/business/tourism/story/2019-07-05/comic-con-is-staying-in-san-diego-at-least-through-2024

Wiedeman, Reeves. "#Activism." *The New Yorker,* December 22, 2014. http://www.newyorker.com/magazine/2014/12/22/activism

Wilcox, Rhonda. "Whedon, Browncoats, and the Big Damn Narrative: The Unified Meta-Myth of Firefly and Serenity." In *Science Fiction Double Feature: The Science Fiction Film as Cult Text,* edited by J.P. Telotte and Gerald Duchovnay, 98–114. Liverpool: Liverpool University Press, 2015.

Winterwood, Lily. "Discourse Is the New Wank: A Reflection on Linguistic Change in Fandom." *Transformative Works and Cultures,* Special issue: Tumblr and Fandom, edited by Lori Morimoto and Louisa Ellen Stein, no. 27 (2018). https://journal.transformativeworks.org/index.php/twc/article/view/1276/1724

Wollheim, Donald, and John B. Michel. "Convention Booklets." *Science Fiction Progress,* no. 2 (September 1939).

_____. "Futurian House." *Science Fiction Progress,* no. 2 (September 1939).

_____. "The Philadelphia Convention." *Science Fiction Progress,* no. 4 (November 1, 1939).

Woo, Benjamin. "The Invisible Bag of Holding: Whiteness and Media Fandom." In *The Routledge Companion to Media Fandom,* edited by Melissa Click and Suzanne Scott, 245–52. New York: Routledge, 2018.

Worldcon '75 Organizing Committee. "The Hugo Awards—What's New in 2017." *Worldcon 75,* not dated. http://www.worldcon.fi/wsfs-hugos/hugo-awards/hugo-awards-whats-new/

Xillionous. "Idiot Nerd Girl." *Know Your Meme,* June 9, 2010. https://knowyourmeme.com/memes/idiot-nerd-girl

Yasharoff, Hannah. "How Trans Harry Potter Fans Are Grappling with J.K. Rowling's Legacy After Her Transphobic Comments." *USA Today,* July 31, 2020. https://www.usatoday.com/story/entertainment/books/2020/07/31/harry-potter-fans-grapple-j-k-rowling-transgender-remarks/5471834002/

Yost, Karen Ann. "It Is Better to Give... a Look at Fandoms and Their Relationships with Charities." *Strange New Worlds,* March 1994. http://www.strangenewworlds.com/issues/fandom-12.html

Young, Iris Marion. "The Ideal of Community and the Politics of Difference." *Social Theory and Practice*, no. 12.1 (1986): 1–26.

Film, Video, Television, Radio, Music

Abbott, Paul. *Shameless*. Showtime, 2011–2021.
Anders, Adam, et al. "Loser Like Me." Columbia, 2011.
Black, Dustin Lance. *El SMS*. Coca Cola, 2015.
Brownwell, Ian, Harry Potter Alliance, and Walmart Watch. *Harry Potter and the Dark Lord Waldemart*. 2006. https://www.youtube.com/watch?v=no0WqYWdH74
Columbus, Chris, et al. *Harry Potter 1–8*. Warner Bros, 2001–2011.
Davies, Russell T. "Day Five." *Torchwood: Children of the Earth*. BBC, July 10, 2009.
Faust, Lauren. *My Little Pony: Friendship Is Magic*. Discovery Family, 2010–2019.
Feig, Paul. *Ghostbusters: Answer the Call*. Columbia Pictures/Sony Pictures, 2016.
"Glee: Keep on Believin'." *Biography*. BIO Channel (now fyi), April 10, 2012.
"The Glee Project Casting Promo." Oxygen, August 2011.
Goss, James. "The House of the Dead." *The Lost Files*. BBC/AudioGo, 2011.
Handler, Chelsea. "Guest: Chris Colfer." *Chelsea Lately*. E!, December 3, 2009.
Harmon, Dan. *Community*. NBC/Yahoo!, 2009–2015.
The Harry Potter Alliance. "The Hunger Games Are Real," 2013. https://www.youtube.com/watch?v=BmVJaBuoEYA
Hirsch, Lee. *Bully*. Where We Live Films/Weinstein Company, 2011.
"I Heart Glee." Sky 1, March 10, 2013.
Kaplan, Jeff, et al. *World of Warcraft*. Blizzard Entertainment, 2004.
Kelly, Gene, and Stanley Donen. *Singin' in the Rain*. MGM/Loew's, 1952.
Lady Gaga. "Born This Way." Streamline/Kon Live/Interscope, 2011.
Lawrence, Francis. *The Hunger Games: Catching Fire*. Lions Gate Films, 2013.
_____. *The Hunger Games: Mockingjay Part I*. Lions Gate Films, 2014.
_____. *The Hunger Games: Mockingjay Part II*. Lions Gate Films, 2015.
Lin, Justin. *Star Trek Beyond*. Skydance Media/Paramount Pictures, 2016.
Lucas, George. *Star Wars IV: A New Hope*. Lucasfilm/20th Century Fox, 1977.
lulzychan. "How Klaine Changed the World." *YouTube* 2012. https://www.youtube.com/watch?v=szyXsExkvyw&index=1&list=PLf6tiuNIg1FUvQfNHduwyex_Fbrk9TJlR (taken down for copyright violation).
Murphy, Ryan. "Extraordinary Merry Christmas." *Glee*. FOX, December 13, 2011.
_____. "Theatricality." *Glee*. FOX, May 25, 2010.
Murphy, Ryan, and Alfonso Gomez-Rejon. "Born This Way." *Glee*. FOX, April 26, 2011.
Murphy, Ryan, and Brad Falchuk. "The New Rachel." *Glee*. FOX, September 13, 2012.
_____. "New York." *Glee*. FOX, May 24, 2011.
_____. "Preggers." *Glee*. FOX, September 23, 2009.
Murphy, Ryan, and Bradley Buecker. "The First Time." *Glee*. FOX, November 8, 2011.
Murphy, Ryan, and Elodie Keene. "Mash-Up." *Glee*. FOX, October 21, 2009.
Murphy, Ryan, and Eric Stoltz. "Opening Night." *Glee*. FOX, April 22, 2014.
Murphy, Ryan, and John Scott. "Acafellas." *Glee*. FOX, September 16, 2009.
Nolan, Christopher. *The Dark Knight*. Warner Bros., 2008.
Persichetti, Bob, Peter Ramsey, and Rodney Rothman. *Spider-Man: Into the Spider-Verse*. Columbia Pictures/SONY, 2018.
Roddenberry, Gene. *Star Trek—The Next Generation*. CBS, 1987–1994.
_____. *Star Trek*. NBC, 1966–1969.
Ross, Gary. *The Hunger Games*. Color Force/Lions Gate Films, 2012.
Screen Junkies. "Honest Trailers—Twilight." *YouTube*, March 22, 2012. https://www.youtube.com/watch?v=0gugBiEkLwU
Spielberg, Steven. *A.I.—Artificial Intelligence*. Amblin Entertainment/Warner Bros., 2001.
Stewart, Jon. "The Daily Show." *The Daily Show*. Comedy Central, April 27, 2015.
Tancharoen, Kevin. *Glee: The 3D Concert Movie*. Ryan Murphy Productions/20th Century Fox, 2011.

Teng, Larry. "Hana I Wa 'Ia." *Hawaii Five-0.* CBS, January 21, 2013.
Wachowski, Lana and Lilly. *The Matrix.* Village Roadshow Pictures/Warner Bros., 1999.
_____. *The Matrix Reloaded.* Village Roadshow Pictures/Warner Bros., 2003.
_____. *The Matrix Revolutions.* Village Roadshow Pictures/Warner Bros., 2003.
Weitz, Chris. *The Twilight Saga: New Moon.* Temple Hill Entertainment/Summit Entertainment, 2009.
Whedon, Joss. *Buffy the Vampire Slayer.* The WB/UPN 1997–2003.
_____. *Firefly.* FOX, 2002–2003.
_____. "Safe." *Firefly.* FOX, November 8, 2002.
_____. *Serenity.* Universal Pictures, 2005.
Yates, David. *Fantastic Beasts and Where to Find Them.* Warner Bros., 2016.
_____. *Fantastic Beasts: The Crimes of Grindelwald.* Warner Bros., 2018.

Index